day trips® se

day trips® from kansas city

seventeenth edition

 getaway ideas for the local traveler

diana lambdin meyer

Globe
Pequot

Essex, Connecticut

All the information in this guidebook is subject to change. We recommend that you call ahead to obtain current information before traveling.

Globe Pequot

An imprint of Globe Pequot, the trade division of
The Rowman & Littlefield Publishing Group, Inc.
4501 Forbes Blvd., Ste. 200
Lanham, MD 20706
www.rowman.com

Distributed by NATIONAL BOOK NETWORK

British Library Cataloguing in Publication Information available

Library of Congress Cataloging-in-Publication Data

ISBN: 978-1-4930-7026-8 (paperback)

ISBN: 978-1-4930-7027-5 (electronic)

♾™ The paper used in this publication meets the minimum requirements of American National Standard for Information Sciences—Permanence of Paper for Printed Library Materials, ANSI/NISO Z39.48-1992.

>> contents

day trip 04

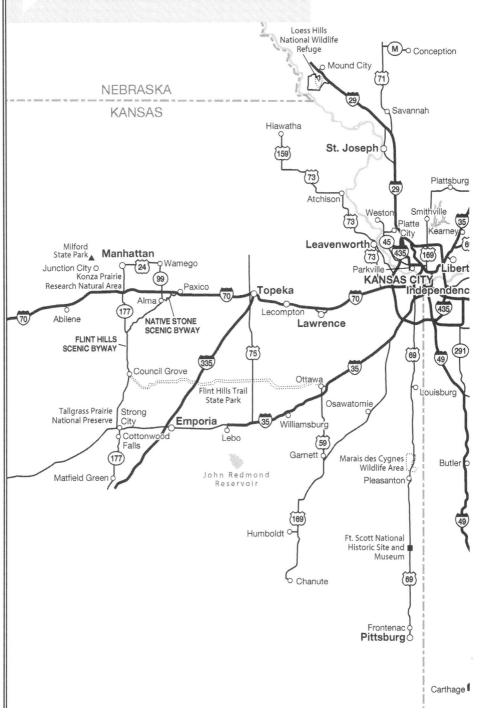

day trips from kansas city

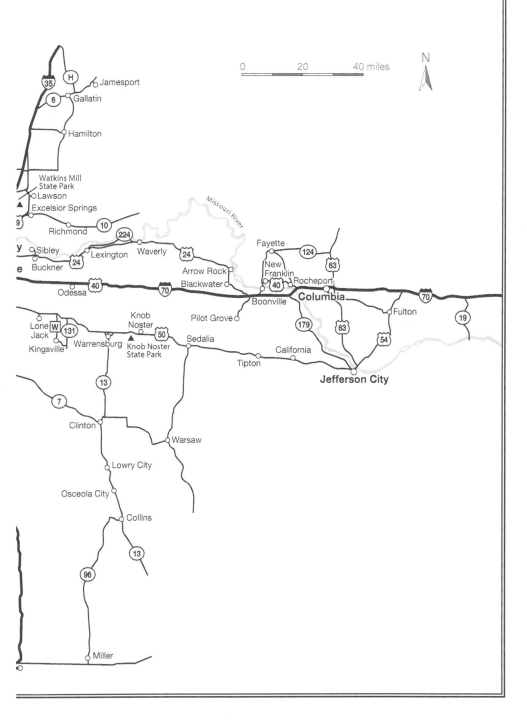

about the author

Diana Lambdin Meyer of Parkville has contributed to dozens of travel guidebooks and written thousands of articles for newspapers, magazines, and websites during her freelance writing career that spans three decades. She is an award-winning member of the Midwest Travel Journalists Association and the Society of American Travel Writers. She and her husband, Bruce, a professional photographer, travel the world in search of stories, education, and adventure, but the Midwest remains their home and their heart in all professional pursuits. Follow their work at MojoTraveler.com.

acknowledgments

I knew the name and the work of Shifra Stein long before I knew her cackling laugh, her energetic wit, and the warmth of her friendship. Although I didn't know it, my life became much richer and much more complex the day she and I met for the first time for lunch in the River Market. I don't even remember the day or the year. She and her husband/photographer, Bob Barrett, became a meaningful force in my life and that of my husband/photographer, Bruce. Although I worked with Shifra behind the scenes on several editions of *Day Trips* before her death In 2008, and my name now appears as the sole author, this is and always will be Shifra Stein's *Day Trips from Kansas City*.

introduction

Day Trips from Kansas City has had a long and happy life. It was first published in 1980, the year I graduated from college, having been written on an old electric typewriter. The Internet was limited to molasses-in-January-like communication among a few scholarly communities. Cordless telephones were rare indeed and the concept of cellular phones was all but unknown. Global Positioning Systems (GPS) were high-tech pieces of equipment costing thousands of dollars that helped airline pilots arrive at their assigned destinations. Mark Zuckerberg, who launched the world of social media, was not yet born.

That was the environment in which *Day Trips* was born, a world much different from that which we experience today. But one thing has not changed—a desire to throw off the shackles of the everyday and get away to refresh our spirits, if just for a few hours. Otherwise, we become stale, monotonous, and boring company.

During its lifetime, *Day Trips* has been updated and revised every couple of years, incorporating numerous suggestions from readers and travelers who excel in exploration far from the madding crowds, a destination first identified by the poet Thomas Gray in 1751. Even then, the peace and quiet and change of pace were valued among sensitive souls.

That's where this *Day Trips* takes you—to places where the whippoorwill calls and the tallgrass prairie whispers from its untouched pastures. Wrapped in these pages are lessons in history and tutorials in human nature, inspirational locations that will stir your creative spirit, and quirky places that should make you smile.

We're uniquely fortunate here in America's heartland that so much of the world has traveled here before us, albeit in covered wagons, steamboats, and coal-fired locomotives. However, it's time you make your own trail. This copy of *Day Trips from Kansas City* will hopefully help you find your way.

But perhaps you'll seek your own road to places you've never been before. Having seen them, please let us know. We're always open for new places to call our own.

using this guide

Day Trips from Kansas City is organized by general direction from the downtown area: northeast, east, southeast, south, southwest, west, and northwest. It by no means purports to cover every worthy destination, but offers 22 complete trips that will appeal to couples, families, friends, and fellow travelers.

hours & prices

In the interest of accuracy and because they frequently change, hours of operation and attraction prices are given in general terms. (Note: Most attraction listings mention only that there is an admission fee.) Always remember to call ahead to get the most up-to-date information, as websites are not always reliable. If you have questions, contact the establishments for specifics.

pricing key

The price codes for accommodations and restaurants are represented as a scale of one to three dollar signs ($). You can assume all establishments listed accept major credit cards unless otherwise noted. For details, contact the locations directly.

accommodations

The price code reflects the average cost of a double-occupancy room during the peak price period (not including tax or extras). Please also note that during peak season in some areas, a two-night stay (or more) is required. Always check online or call to find out if any special discounts are available.

$	Less than $100
$$	$100 to $175
$$$	More than $175

restaurants

The price code reflects the average price of dinner entrees for two (excluding cocktails, wine, appetizers, desserts, tax, and tip).

$	$10 to $20
$$	$20 to $40
$$$	More than $40

Wheelchair accessibility: The designation is provided only for those wildlife areas and historic sites that provide amenities for those with mobility Issues.

Lewis and Clark Trail: The designation is provided to highlight sites associated with the Corps of Discovery journey through this region in 1804–1806.

where to get more information

Day Trips attempts to cover a variety of bases and interests, but if you're looking for additional material, plenty is out there. Each state and most communities have their own tourism bureaus. For most trips, they are listed as a first "Where to Go" location. They are a good place to start, often offering comprehensive websites and welcoming calls, emails, or requests for printed visitor guides, brochures, and maps. Nearly all of these tourism bureaus have a social media presence as well, where you can often find the latest happenings and information. In addition to the resources in this book, some additional sources of information include:

kansas

Kansas Historical Society
6425 SW Sixth Ave.
Topeka, KS 66615
(785) 272-8681
kshs.org
Facebook: @KansasHistorical
Twitter: @kansashistory
Instagram: @kansas_history

Kansas Tourism
1000 SW Jackson, #200
Topeka, KS 66612
(785) 296-8478
travelks.com
Facebook: #TravelKS
Twitter: @TravelKS
Instagram: @TravelKS

Kansas I-70 Association
kansasi70.com
Facebook: @KansasI70
Twitter: @travelKansasi70

missouri

Missouri Department of Conservation
PO Box 180
Jefferson City, MO 65102-0180
(573) 751-4115
mdc.mo.gov/

Kansas City Office
8616 E. Sixty-Third St.
Kansas City, MO 64133
(816) 356–2280

Missouri Department of Natural Resources
Division of State Parks
PO Box 176
Jefferson City, MO 65102
(800) 334-6946
mostateparks.com
Facebook: @mostateparks
Twitter: @mostateparks

Missouri Department of Tourism
PO Box 1055
Jefferson City, MO 65102
(573) 751-4133 or (800) 519-2100
visitmo.com

Facebook: @VisitMO
Twitter: @VisitMO
Instagram: @VisitMO

Missouri Historical Society
PO Box 775460
St. Louis, MO 63177
(314) 746-4599
mohistory.org
Facebook: @statehistoricalsocietyofmissouri
Twitter: @SHSofMO
Instagram: @SHSofMO

Platte County Convention and Visitors
Bureau
11724 NW Plaza Circle, #200
Kansas City, MO 64153
(816) 270-3979 or (888) 875-2883
visitplatte.com
Facebook: @PlatteCountyVisitorsBureau

Kansas City Regional Destination Alliance
kcdestinations.com
Facebook: @KCdestinations
Instagram: @KCDestinations

Lewis and Clark Trail
nps.gov/lecl

Freedom's Frontier National Heritage Area
PO Box 526
Lawrence, KS 66044
(785) 856-5300
freedomsfrontier.org

northeast

day trip 01

northeast

city by the lake:
smithville, mo; plattsburg, mo

smithville, mo

Humphrey Smith came to Clay County in 1822 and built the first grain mill north of the Missouri River on the Little Platte River. The town that developed was known as Smith's Fork but later was incorporated as Smith's Mill. At some point, the town became Smithville, which it remains today.

Most people envision Smithville Lake when they think of this community about 20 minutes north of downtown Kansas City. The lake was created in the late 1970s and is managed by the US Army Corps of Engineers. Many flights coming into Kansas City International Airport circle over the lake to get a perfect view of this long, narrow body of water that stretches 18 miles north of Smithville.

The focal point of most community activities is the downtown square, which is lined with a variety of antiques and gift shops and a few thrift stores that are always worthy of investigation. A farmers' market operates here Wednesday evenings from May through Oct, and a number of special events keep the square lively throughout the year.

getting there

From downtown Kansas City, take the Buck O'Neil Bridge, aka US 169, and head straight north for about 25 minutes, depending on how fast you drive.

2

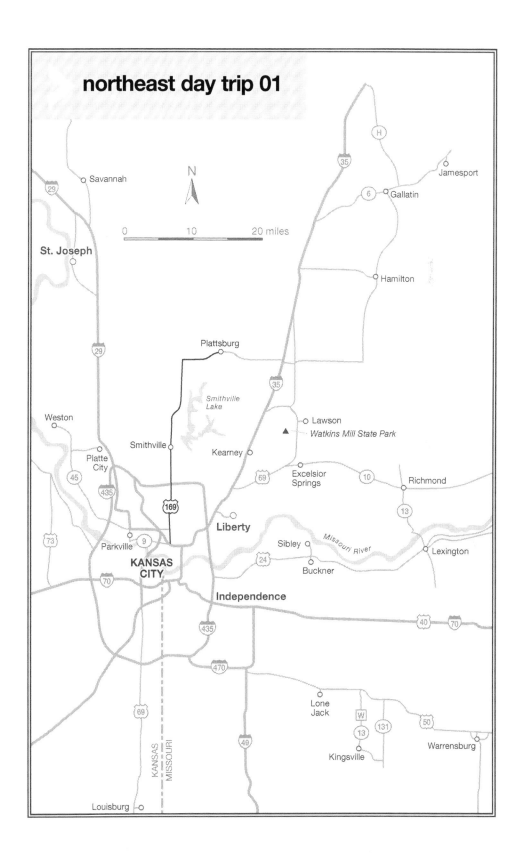

northeast day trip 01

where to go

Smithville Chamber of Commerce. 105 W. Main St.; (816) 532-0946; smithvillechamber
.org.

Comanche Acres Iris Gardens. 12421 SE MO 116, Gower; (816) 424-6436; comanche
acresiris.com. Travel about four miles north of Smithville on US 169, then turn left on MO 16
to the beautiful eight acres of Comanche Acres Iris Gardens. Before the land was flooded
to form Smithville Lake, Jim and Lamoyne Hedgecock scoured the old homesteads for iris
rhizomes, which they replanted. Jim has bred more than 4,600 new types of flowers, which
they sell around the world through a catalog company—and to anyone who happens by.
Their irises have won dozens of awards around the world. Spring is the most impressive time
for a visit. You can wander through the flowers without charge and enjoy the guinea hens,
turkeys, and ducks that eat the bugs from the blooms, but please don't bring your dog.

The Jerry L. Litton Visitor Center. SR 92 east from Kearney or US 169 north from Kansas City to 16311 Hwy. DD (south end of dam), PO Box 428; (816) 532-0174; nwk.usace
.army.mil/sm. Named after the late sixth district congressman, this center offers exhibits and
artifacts concerning the Missouri Valley and the Native Americans who inhabited it. There's
information about the lake and dam and on the life of Litton. Pick up information about other
Corps of Engineer lakes in the region and climb the tower for a fabulous view of the lake.
Free. Open 8 a.m. to 4 p.m., Mon through Sat.

never forget

*The downtown square of Smithville, the location of many community activities,
is a spacious plaza-style setting with picnic tables, benches, potted plants, and
grand shade trees. Here, you'll find a steel beam from the World Trade Center
fabricated into a memorial for the events of September 11, 2001. Take note also
of the public stage. It is dedicated to the memory of Allie Kemp, a Leawood teen-
ager who was tragically murdered in 2003. She has family members in Smithville.*

Smithville Lake and Clay County Parks (Camp Branch, Little Platte Park, and Crow's
Creek Area). Two miles east of US 169 on NE 180th Street; (816) 407-3400; claycountymo
.gov. Located amid rolling hills and grassland, the 7,200-acre lake is just 20 miles from
downtown Kansas City and is surrounded by 27 miles of horseback-riding trails along with
24 miles of walking/biking trails and an 11-mile mountain-biking trail. Clay County operates recreation areas on the lake, leasing nearly 5,500 acres from the US Army Corps of

Engineers. The recreation areas include 777 campsites for tents and RVs, 2 swimming beaches, 200 picnic sites, 11 shelter houses, 3 disc golf courses, and 2 full-service marinas. Favorites with anglers are bass, walleye, crappie, and catfish.

Golfers are offered challenging play on two par-72, award-winning 18-hole championship golf courses. The Sand Bar, located in Little Platte Park, is open from May through Sept (816) 407-3481.

The Kansas City Trapshooters Association offers the public a chance to do some of the finest trap and skeet shooting in the Midwest. This well-equipped facility includes 11 trapshooting pads, 2 skeet fields, and a recently remodeled clubhouse and pro shop. Admission fee; (816) 532-4427; kctraps.com.

In addition to all campground restrooms, Crow's Creek Area offers a wheelchair-accessible fishing dock and picnic shelter. Most of the walking trails have been paved in recent years.

Woodhenge. (816) 407-3400. Located on the west side of Smithville Lake in Little Platte Park, this is a working replica of the only known square prehistoric Native American solar calendar. The original site was flooded when Smithville Lake was created in the late 1970s. It's an interesting place to visit if you're already at the lake. Open year-round. Free with admission to the park.

where to eat

Chop's BBQ. 109 E. Main St.; (816) 866-4337; chopsbbqandcatering.com. In addition to the yummy barbeque basics of pulled pork, brisket, and burnt ends, Chop's has a pork tenderloin worth the drive to Smithville. You'll also find menu items to meet gluten-free and vegan needs. Consider the spicy fried pickles. They're something you'll remember. Closed Mondays. $

Humphrey's Bar & Grill. 111 N. Bridge St.; (816) 532-1525; humphresbarandgrill.com. This fun local spot is the place to join friends to watch a Royals or Chiefs game or the Jayhawks win another national championship. The décor includes some historic images of the area, lots of big screen TVs, and a couple of basketball hoops to keep the energy flowing. A big stage near rollup floor-to-ceiling windows is where you'll find some of the area's best garage bands in action. Tuesdays are for Texas Hold'em Tournaments and Thursdays are for tacos and margaritas. $

plattsburg, mo

Plattsburg was home to David Rice Atchison, the Missouri senator who was president pro temp of the US Senate, who on March 4, 1849, served as president of the United States for less than 24 hours. Although there is some historical argument over the details, nonetheless, a large bronze statue of Atchison graces the grounds of the Clinton County Courthouse in downtown Plattsburg. The city of Atchison, Kansas, is named for this Plattsburg senator. He is buried at the Greenlawn Cemetery in Plattsburg.

Throughout the mid-1800s, Plattsburg enjoyed great prosperity due to hemp, tobacco, and cattle production. As a result, the small community of about 3,000 people today has a number of well-maintained Victorian homes. Driving around the streets of town is a celebration of color, turrets, and gingerbread details.

Plattsburg is home to Ulysses "Slim" Hollimon, a pitcher in the Negro Leagues. In 2008, the MLB held a special draft where today's teams could symbolically draft surviving members of the Negro Leagues. The Kansas City Royals chose Hollimon as its pitcher. He coached Little League Baseball in Plattsburg for many years.

The city hosts a Wine Walk the third Saturday of May each year to raise funds for a fall festival in October.

getting there

Head north out of Smithville on US Highway 169. Go 12 miles to MO 116 and turn right. Continue six miles to Plattsburg.

where to go

Plattsburg Chamber of Commerce. 114 W. Maple St.; (816) 539-2649; plattsburgchamber.org. Stop in to pick up brochures for walking tours of the Victorian homes in town.

Hartzell and Co. 104 W. Locust St.; (no phone); shophartzellco.com. Kami Hartzell, who spends much of her day teaching school, loves to create, and this fun shop is the result of her creativity and that from other makers in northwest Missouri. You'll find home décor, women's fashions, and a few other treats, all handcrafted locally. Kami's hours vary, but you'll mostly find her on weekends, in the summer and a few evening hours.

Plattsburg Artist Coalition. 202 N. 2nd St.; (816) 304-4387; plattsburgartists.com. Each November for more than 20 years, the Plattsburg Artist Coalition has hosted an open house and show featuring dozens of northwest Missouri's finest artists. You'll find oils, pastels, sculptures, photography, and so much more. Check the website for ideas and feel free to reach out to individual artists prior to November.

Tigers on Main. 111 N. Main St.; (816) 539-2187. This incredibly interesting shop is operated by students and teachers in the Clinton R-III, with products the students make themselves. It started as a project to create and sell Tiger T-shirts, but just grew from there. The hours tend to vary a bit, so be understanding if the store is not open when you arrive. But the teachers say they hope to keep the store open Mon through Fri, 9 a.m. to 3 p.m.

The Tin Cottage. 102 N. Main St.; (816) 723-7359; tin-cottage.com. Some of the cutest children's gifts, bath and body products, fun hats and sunglasses, a little locally made jewelry, some home décor items, and a few other goodies for yourself fill this colorful shop on Main St. It's just a mishmash of fun shopping. In the back is a paint-your-own pottery studio.

Shatto Milk Company. 9406 N. MO 33, Osborn; (816) 930-3862; shattomilk.com. Head east out of Plattsburg 2.5 miles, then turn left or north on MO 33 for nine miles. Look for signs. This century-old family-owned dairy produces hormone-free milk bottled in glass, as well as cheese curds, butter, and ice cream. Enjoy a fresh-baked chocolate chip cookie and a glass of cold milk at the end of your tour. Open daily. Farm tours are Tuesday through Saturday. Reservations needed. There is a small fee for the tour, but kids two and under are free. Watch the bottling operation from the store without a charge. Check the website for special events, such as Easter egg hunts and family fun days at the farm.

where to eat

Lucila's on Main/The Backyard. 104 N. Main St.; (816) 723-7359; lucilasonmain.com. These two restaurants-in-one are based on the season and your desire to dine indoors or gather in the backyard with friends, games, and occasional music. The restaurant is known for burgers and Bourbon slushies, along with some really good fish tacos, salads, and other sandwiches. Open 11 a.m. to 7 p.m., Wed through Sat. $

Sugar Whipped Bakery. 107 N. Main St.; (816) 930-0014; sugarwhippednyc.com. Not just another bakery, this is a destination created by Melissa Fahlstrom, a Platte County native who spent 16 years in New York perfecting her craft before returning to northwest Missouri. The space is just as cute and yummy as the display case filled with elaborately decorated doughnuts, cupcakes, cookies, and more. But take a look around at the whimsical and meaningful décor. The grandfather clock is a bookcase filled with children's books. Take one and snuggle up on the overstuffed couch for a read. Examine the chandelier over the display case. It's made of her grandmother's and sister's wedding china. And look closely at the crown molding. The names etched there are friends, family, and complete strangers who contributed to Go Fund Me to help Melissa's dream come true. Open Wed through Fri, 7 a.m. until sold out; Sat, 8 a.m. until sold out. $

day trip 02

northeast

jesse james country:
liberty, mo; kearney, mo; excelsior
springs, mo; richmond, mo

liberty, mo

One of the most famous robberies attributed to the notorious James Gang was the daylight holdup of Clay County Savings in Liberty in 1866. The robbers took $60,000 in gold and currency, and none of the money was ever recovered. Others who put Liberty on the map are Joseph Smith, the Mormon prophet who was jailed here, and Alexander Doniphan, who took up the practice of law in Liberty in 1833. During his residence of 30 years, he became a leading citizen, orator, jurist, statesman, and soldier, eventually leading his famous expedition to Old Mexico in 1846–1847, the longest military march ever made.

By 1820, Clay County was formed and named in honor of Henry Clay, the congressional leader who crafted the Missouri Compromise. Liberty, selected as the county seat, was established that same year. Two years later, a college grew under the supervision of Dr. William Jewell, and today the lovely campus is still a fine center of higher learning. In recent years, the city has invested In public art around the historic square, making a stroll on a sunny day all the more pleasant. You can also explore the town by Bird scooters, positioned around the square. For more information: Liberty Area Chamber of Commerce, 1170 W. Kansas St., #H, Liberty; (816) 781-5200; libertychamber.com. Liberty has 17 public electric car charging stations.

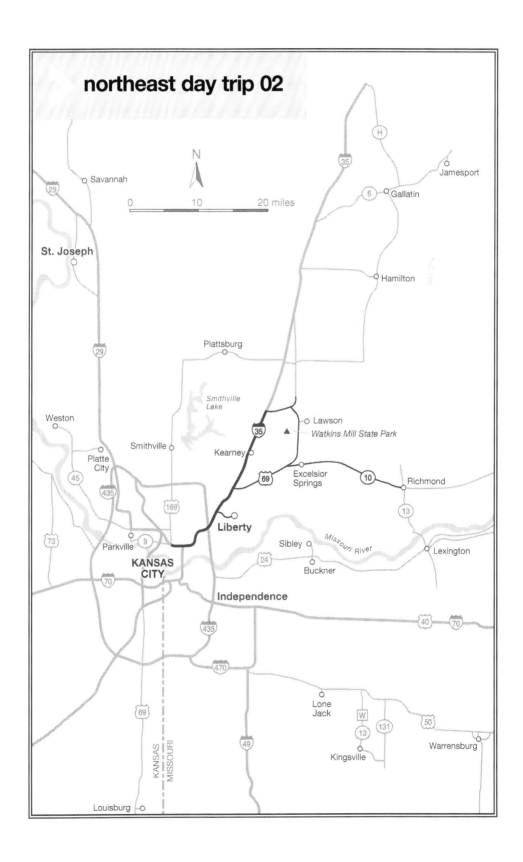

getting there

From downtown, take I-35 north toward Des Moines. Travel 16 miles and exit right on MO 152. Follow Kansas Street to the historic square.

where to go

Belvoir Winery. 1325 Odd Fellows Rd.; (816) 200-1811; belvoirwinery.com. The old Odd Fellows Complex, built in the 1900s, began its life as a home for orphans and the elderly. Many of the old buildings remain and have become popular destinations for ghost hunting events. The property is one of the most spectacular settings in the Northland and particularly popular for weddings. The inn has nine rooms. Hint: Room 7 is considered the most active for ghosts. Enjoy wine tasting seven days a week, as well as ice cream and deli snacks.

Bratcher Cooperage. 109 S. Water St.; (816) 781-3988; bratchercooperage.com. Stop in this fun shop, a former gas station, to see one of the nation's top craft artisans at work. Doug Bratcher has been handcrafting barrels, buckets, kegs, and churns in the traditional style for more than 30 years. If he's not in the shop when you come by, it's because he is at Silver Dollar City, where he is a featured craft artisan. You'll also find his work in many state and national parks, at Civil War reenactments, and in lots of movies, such as *Far and Away* with Tom Cruise and Nicole Kidman. You'll enjoy a visit with Doug's wife, Jan, who runs the gift shop. Open 10 a.m. to 5 p.m., Mon through Sat. Closed Sun.

Clay County Museum and Historical Society. 14 N. Main St.; (816) 792-1849; claycountymuseum.org. Housed in an 1877 drugstore, the museum collection focuses on Clay County history. It features a restored doctor's office, prehistoric Native American relics, toys, tools, arrowheads, and artifacts relating to the operation of a 19th-century drugstore. The third Thursday of each month, the Historical Society hosts a program featuring various aspects of Clay County and Missouri history. Open Mon through Sat, afternoons. Closed in Jan.

Corbin Theatre Co. 502 N. Water St.; (402) 917-4716; corbintheatre.org. Once the site of all entertainment in Liberty, this historic, circa-1880s theater was renovated in 2007. Theatrical productions are offered four to six times a season, in addition to jazz performances every Monday night. Visit the website for more entertaining events and the children's theater program.

Historic Liberty Jail and Visitors Center (Mormon Jail). 216 N. Main St.; (816) 781-3188. Mormon leader Joseph Smith was imprisoned here in 1838–1839 for his beliefs. Built in 1833, the limestone jail eventually crumbled but was reconstructed by the Church of Jesus Christ of Latter-day Saints in 1963. The jail has cutaway walls so that visitors can see what conditions were like nearly 175 years ago. The center also teaches about the unfairness of persecuting those of different faiths. Guided tours include historical highlights, exhibits, artwork, and interactive video displays. Open daily, 11 a.m. to 5 p.m. Free.

Jesse James Bank Museum. 103 N. Water St. (the northeast corner of Courthouse Square); (816) 781-4458. Frank and Jesse James were responsible for the first successful daylight bank robbery during peacetime. The James boys made a bank "withdrawal" of $60,000 from the Clay County Savings Association on February 13, 1866. A William Jewell College student who witnessed the event was shot and killed. No one was ever convicted. Today, you can take a glimpse into the workings of a 19th-century bank and view a number of artifacts related to Jesse James. The original bank vault and a rare Seth Thomas calendar clock are part of the tour. The building is listed on the National Register of Historic Places. Closed Sun. Admission fee.

Martha Lafite Thompson Nature Sanctuary. 407 N. LaFrenz Rd. (0.5 mile southeast of William Jewell College); (816) 781-8598; naturesanctuary.com. This 100-acre sanctuary is filled with wildlife that inhabits prairies, woodlands, meadows, and marshes. White-tailed deer, raccoons, foxes, squirrels, birds, and butterflies delight the eyes. The visitor center features educational exhibits for children and has organized activities such as wildflower and full-moon hikes. There are also two geocaches on-site. The visitor center is closed Sun and Mon, but the four miles of hiking trails are open daily from 8 a.m. to sunset. Donations accepted.

where to shop

Anna Marie's Teas. 9 W. Franklin; (816) 792-8777; annateashop.com. For those who love tea, iced or hot, this place has dozens of rooibos, herbals, and other loose leaf teas, as well as tea ware and gifts for the tea lover. Sign up for the monthly tea party. How fun is that!

Catfish and Tater. 4 N. Main St.; (816) 415-3677; catfishandtater.com. Are you looking for a dress, a handbag, or jewelry like no one else has? You'll find it in Heather Chaney's intimate boutique on the square. Or if you would like some clothing to match your latest tattoo, you can find that here as well. Heather's husband is a tattoo artist and transfers many of his designs to her clothing and home décor items. Or if you simply prefer clothing that comes from recycled and sustainable resources, you'll find that here as well.

Classy Chocolate. 18 W. Kansas St.; (816) 781-2260; classychocolate.com. You know you've entered a special place when the outdoor sign reads EXPERTS IN DECADENCE. Come in to satisfy your craving for chocolate-dipped strawberries or grapes or cashews or cookies. You name it, they dip it in chocolate here. Cupcakes, cheesecakes, wedding cakes, brownies. You get the idea. This is the place to blow your diet, increase your cholesterol levels, and enjoy life just a little more.

Quilting Is My Therapy. 2 E. Franklin St.; (816) 866-0126; quiltingismytherapy.com. Angela Walters absolutely loves quilting, and if you spend just a minute in her colorful shop, you'll love quilting, too. So many choices of fabrics and colors and ideas. Angela and her team can walk you through them all. Watch several long-arm quilting machines in action or browse some of the other gift items in the shop. And check out Angela's YouTube channel "The Midnight Quilter." Closed Sun and Mon.

where to eat

Huey's on the Square. 18 N. Main; (816) 415-4727; hueyscafe.com. Breakfast is served all day long in this cute little place on the square, including burritos, chicken, and waffles. For lunch, enjoy deli favorites like roast beef, corned beef, and Reubens. Open for breakfast and lunch only, Mon through Sat. $

where to stay

Belvoir Winery and Inn. (See listing above under What to Do.)

kearney, mo

Kearney is best known as the birthplace and burial place of outlaw Jesse James. A festival each September celebrates the city's most renowned resident (jessejamesfestival.com). The first thing to know about the community is that it's pronounced "Karn-knee," not "Ker-knee." Many assume the town was named after Kearney, Nebraska, and there's some evidence to support that. However, more likely is that it was named for Charles Esmond Kearney, an Irish immigrant who lived a colorful life after coming to the New World. Among his business ventures was a railroad partnership with Joseph Van Horn and Kersey Coates, names etched into Kansas City's history. A railroad stop was needed to ship the many cattle raised in this part of Clay County, and since Charles Esmond Kearney was president of the company, that's probably how the town got its name. For more information, contact the Kearney Chamber of Commerce; (816) 628-4229; kearneychamber.org. Kearney has 20 electric car charging stations.

getting there

It's a quick 10-minute drive from Liberty to Kearney. The easiest route is straight up I-35 to exit 26. Or for a more scenic route, drive the back roads along MO 33. Leave downtown on Kansas Avenue and just follow the signs.

where to go

Jesse James Farm and Museum. 21216 James Farm Rd. (three miles east of Kearney on MO 92); (816) 736-8500; jessejamesmuseum.org. This is the birthplace of Jesse James, where he and his brother Frank grew up during the mid-1800s. The house, listed on the National Register of Historic Places, has been authentically restored. The museum features the world's largest collection of James family artifacts, including guns, saddles, and boots. The quilt, handmade by Frank's wife, Annie, remains on the bed in which he died. Open year-round. Admission fee.

Jesse James Grave. Mount Olivet Cemetery, west end of MO 92 on the way out of Kearney. Jesse's grave is located between two small evergreen trees on the cemetery's west side. Originally, the outlaw was buried on the front lawn of the farm so that his family could protect his remains from grave robbers and curiosity seekers. For years Jesse's mother, Zerelda, sold pebbles off the grave to tourists. Later, his body was moved to Mount Olivet. A relatively small marker identifies the grave as that of Jesse James and his wife, Zerelda. Yes, both his wife and mother were named Zerelda. Jesse's marker reads: BORN: SEPTEMBER 5, 1847. ASSASSINATED: APRIL 3, 1882. To the left and right of Jesse's grave stand taller monuments inscribed SAMUEL, where the outlaw's mother and stepfather are buried. Also nearby is the grave of young Archie Samuel, Jesse's half-brother who was killed when Pinkerton detectives bombed the James farm in Jan 1875. Open daily. Free.

Kearney Museum. 101 S. Jefferson St.; (816) 903-1856. This small museum strives to compile a history of the community. Perhaps of greatest interest to those from outside the area is a bank vault that was not robbed by the James brothers but instead contained the cremated ashes of Frank James for almost 30 years before they were interred beside his wife in an Independence, Missouri, cemetery. Open Fri through Sat, 10 a.m. to 2 p.m. Admission fee.

Tryst Falls Park. Located five miles east of Kearney on MO 92; (816) 407-3400. The Clay County Parks and Recreation Department runs this 40-acre park, which includes the area's only waterfall open to the public. It's a great place to picnic because of the many shelters and grills and the modern playground. Jesse James's father, a Baptist minister, baptized Walthus Watkins, owner of Watkins Mill, at Tryst Falls. Swimming is dangerous and not allowed here because of the rocks. Fishing is not allowed. The park makes a sightseeing stop in your tour of Jesse James Farm or Watkins Mill State Park. Open daily.

Watkins Woolen Mill State Historic Site and Park. Located 6.5 miles north of Excelsior Springs and seven miles east of Kearney, off MO 92 at Highway RA, Lawson; (816) 580-3387; mostateparks.com. This is the last 19th-century woolen mill in America with original equipment. The mill heralds the beginning of the industrial age and still contains 60 of the original machines and a steam engine. The Watkins home, smokehouse, summer kitchen, and fruit dry house, along with an octagonal school and a church, add interest. The original farm was 3,550 acres, but the park is now 1,500 acres and includes the original sawmill, gristmill, and brick kiln built by the Watkins family.

The state park features picnicking, camping, hiking, fishing, and swimming in the lake. Bring your bike along and enjoy the 3.5-mile bike/hike trail around the shoreline. Bring food and drink; there are no concessions here and water is turned off from Nov 1 to Apr 1. Open daily. Free.

where to eat

D'Creamery. 105 S. Jefferson St.; (816) 635-2479; dcreamery.com. This family-owned business is best known for its small-batch homemade ice cream and bakery. Open for breakfast, lunch, and dinner, you'll enjoy personal, attentive service, as well as some good BBQ, burgers, and salads. Pork tenderloin fans know to come on Thursday for the special. Check out the colorful collection of cookie jars lining the walls. $

Diddy's Kitchen BBQ & Brewery. 103 S. Jefferson St.; (816) 635-7026. Open mic nights on Wednesdays. The BBQ comes from Wolfpack BBQ in North Kansas City, a competitive team with plenty of trophies to show for it. But Diddy's rocks most nights with local live bands in what was originally the Kearney Methodist Church, built in 1865. Check out the collection of growlers from craft brewers around the country. Open daily, except for Tues, 3 to 9 p.m. $

where to shop

Paisley Candle and Home. 400 S. Jefferson St.; (816-635-7017); paisleycandle.com. The many scents of candles are created daily in a back room of this charming little business. The scents vary seasonally. You'll also find adorable home décor items. Just across the parking lot is Paisley Perks, a coffee shop that also smells pretty good. Closed Sun.

excelsior springs, mo

Long revered as a haven of health, Excelsior Springs has attracted thousands of people to its mineral waters since 1881 and still offers historical insight into the healing powers of the waters. Excelsior Springs now has more than 40 springs and wells. These springs have four distinct mineral groupings, giving Excelsior Springs the distinction of the most mineral groups of any town in the world. A summer festival celebrates the influence of the waters in this town. For more information: Excelsior Springs Chamber of Commerce, 426 S. Thompson Ave.; (816) 630-6161; exspgschamber.com.

getting there

A 12-mile drive north on US 69 takes you to historic Excelsior Springs in about 20 minutes.

where to go

Atlas Saloon. 100 Broadway; (816) 630-9229; atlassaloon.com. This bar has been open in this spot since 1894 and is the fifth oldest continuously operating bar in Missouri. However, what makes it really interesting is the bar itself. Schlitz Brewing Company out of Milwaukee built this bar and brought woodworkers from Germany to build bars in pubs across the Midwest. This one is pure walnut and absolutely beautiful. Having been owned by Schlitz, the Atlas is what's known as a "tied house." There's a shuffleboard and billiards table inside, and live bands frequently make the space a little more lively.

Christmas Ranch Tree Farm. 24818 NE 148th St.; (816) 630-5086; christmasranchtreef-arm.com. This lovely family farm makes for a perfect holiday getaway to visit with Santa and to walk among 25 acres of Christmas trees. You'll have plenty of help from the many elves around. Are you a fan of holiday movies on the Lifetime Channel? Watch for *My Sweet Holiday*. It was shot, in part, on the Christmas Tree Ranch. Open in November. Check website for exact date.

Historic Hall of Waters. 201 E. Broadway; (816) 631-2811. The Historic Hall of Waters was the central dispersal site of the five mineral waters found here and focused on the development of equipment for the use of water in therapeutic treatment. Siloam Springs remains today as the only natural supply of iron manganese mineral water in the country and is one of five recognized in existence worldwide. The space now serves as the visitor center, but it doesn't take much imagination to see how lively the building was when individuals came here to drink, just as some do in bars and pubs. Fans of art deco architecture will love the building with the beautiful Mayan Indian design inside.

Slightly Off Broadway Theatre. 114 N. Marietta St.; (816) 637-3728; sobtheatre.org. A historic church, built in 1903, is home to this energetic community theater, which offers six shows a year. Performances Fri through Sun. $

Trolley Tours. (816) 630-6161; estrolley.com. A fun way to experience the community with a large group of friends. The company offers wine and spirits tours, a ghost tour and a coffee trolley, and more according to the season.

Willow Springs Mercantile. 249 E. Broadway; (816) 630-7476; shopthemercantile.com. Made in Missouri products are among the reasons to visit the mercantile. While the store carries plenty of home décor and gift items, its specialty is Missouri wines and beers and gourmet food products. Downstairs is a little bistro that serves a light lunch and hosts monthly wine dinners. $$

where to eat

Ventana Gourmet Grill. 117 W. Broadway; (816) 630-8600; ventanagourmetgrill.com. A relaxing spot for lunch or a destination for dinner, the Ventana has brought fine dining to Excelsior Springs. Lunch offers a variety of soups, salads, and sandwiches, including a yummy Cajun shrimp BLT. Dinner is all about the beef, from a 16-ounce prime rib to a 12-ounce KC strip. This is where locals come for a good steak. The wine selection is extraordinary, as is the dessert menu. Check out the Dinner & a Show specials in conjunction with the Slightly Off Broadway Theatre. $$

where to stay

The Elms Resort and Spa. Regent Street and Elms Boulevard; (816) 630-5500; elms hotelandspa.com. The Elms Resort has once again undergone a major renovation, thus maintaining its status as a premier retreat and conference center in the Kansas City area. Al Capone still has a room named for him here, as does Harry Truman. It was here on election night in 1948 that Truman learned he did indeed defeat Dewey. Casual and fine dining options, indoor and outdoor swimming, and hiking and biking trails are all amenities above and beyond the well-appointed guest rooms and spa. Even if you don't spend the night, come for a ghost tour. $$$

The Inn on Crescent Lake. 1261 St. Louis Ave.; (816) 630-6745; crescentlake.com. This country inn makes a great romantic getaway or a pleasant alternative for businesspeople tired of the motel shuffle. The three-story Georgian colonial mansion is nestled on 22 acres and surrounded by two ponds and a lawn designed for strolling and relaxing. A full breakfast might include quiche, scones, waffles, French toast, and other delights.

Each of the 10 guest rooms has a private bath, including a whirlpool or claw-foot tub. The downstairs guest room is wheelchair-accessible, with its own separate entrance, and is adjacent to the kitchen. The ballroom-size third floor features a king-size bed, a separate sitting area, a whirlpool bath, and a custom marble shower big enough for two.

An outdoor swimming pool makes a summer stay even more delightful. The ponds are stocked with bass and catfish, and the inn will supply a boat. $$$

richmond, mo

Located 11 miles north of Lexington on MO 13, Richmond touts itself as the "Mushroom Capital of the World." Time your trip so that it coincides with Richmond's annual mushroom festival the first weekend in May. This is when those hard-to-find morel mushrooms pop up, begging to be sautéed in butter and wine. The mushrooms are plentiful enough around here for a celebration in their honor. Richmond folks will sell you some morels to take back home, but they won't reveal their secret mushroom spots. If you want to go searching in the woods, you're on your own.

Fans of Jesse James lore come to Richmond to visit the grave of Robert Ford, the man who shot the outlaw in the back. Bob Ford and his brother Charley, who was in on the plan to shoot James, are buried in the Sunnyslope Cemetery. Also buried here is Joseph Smith, the founder and First Prophet of the Church of Jesus Christ of Latter-day Saints.

getting there

It will take about 30 minutes to reach Richmond from Excelsior Springs, but it is a pleasant 15-mile drive in the country along MO 10.

where to go

Richmond Chamber of Commerce. 104 N. Main St.; (816) 776-6919; richmondchamber .org.

The Farris Theatre. 301 W. Main St.; (816) 776-6684; farristheatre.com. Look closely at this structure and see if it reminds you of the Folly Theatre in downtown Kansas City. Originally built in 1901 as an opera house, the Farris was modeled after the Folly. The Farris Theatre has been fully restored for use as a performance theater, movie house, and community center by a not-for-profit group called Friends of the Farris. The Saturday morning cartoon series is a lot of fun for kids.

Of the Earth Farm + Distillery. 17190 Highway 13; (660) 232-1096; oftheearthfarm.com. You might have first found Of the Earth apple brandy at the City Market in downtown Kansas City, but now Jim and Sarah Pierce have a tasting room on the farm in Ray County. Come sample all of their fruit brandies, as well as gin, liqueurs, and other spirits, and enjoy the peaceful setting of the farm and orchard. Open Fri through Sun, 2 to 8 p.m.

Ray County Museum. 901 W. Royal St.; (816) 776-2305. This odd-looking Y-shaped building, constructed in 1910, was designed so that all 54 rooms would have lots of sunshine. It was first the county poor farm. Today, it is home to a number of artifacts that tell the story of this region, including Native American, Civil War, and Mormon history. It is open year-round, Wed through Sat, 10 a.m. to 4 p.m., and closed on holidays. Free.

United Methodist Church. 212 Main St.; (816) 776-2122. This lovely limestone church is remarkable for its 15 stained-glass windows of various sizes. But unique to a church in 1918 was the inclusion of an in-ground swimming pool and library, both open to the public. Although neither exists today, the public is welcome to visit anytime to see the windows and lovely woodwork rarely found in construction projects today.

where to eat

Branded Steakhouse, Oink & Moo BBQ & Taproom. 708 Wollard; (816) 776-6465. The fun and friendly restaurant is not going to disappoint, whatever your cravings. Good steak and BBQ are always available, but daily specials run the gamut from lobster bisque to lasagna to fried chicken and wings. Give these folks a try. They opened in the middle of the pandemic and there's no looking back. $$

day trip 03

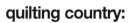

quilting country:
jamesport, mo; gallatin, mo; hamilton, mo

jamesport, mo

In Jamesport, the Amish community offers a glimpse into a lifestyle much different than what many of us live. The Amish who call the Jamesport area home are part of the Old Order Amish, who are direct descendants of the Mennonite Anabaptists, a group that developed during the Reformation in Germany and Switzerland. In the early 1950s, the Amish immigrated to Jamesport, now the largest settlement west of the Mississippi. Currently, about 2,200 Amish reside on the rich farmland of the area.

They shun the use of modern conveniences and travel by horse-drawn vehicles. Their peaceful lifestyle revolves around a close-knit family, their faith, and farming. They use no electricity, cars, televisions, radios, or Internet. Their education ends at the eighth grade. Many of the Amish farmhouses now have indoor plumbing, and most Amish families use oil furnaces, kerosene- or wood-burning stoves, and kerosene lamps.

Amish men are expert farmers who use plows pulled by horses to till their fields. They dress modestly in black broad-brimmed hats, white shirts, and black trousers.

The women excel in the home arts. They wear plain, long cotton dresses held together with pins (they consider buttons worldly). On their heads they wear white prayer caps at all times. Their conversation often lapses into something called "Ferhoodled English," a combination of German, Dutch, and English.

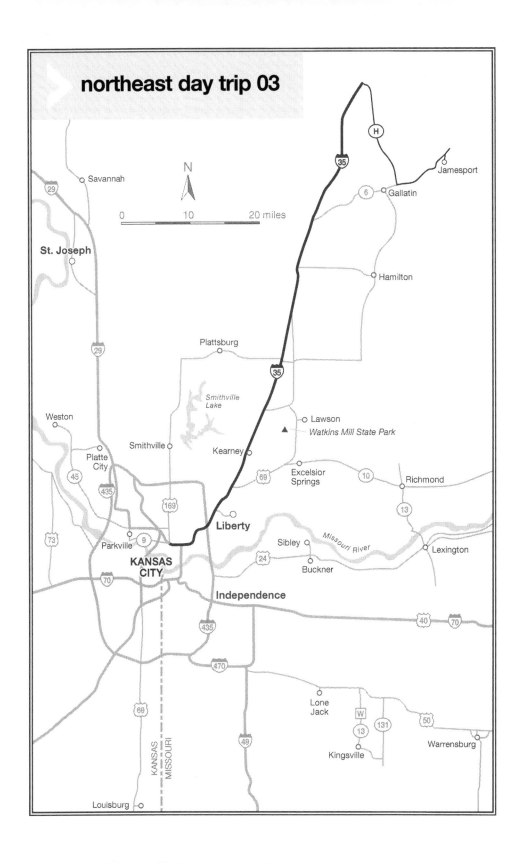

northeast day trip 03

Jamesport has prospered as a tourist attraction because of the Amish, and they, in their practical way, have taken advantage of public curiosity. The Amish typically do not want their pictures taken since it violates their religious beliefs. As a courtesy, ask permission before you shoot.

If you're looking for authentic Amish foods, goods, and services, be aware that "Amish style" does not necessarily mean that something is Amish made.

A visit to Jamesport can be fun if you tour it with the idea that there are two separate reasons for coming here. The first is to visit the Amish-owned stores, where you will find authentic Amish foods, quilts, and other items. The second reason is to enjoy the antique, craft, and specialty shops; restaurants; and bed-and-breakfasts, most of which are not Amish owned.

If you want to determine whether an establishment is Amish or Mennonite, check the days it is open; Amish shops close on Thursday and Sunday. If you like to preserve your own fruits and vegetables, plan your visit to Jamesport to coincide with the **Produce Auction.** The days of the week vary, depending on the growing season. Anyone can attend, but all produce is sold in larger quantities. Call for details at (660) 684-6844.

Many farm stores and related businesses are found along gravel country roads, and street addresses are ineffective for those locations. Therefore, pick up a free map of the area at any of the local businesses. Siri is of no help here.

For more information, contact the Jamesport Community Association, PO Box 215, Jamesport, MO 64648; (660) 684-6146; jamesportmissouri.org.

getting there

From downtown, take I-35 north about 75 miles to exit 84, which is Highway H. Turn right, heading east about eight miles. There will be lots of signs for Jamesport. Be alert to horse-drawn buggies.

where to shop

The Farmhouse Collection. 113 S. Broadway; (660) 684-6704; jamesport-farmhouse .com. Actually five buildings connected, this store has almost 9,000 square feet of home décor and handmade furniture. Come early in the day and you might catch the owners in the process of pouring hand-dipped candles, something they do every morning. You'll also find nice collections of handmade soaps and lotions here.

Homestead Creamery. East on County Road F, then south on County Road U; (660) 684-6970. This family dairy farm is picturesque in its own right, but come on Tuesday to witness the cheese-making process, directly from the milk from the Jersey cows in the adjacent pastures. Otherwise, bring a cooler to fill up from the gift shop. Closed Thurs and Sun.

Jamesport Country Store. Located two miles west on County Road NN; (660) 684-6664. You may need a map to find this place, but it's so worth it to get out on the country roads and see the Amish homes and farms. This Amish-owned store carries natural farm-raised meats, homemade goodies, and crafts. Open Mon, Wed, and Fri.

Pastime & Carlyle's. 100 Auberry Grove; (660) 684-6222. Early country furniture and decorative items, plus original painted furniture, are sold here along with old-fashioned candy and collectibles. You can also order custom-made furniture for your home. Closed Sun.

where to eat

Anna's Bake Shop. 1005 Old Hwy. 6; (660) 684-6810.This Amish shop is worth the drive to Jamesport just for the mouthwatering fresh-baked doughnuts, pies, breads, and cinnamon and dinner rolls. Closed Christmas through Feb 1 and the rest of the time when the day's goods are sold out. According to the owner, the phone works only "when the weather is above 20 degrees." $ (cash only)

Countryside Bakery. 21870 MO 190; (660) 684-6767. Leave room in your tummy and your car for some delicious, authentic Amish homemade baked goods. Or if you are inspired to do the baking yourself, you can choose from a number of cookie mixes already packaged for you. Closed Thurs and Sun. $ (cash only)

Gingerich Dutch Pantry. 107 Auberry Grove; (660) 684-6212; gingerichdutchpantry.com. Located at the four-way stop in downtown Jamesport, this Mennonite-owned restaurant specializes in Mennonite cooking using Old Dutch recipes. Homemade pies, breads, cinnamon rolls, and other baked goods are featured. However, on Monday evenings, the menu turns to Mexican dishes. Closed Sun. $

where to stay

Country Colonial Bed & Breakfast. 106 E. Main St.; (660) 684-6711; jamesport-mo.com/cc/. Sleep tight in an original pre–Civil War rope bed, the kind that instigated the term "sleep tight," in this three-bedroom inn that is filled with antiques throughout. But don't snuggle in too tightly before enjoying a moonlight, horse-drawn carriage ride through the Amish countryside. And don't sleep too late or you'll miss Nina den Hartog's fabulous cinnamon raisin French toast. $$

Marigolds Inn and Gift Shoppe. 305 W. Auberry Grove; (660) 684-6122. Located three blocks west of downtown Jamesport. If you like handmade quilts, you'll enjoy a stay in one of the 12 individually decorated rooms at Marigolds. Several have a garden theme; others have a western or bunkhouse look to them—all based on the bed coverings. And if you appreciate the craftsmanship of Amish carpenters, take a close look at the quality in this building constructed by local Amish. Breakfast is on your own, but with so many wonderful bakeries nearby, you won't go hungry. $

getting squirrelly in daviess county

*About halfway between Jamesport and Hamilton is the town of **Gallatin**, a nice little community with about 1,800 mostly nice people. Gallatin is often visited today because of the Daviess County Squirrel Cage Jail. Listed on the National Register of Historic Places, the jail was completed in 1889. It is an octagonal shape on the outside, but on the inside, the pie-shaped jail cells rotate on an axis, thus allowing only one cell to be at the door and opened at a time. The idea was to make breaking out or breaking in nearly impossible, but in case of fire or natural disasters or other emergencies, it was also impossible to get inmates out in a timely manner. It was one of the first jails in the country to have indoor plumbing and operated until 1975. A company out of St. Louis designed 18 similar jails, but only three remain in existence. One is in Council Bluffs, Iowa, the other in Crawfordsville, Indiana. The jail is located at 310 Jackson Street in Gallatin and you can drive by any time of the day or night for a look from the outside. For an interior tour, call ahead at (660) 663-7342.*

hamilton, mo

Fans of the globally popular Broadway musical *Hamilton* will be pleased to know that the town was named, in part, to honor Alexander Hamilton, the "ten dollar founding father," George Washington's "right-hand man," and the first treasury secretary of the United States.

Until 2008, sleepy little Hamilton was best known as the birthplace of retail giant J.C. Penney, who was born on a farm near here in 1875, one of 12 children. The high school in Hamilton is named for Penney, as is a quilt shop.

But for many people, Hamilton is now known as home to the largest quilting retailer in North America. The company is the Missouri Star Quilt Company, owned and operated by Jenny Doane, a popular YouTube personality who teaches you how to make a quilt in a day. She is considered the "world's most famous quilter," and the company's presence in the town of 1,600 cannot be missed. Among the many attractions is the world's largest spool of thread, some great murals, and many other shops and restaurants.

For information all events and other things to do in the Quilting Capital of the World, visit visithamiltonmo.com.

getting there

From Jamesport, head south on MO 6 ten miles to Gallatin, then south 14 miles on MO 13 to Hamilton.

where to go

J.C. Penney Birthplace and Museum. 312 N. Davis St.; (816) 583-2168. Opened in 1976, five years after James Cash Penney died in New York, this little museum is a result of a community effort to remember one of their own who had such an impact on retail shopping. Get a selfie with a life-size, well-dressed version of Penney. You'll see old cash registers from his stores, be able to sit in his office chair, and see an entertaining selection of advertising memorabilia and items sold in the first Penney's store. Two blocks away is the small, simple home where Penney was born and raised. Open Tues through Fri, 9 a.m. to 5 p.m.; Sat, 9 a.m. to noon.

Missouri Star Quilt Company. 114 N. Davis; (888) 571-1122; missouriquiltco.com. This is the anchor store, the first of 12 in Hamilton, of the Missouri Star Quilt Company. Each shop has a slightly different theme—florals, batiks, seasonal fabrics, kids and babies, and modern designs. Stroll through them all and let the colorful energy of the fabrics, the designs, and the interesting people convince you that quilting is your favorite hobby. Of course, you can buy finished quilts, but the joy is creating something unique for yourself and your loved ones. All of the shops are on and around the anchor store, within easy walking distance. Open Mon through Sat, 9 a.m. to 5 p.m.

Levi Garrison & Sons Brewing Co. 105 W. Bird; (816) 679-7596; lgsbrewingco.com. If someone local suggests you head to the Moose, they are referring to this place, which started its life as Ninja Moose Brewing. After a nasty trademark dispute, owner Scott Falley changed the name to Levi Garrison to honor his great-grandfather. While the craft beer is good, as is the weekend live music, many people come to this little craft brewery to see the building in which it is housed, which is the former AT&T building. Built in 1913, the owners saved many of the original features from back in the day when operators actually connected your phone call. Open Tues through Sat, noon to 8 p.m.

where to eat

Country Cabin Bake Shop & Chuckwagon Dinner. (816) 284-3556; countrycabinvillage.com. Four miles west of Hamilton on US 36. More than a place for super big muffins, cookies, cakes, and pies, the Country Cabin Bake Shop also serves a healthy selection of salads and sandwiches. The fried egg and grilled cheese sandwich, served on a croissant, is so good, as is the turkey cranberry wrap. But hang around on a Saturday night in warm weather months for a chuckwagon supper. Even though it's not really served from a chuck-wagon, it is an opportunity to enjoy an incredible chicken fried steak or a super thick pork chop with all of the fixins. You may choose to eat outside or in one of the three log cabins on the property. Sometimes there's live music and other entertainment. Call for reservations for the chuckwagon dinner. Open Tues through Sat, 8 a.m. to 4 p.m. $

east

day trip 01

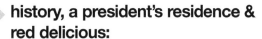

>>>

history, a president's residence & red delicious:
independence, mo; sibley, mo; lexington, mo; waverly, mo

independence, mo

Founded in 1827, Independence became known as the Queen City of the Trails, heading three dominant routes west—the Santa Fe, California, and Oregon trails. The Santa-Cali-Gon Festival, held annually on Labor Day weekend, commemorates the opening of these prairie pathways.

Fortunes were made here during the westward expansion and Victorian periods, and many of the charming homes built during these times have been designated with historic markers. Today, Independence is best known as the home of the 33rd president, Harry S. Truman. Places related to his life here include his home, courtroom, and office, as well as the Harry S. Truman Museum and Library.

Just a few blocks from the Harry S. Truman National Historic Site (Truman home) is Independence Square, filled with restaurants and shops housing arts, crafts, antiques, and memorabilia. It's fun to go exploring around a historic area that has a great past. Smack in the middle of the square is the Jackson County Courthouse. Built in 1836, it was renovated in 1933 during the administration of Jackson County Judge Harry S. Truman.

On the east side of the courthouse is a full-size statue of Harry himself. *The Man from Independence*, a multimedia show highlighting Truman's life before his presidency, is shown on the hour inside the courthouse.

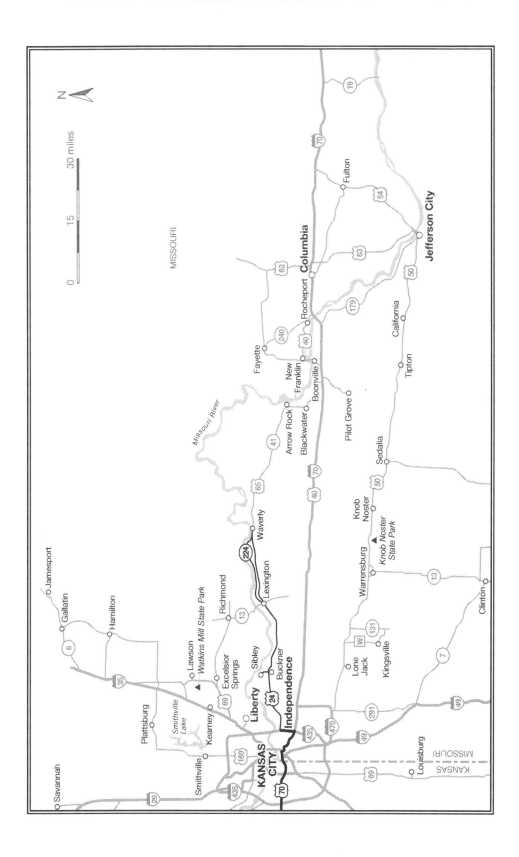

Independence has three walking trails for historically minded leisure walkers. The Swales Walking Trail at the Bingham-Waggoner Estate winds along a quarter-mile paved surface through the grounds, and nine interpretive signs focus on wagon ruts that follow the Santa Fe trade route west. The second trail begins in front of the Harry S. Truman National Historic Site Visitors Center. This 2.7-mile trail features 43 brass plaques embedded in the sidewalks throughout the Truman neighborhood. Finally, the Missouri Mormon Walking Trail begins on the corner of Walnut and River and explores the religious history of the Mormons, illustrated by 14 brass sidewalk markers at locations of significance in the early days of the church.

getting there

From downtown, take I-70 East to I-435 North and the Truman Road exit; then take Truman Road east to Independence.

where to go

Independence Tourism. 210 W. Truman Rd.; (816) 325-7890; visitindependence.com. Pick up brochures for the walking tours here, as well as the latest news in town. Or simply download the "Find Your Independence" app on your phone. Another option is to take a ride on the Truman Trolley between May and Sept. Independence has 26 electric car charging stations.

The Auditorium. 1001 W. Walnut St.; (816) 833-1000, ext. 3030; cofchrist.org. This is part of the world headquarters for the Community of Christ. The 6,000-seat chamber features a world-famous 111-rank, 6,334-pipe Aeolian-Skinner organ, one of the largest church organs in the nation. Guided tours and organ recitals are available daily upon request.

Bingham-Waggoner Estate. 313 W. Pacific Ave.; (816) 461-3491; bwestate.net. Built in 1855, this private home eventually became the residence of Missouri artist George Caleb Bingham, who lived here with his wife, Eliza, until 1870. In 1879, the home was purchased by Peter and William Waggoner, who remodeled the original structure. The house served as the Waggoner family home until 1976. The 26-room residence is open to tour from Apr 1 to Oct 31 and throughout the month of Dec. Admission fee. Stop in for some shopping at the Carriage House Boutique, Thurs through Sun. No sales tax in the boutique.

1859 Jail, Museum. 217 N. Main St.; (816) 252-1892. Four buildings constitute this museum operated by the Jackson County Historical Society. These include the jail that held the outlaw Frank James, the marshal's restored home, a one-room schoolhouse, and a county museum. Open daily Apr 1 to Oct 31 and in the month of Dec. The complex is closed in Nov and Jan through Mar. Ask about the paranormal tours. Admission fee.

George Owens Nature Park. 1601 S. Speck Rd.; (816) 325-7115; georgeownesna-turepark.org. This 85-acre gem of the Jackson County Parks system has two fishing lakes stocked with bass, channel cat, bluegill, and bullheads. A fishing license is required for people ages 15 through 64. There are four miles of nature trails for hiking, one of them wheelchair-accessible, as well as a nature center whose outdoor habitat is filled with live deer, bats, geese, and snakes. Open daily May 1 through Sept 30. Free.

Harry S. Truman Courtroom and Office. Independence Square Courthouse, Rm. 109, Main at Maple Street; (816) 252-7454. This is where the 33rd president of the United States began the political career that led him to the White House. You'll see Judge Truman's restored quarters and an audiovisual presentation about his life and courtship with Bess. Open Mon through Fri, 10 a.m. to 3:30 p.m. Admission fee.

Harry S. Truman Presidential Museum and Library. US 24 and Delaware Street; (816) 268-8200; trumanlibrary.org. One of 15 presidential libraries administered by the National Archives and Records Administration, this library houses exhibits and memorabilia of the Truman years, as well as a research facility. The Covid pandemic coincided with the museum and library being closed for a $25-million, two-year renovation. Visitors are now able to explore deeper into the time period that was Truman's life, from his days as a farm boy and haberdasher, to the steps that led him to the White House. Walk through the muddy trenches where Truman served in World War I, sit in the hot seat of a McCarthy-era communist inquiry, and climb into a C-54 cargo plane during the Berlin Airlift. Of course, Truman will forever be known as the president who dropped the atomic bomb. Try to put yourself in Truman's shoes to make that decision. The Thomas Hart Benton Mural no longer greets visitors upon entry, but it's still there, in a gallery focusing on "Truman's Independence." In 2018, the Truman Library became the recipient of several thousand items from the now defunct Korean War Veterans National Museum and Library in Springfield, Illinois. Those are now highlighted in a gallery devoted to the Korean War.

The graves of President and Mrs. Truman are located in the library's courtyard. Visit on May 8, Truman's birthday, for cake and other events. Open daily. Admission fee.

Harry S. Truman National Historic Site. 219 N. Delaware St.; (816) 254-2720; nps.gov/hstr. Located in the Harry S. Truman National Landmark District, this was the home of the former president and his wife, Bess Wallace Truman, until their deaths. Informative tours include a 12-minute slide show at the ticket center and a 15-minute tour of the residence. Individuals must reserve their tickets in person on a first-come, first-served basis on the day of the tour at the Truman Home Ticket and Information Center, 223 N. Main St., adjacent to Independence Square. Open daily Memorial Day through Labor Day. Closed Mon from Labor Day through Memorial Day. Admission fee.

Mormon Visitors' Center. 937 W. Walnut St.; (816) 836-3466. Operated by the Church of Jesus Christ of Latter-day Saints (Mormons). The high-tech exhibits document the doctrines of the church. Visitors enter through a covered wagon and see the daily life of the Saints portrayed in a log cabin. Open daily. Free.

National Frontier Trails Museum. 318 W. Pacific Ave.; (816) 325-7575; frontiertrailsmuseum.org. This acclaimed museum, library, and archival center is located at the principal jumping-off point of the Santa Fe, Oregon, and California trails. It is the only interpretive center in the nation devoted to all three trails. The gripping story of the exploration and settlement of the American West is shown in an award-winning introductory film that prepares visitors for their interesting trip through the museum's many exhibits, which feature memorabilia and relics from the prairie pathways. The two-story Chicago and Alton Depot, restored from the 1890s, is located on the grounds. Open Thurs through Sat. Admission fee.

The Temple. 201 S. River St.; (816) 833-1000, ext. 3030. This unusual architectural structure is part of the Community of Christ World Headquarters complex. It includes two visitor theaters, a lecture hall, and classrooms, plus a museum, a bookstore, a library, and a chapel with an adjacent meditation garden, along with administrative offices. Highlighting the building is a 1,600-seat sanctuary and a 102-rank, 5,686-pipe organ built by Casavant Frères Limitée of Quebec, Canada. Fashioned after the nautilus seashell, the 150-foot spire rises from the sanctuary and can be seen from many areas of the city. The public is invited to attend the programs dedicated to peace and reconciliation, along with a daily prayer for peace, offered in the temple sanctuary at 12:30 p.m. Public organ recitals are offered at 3 p.m. daily June through Aug and on Sun only the remainder of the year. Free.

Vaile Mansion–DeWitt Museum. 1500 N. Liberty St.; (816) 325-7111; vailemansion.org. One of the best examples of Victorian architecture in the United States, this 1882 mansion has a second-floor smoking room where woodwork is painted with dozens of little faces and animals. The home also has nine beautiful fireplaces and an indoor water tower. Open Thurs through Sat Apr 1 to Oct 31, when it closes for a month to decorate for the Christmas holidays. The home is open throughout Dec. Admission fee.

where to shop

Scandinavia Place. 209 N. Main St.; (816) 461-6633. Nina Anders's shop on the Independence Square is about as close as you can get to visiting Iceland without a passport. A native of Iceland, Nina has a mission, albeit a small one, to help others better understand and appreciate Scandinavian countries. In her little shop, you can buy rosette and almond cookies, Dala horses, lingonberry jam, and other goodies that speak to those northern countries. Find flags, storybooks, and holiday ornaments unique to Scandinavian cultures. Nina's shop is one of the few places in the Midwest that carry these specialty items. Open daily.

Wild About Harry. 104 W. Maple St.; (816) 252-0100; wildaboutharryind.com. Before dabbling in politics, Harry Truman operated a haberdashery in downtown Kansas City. Haberdashery is a word that's fallen out of favor in the English language, but it's basically a men's clothing and accessory store, and that's what Wild About Harry is, with a modern twist. Yes, you can find men's ties, but they are the line Ties That Don't Suck. There are some cool hats and backpacks made from recycled canvas tarps. You can find manly hand lotions, drink decanters, and all sorts of offbeat gift items for men and women. Closed Sun.

where to eat

Courthouse Exchange Restaurant and Lounge. 113 W. Lexington Ave.; (816) 252-0344. Located right across the street from the old courthouse, this restaurant has been serving up good Midwestern fare since 1899. Open for lunch and dinner, the Courthouse Exchange offers everything from prime rib to homemade cinnamon rolls. The tenderloin sandwiches here are famous. Closed Sun through Mon. $–$$

Ophelia's. 201 N. Main St.; (816) 461-4525; opheliasind.com. Located on historic Independence Square, this trendy restaurant offers American cuisine, with the highest-quality seafood, steaks, chops, and pastas available for lunch and dinner. Closed Sun through Mon. $–$$

where to stay

The Inn at Ophelia's. 201 N. Main St.; (816) 461-4525; opheliasind.com. Seven rooms and one suite afford the business or leisure traveler gracious accommodations, complete with private baths, voice messaging, modem capability, hotel amenities, and down comforters and pillows to make you feel at home. $$–$$$

Serendipity Bed and Breakfast. 116 S. Pleasant St.; (816) 833-4719; serendipitybedandbreakfast.com. Housed in an 1887 home, this bed-and-breakfast features antique furnishings along with Victorian children's books and toys, china figurines, glassware, and books for guests to peruse. The backyard garden provides a hammock and swing for peaceful relaxation. Accommodations include the carriage house, with king and twin beds, a kitchen, and a sitting room on the ground level, as well as two-room suites, one with a kitchenette. All six rooms have private baths. A full breakfast is served in the main dining room. The home also offers a Tour and Tea and antique car rides, weather permitting, for a fee. $–$$

Woodstock Inn Bed and Breakfast. 1212 W. Lexington Ave.; (816) 833-2233. Located near Independence's historic sites, this inn offers 10 rooms with private baths and 2 elegant suites. You can choose from king-, queen-, and double-bed accommodations that also include fireplaces and Jacuzzis. Breakfast is whatever you would like it to be, and many choose to enjoy it at tables outside in the flower garden. Lunch and dinner are available by request. $$–$$$

sibley, mo

Snuggled in on the banks of the Missouri River, Sibley is a great destination for fresh fruit and produce. The rolling hills and open farmland of eastern Jackson County are filled with orchards and gardens that provide everything from strawberries, peaches, and apples to asparagus, tomatoes, and green beans.

getting there

As you leave Independence, ignore I-70 and follow US 24 east, about an 18-mile drive that will take you about 30 minutes.

where to go

Fort Osage National Historic Landmark. 105 Osage St.; (816) 650-3278; fortosagenhs .com. When the Lewis and Clark expedition passed this bluff on the Missouri River in June 1804, William Clark noted in his journal that it would be a prime location for a military outpost. In 1808 he returned to supervise the building of this, the second outpost in the Louisiana Purchase. It operated as Fort Clark for several months but then became Fort Osage until it ceased operation in 1827. The fort is also a stop on the Santa Fe Trail. An impressive 15,000-square-foot visitor center explores the geology, flora, and fauna of the Missouri River basin, as well as the prehistoric Hopewell Indians and the namesake Osage Indians. A wide veranda filled with rocking chairs and benches provides wonderful views of the Missouri River and a place to contemplate this spot's role in American history. Open Tues through Sun year-round. Admission fee. The visitor center is wheelchair-accessible, but many of the buildings—to retain their authenticity—are not.

Sibley Orchards. 3717 Buckner-Tarnsey Rd.; (816) 650-5535; sibleyorchards.com. Located three blocks from historic Fort Osage, the orchard offers blackberries and peaches in summer, along with sweet corn, tomatoes, and other seasonal vegetables. Peaches and apples are sold here in July. In the fall, apples, apple cider, and pumpkins are available. For barbecue enthusiasts, you can buy applewood chips here to enhance the smoking flavor. Evening hayrides take visitors through the orchard. Open daily June through Nov.

lexington, mo

Lexington was once one of the great river ports of this state. River trade made it a fine commercial center and an outfitting point for those heading west. A US land office was established in 1823, followed by a courthouse, a bank, churches, colleges, and more than 120 lovely antebellum and Victorian homes and buildings. Lexington has four historic districts on the National Register of Historic Places. More than 120 antebellum and Victorian homes and buildings are listed on the register. The Vintage Homes Tour, held in September of odd-numbered years, allows the public a glimpse of the interiors of these elegant historic structures.

The cannonball embedded in one of the courthouse columns is a relic of the Confederate victory in the 1861 Battle of Lexington. The Anderson House, built in 1853 and located on the battlefield, was used as a field hospital and has been restored to its original elegance.

getting there

The historic town of Lexington can be reached by meandering along MO 224, which is a designated Missouri Scenic Byway. The 38-mile route follows the curves of the Missouri River and could take you an hour or more, depending on farm traffic at the time. Note: If the Missouri River has been out of its banks, the road will be closed or at least not very pretty as a result of the high water. A faster route is along US 24. It will take you about 30 minutes to drive the 24 miles.

where to go

Lexington Tourism Bureau. 927 Main St.; (660) 251-3270; visitlexingtonmo.com.

Battle of Lexington State Historic Site. Northwest edge of town on 13th Street; (660) 259-4654; mostateparks.com/lexington. Between September 18 and 20, 1861, Union forces suffered a major defeat when the pro–Southern Missouri State Guard, commanded by former Missouri governor Major General Sterling Price, led 12,000 men against the Union outpost at Lexington. The siege ended when the Union troops ran out of food, water, and ammunition. This is one of the few Civil War battlefields that has never been cultivated. Outlines of the trenches are still visible on the self-guided walking tour.

Also on the grounds is the Anderson House, which was used a field hospital during the Civil War. It was originally built in 1853 as a private home for Colonel Oliver Anderson. Battle damage is still visible inside and outside the home. There is a fee for guided tours of the home, but otherwise the state historic site is free. The visitor center is open daily and has a 15-minute film that explains why this has become known as the Battle of the Hemp Bales.

Lexington Historical Museum. 112 S. 13th St.; (660) 259-4711; visitlexingtonmo.com. Built originally as the Cumberland Presbyterian Church in 1846, the museum contains an extensive exhibit on the Pony Express, along with Civil War artifacts from the Battle of Lexington, a coal-mining display, and a fine collection of early Lexington photographs. Open daily during summer; other times by appointment only. Admission fee.

the williamsburg of the west

Lexington at times has been called the "Williamsburg of the West" because of its numerous historic homes and the dedicated efforts of the community to preserve the city's historic and cultural integrity. Early settlers built a performing arts school and three women's colleges to cultivate the finer elements of life.

A modern-era concert series known as "Live! in Lexington" brings renowned performers such as the Kansas City Symphony and the St. Louis Philharmonic to this small river town an hour east of downtown Kansas City.

Despite its early emphasis on culture, Main Street Lexington was once known as Block 42 because of the number of saloons that thrived here. It has been said that proper women and children never were seen on the sidewalks of Block 42, which is now home to lovely shops and restaurants that do indeed reflect the finer elements of life.

Madonna of the Trail. At the corner of Highland Avenue and Cliff Drive. This monument is one of 12 placed in every state crossed by the national Old Trails Road, the route of early settlers from Maryland to California. It honors the pioneer women who made the journey west.

Saluda Memorial at Heritage Park. (660) 259-4711. In 1852 the *Saluda* steamboat's boilers exploded while it was docked at Lexington, killing approximately 100 people. The people of Lexington responded, providing medical care and housing and in some cases, adopting the children of those adults killed in the accident. The memorial was dedicated in April 2002 on the 150th anniversary of the accident.

where to shop

Main Street Lexington is peppered with more than a dozen interesting boutiques, specialty shops, and quality antiques stores. Come with plenty of cash in your pocket or an extended limit on your credit card because it's almost impossible to go away with your vehicle empty. A couple choice suggestions:

Blackthorn Antiques. 115 Main St.; (660) 259-4231; blackthornantiques.com. Straight from many old homes, barns, and businesses in rural Missouri, you'll find lots of primitives, architectural salvage items, and odds and ends. The store has a lovely collection of lighting, fine art, and clocks. Open Tues through Sat.

River Reader Bookstore. 1010 Main St.; (660) 259-4996; river-reader.com. We love an independent bookstore, and this is one of just a handful remaining in Missouri. The River Reader promises you'll find titles here not available at those big guys. In addition, they have a lovely coffee and espresso bar. Open Tues through Sat.

The Purple Turnip. 1109 Main St.; (660) 232-4406. If you love the art of hooked rugs and would like to take a class, Maggie Bonanomi is the woman to see, and her shop here on Main Street is the place to be. The store is open by appointment or chance, so maybe call before you drive to Lexington.

where to eat

Maid-Rite. 1401 Main St.; (660) 259-444. While *Day Trips* is about taking people to places off the beaten path, this little Maid-Rite drive-in is worthy of inclusion simply for its longevity. Since 1946, the people of Lexington have been enjoying Maid-Rite's famous loose meat sandwiches and classic malts and milkshakes. It's quite possible that the sign or the building's exterior has not been refreshed since then, making it an antique, although not quite antebellum. Business continues to hum along, right in the shadow of a more modern set of golden arches. Closed Sun. $

The Spotted Pig. 1211 Franklin Ave.; (660) 259-7768. A place named The Spotted Pig makes you think barbeque, but not in Lexington. This pig is famous for all you can eat peal-and-eat shrimp. The pig also makes some good tacos on Thursday and prime rib, but no barbeque. Check the website for the schedule of live bands. This is a fun and lively local favorite where visitors fit right in. Open Mon through Sat, 11 a.m. to 1:30 a.m.; Sun, 11 a.m. to midnight. $

waverly, mo

US 24 is a Missouri Scenic Byway, and you'll understand why when you drive this road between Lexington and Marshall. The shades of gold from fields of soybeans readying for harvest, punctuated by the hearty reds and greens of apple orchards loaded for the season, are enough to make Monet's garden at Giverny tip its hat in appreciation. This road is also the beginning of the nearly 1,200-mile Santa Fe Trail, which ends in New Mexico. Find more at npw.gov/safe.

Along this roadway, you'll find nearly two dozen farms and orchards that sell everything from blackberries and asparagus to bedding and vegetable plants to Christmas trees. Many of these are you pick, so bring a bucket.

Situated right in the middle of this cornucopia is Waverly, where more than half of Missouri's apple crop is harvested each year. The Apple Jubilee each September features apple judging and apple eating, as well as entertainment, contests, and lots of family fun. Call the Waverly City Hall for details: (660) 493-2551.

getting there

A pleasant 20 miles away along US 24 is Waverly. It should take about 30 minutes to make the drive, unless you get behind a farmer moving equipment from one field to another. Be patient and enjoy.

where to go

Baltimore Bend Winery. 27150 US 24; (660) 493-0258; baltimorebend.com. Harvesting more than three tons of grapes in a season, this little vineyard has made a name for itself with Chardonnet, Cynthiana, and Cabernet grapes. (The Cynthiana, by the way, is the state grape of Missouri.) The tasting room is open seven days a week, Apr through Dec 31.

Five Oaks Christmas Tree Farm. Higginsville; (660) 584-8515; fiveoaksfarm.net. The easiest way to find this cut-your-own Christmas tree farm is to travel east on I-70 to the 49-mile marker and turn north on MO 13. Follow the signs. Open on weekends from Thanksgiving through Christmas. However, you can come early in November and tag your "Griswold Family Tree" to be cut later. The majority of the trees are Scotch and white pine with a few blue spruce. The Raucher family also has beehives on the farm, and this is one place you can buy raw honey on the comb or look for it in area grocery stores under the label Five Oaks Farm.

buried treasure in the missouri river

Most Kansas Citians are familiar with the Arabia Steamboat Museum in the River Market. It is the showplace for a steamboat that sank in the Missouri River near Parkville in 1856. The boat was discovered by the Hawley family of Kansas City, who recovered the contents in 1988. The Hawley family continued to research and explore the Missouri River for other sunken treasures. They have located what they believe to be another steamboat, which sank in 1841, in a farm field near Malta Bend.

Today, a historical marker in the small village of Malta Bend provides additional details. Malta Bend is nine miles east of Waverly on US 65.

As of press time in the spring of 2023, David Hawley has received permission from the landowner and is preparing to dig. Depending on when this occurs, it may be possible for visitors to watch from a distance. Otherwise, take a moment to reflect on the mighty Missouri at this point, how its path has altered over the years and what it must have been like to travel here in the days of steamboats.

Peters Orchards and Market. 32615 US 65; (660) 493-2368; petersmkt.com. Home-grown yellow and white peaches, as well as nectarines, abound here in season, along with delicious fruit butters and locally grown farm produce. Fall brings crops of Red and Golden Delicious apples, together with the popular Braeburn, Fuji, Granny Smith, and Stayman Winesap varieties. Peters holds a flea market in October that offers utility-grade apples at ridiculously low prices. The market carries a delicious selection of canned and baked goods, as well as locally harvested pecans and walnuts. Check the website for the ripening schedule, usually around July 1. That's when Peters opens seven days a week.

Schreiman Orchards. Located two miles west of Waverly on US 24; (660) 493-2477; schreimanorchards.com. This roadside market sells peaches in summer and apples in fall, along with homemade apple butter, raw honey, jams, jellies, applewood chips, cookbooks, and Amish-made foods. The Schreiman family has been in business here for almost 100 years. Open daily from mid-June through mid-Nov.

day trip 02

east

>>> **the katy trail corridor & boonslick country:**
blackwater, mo; arrow rock, mo; boonville,
mo; pilot grove, mo; new franklin, mo;
fayette, mo; rocheport, mo; columbia, mo

It's flat, free, and fun, and it snakes across Missouri for 240 miles from Clinton to 12 miles east of St. Charles. It's Missouri's Katy Trail, the longest rails-to-trails project in the United States. If you've never traveled the Katy Trail, you're missing some of the prettiest country in the Midwest. The Katy Trail can be traveled on foot, on horseback, or on two wheels. All along the way you can see glimpses of dense forests, wetlands, valleys, and rolling farm fields, and always the Missouri River is not far away. In spring there are flowering dogwood and redbud trees. Fall brings crimson colors of maple and sumac, along with an abundance of wildlife that includes woodpeckers, red-tailed hawks, waterfowl, deer, and other creatures.

The section of trail between Boonville and St. Charles has been designated an official segment of the Lewis and Clark National Historic Trail. The entire trail is part of the American Discovery Trail and Millennium Legacy Trail.

The Missouri-Kansas-Texas (MKT) Railroad, known as the Katy, ceased operation in 1986 and donated its right-of-way for the Katy Trail State Park. Almost all the Katy Trail towns have bike-rental shops, and most offer a selection of mountain bikes, tandems, and toddler trailers for a modest hourly cost.

Although the trail is mostly flat, with a grade that seldom reaches more than 5 percent, it is very possible to overextend yourself, especially on a hot Missouri summer day. For in-depth information on the Katy Trail State Park, get a copy of *The Katy Trail Guidebook* by Pebble Publishing (pebblepublishing.com). Otherwise, contact the Department of Natural Resources, (573) 449-7402; mostateparks/katytrail.

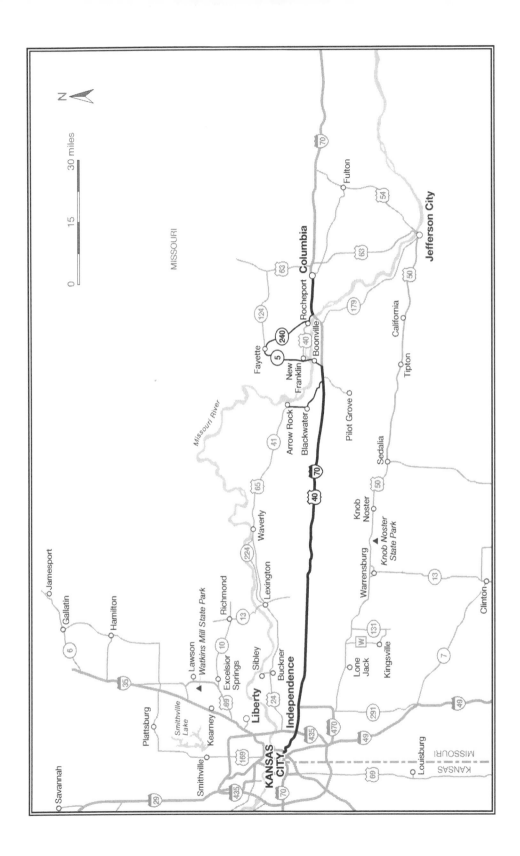

Much of the Katy Trail passes through the **Boonslick region,** which takes its name from a salt lick in southwestern Howard County that was worked, about 1805, by Nathan and Daniel Morgan Boone, sons of the famed pioneer and scout Daniel Boone.

The magic of the Boone name, plus the salt licks and fertile soil, drew early settlers to the area. There has been much speculation since that time as to why the e was left out of Boonslick. It may have been because then, as now, many people placed little importance on accurate spelling.

Boonslick Country is chock-full of history, for many of its towns brought politicians, land speculators, and entrepreneurs who later gained fame, such as painter George Caleb Bingham and frontier scout Kit Carson. Many of the gorgeous old homes in this area are listed on the National Register of Historic Places.

A fun drive through this region is a search for quilt barns. Nearly 60 old barns in Cooper, Saline, and Howard counties have colorful quilt patterns painted on them. Find a map and more information at boonslicktourism.org or call (660) 882-3967. You are encouraged to stop and take pictures, but remember that these barns are on private property so get your photos from the roadside.

blackwater, mo

This little town tucked along the tracks of the Missouri Pacific Railroad almost disappeared off the map until brothers Mark and Bobby Danner, who grew up in Blackwater, returned as adults and harnessed the energy that had been hovering just beneath the surface of dozens of the little town's residents.

In its heyday as a railroad town at the turn of the 20th century, the population was just 600, but it dropped dangerously low in the 1980s as the rural agricultural economy took its toll on small towns. Today, the little green highway sign on Highway K lists the population as 199, but the energy along Main Street today makes it feel more like 200 or more. An extraordinary number of flowers bloom in this little town where an April weekend is dedicated to flower and plant sales. Classic car shows fill the streets the second Saturday of each month May through Oct.

Just about the entire town is the two blocks of Main Street, where you'll find a couple of good-quality antiques and gift shops. For more information, visit blackwatermissouri.com.

getting there

From downtown, take I-70 east almost 100 miles to exit 89 for Arrow Rock and Blackwater. Follow Highway K about three miles and turn right into town.

where to go

Blackwater City Hall. 125 Main St.; (660) 846-4411; blackwatermo.com. Much of Blackwater is self-explanatory, but if you have any questions or just want to chitchat for a while, check in with Karen at City Hall. She'll have brochures about things to do in the community and the latest developments in town.

West End Theatre. 301 Doddridge St. (no phone). This is where the creative talents of Blackwater area residents are often on display with music, theater, poetry readings, and you name it. Visitors may appreciate the original stained-glass windows a bit more than the comfort of the original pews in this theater, located in a former church that dates to 1905. For a schedule of activities, check the city website or call City Hall at (660) 846-4411.

where to stay

Iron Horse Hotel. 101 Main St.; (660) 846-2011; ironhorsehotel.com. The original hotel that housed railroad workers from the 1880s, the Iron Horse is a focal point of the revitalization of the community. From the Katy Trail to the Marrakesh Express, each of the 10 rooms is named for a prominent railroad or rail route. Some rooms have fireplaces and televisions, but all have claw-foot bathtubs and a sense of authenticity to the period and community. The lunch and dinner menus are reflective of much larger communities and the culinary experiences the owners received while living in New Orleans. Open daily from May through Sept, then on weekends or when something is happening in town. $–$$

arrow rock, mo

As the state's first historic site, the Missouri River town of Arrow Rock is the western gateway to Boonslick Country. Founded in 1829, it was an important Santa Fe Trail rendezvous point and home of several distinguished Missourians, including three Missouri governors, painter George Caleb Bingham, and Dr. John Sappington, who pioneered the use of quinine for treating malaria.

On their epic expedition upriver in 1804, Lewis and Clark made note of the area, and later William Clark termed it a "handsome spot for a town." Just 25 years later, in 1829, a town was founded here. Indeed, Arrow Rock was then, as it is now, a beautiful place, and it has somehow retained its peaceful country character and managed to keep the look and feel of 19th-century America.

Once a bustling frontier village with a population of 1,000, it has 62 year-round residents today. The entire town is a National Historic Landmark. Each October during the annual Arrow Rock Craft Festival, that number increases as visitors come to enjoy historically authentic crafts interpreted in a period setting. The town hosts a variety of other events, including the Traditional Folk Music Festival in September and an antique show in May.

For information about driving and walking tours, call (660) 837-3231; arrowrock.org.

getting there

From Blackwater, go back to Highway K and follow it five more miles to MO 41, which will lead you right into Arrow Rock.

where to go

Arrow Rock State Historic Site Interpretive Center. 39521 Visitor Center Dr.; (660) 837-3330; mostateparks.com. This center is expansive not only in physical size but in the periods of history covered. Starting with the Osage and Missouri Indians through the Lewis and Clark expedition to the Civil War and finishing with issues of the 20th century, this facility provides a fascinating and in-depth interpretation of the region. From here, you can also sign up for guided tours of the village of Arrow Rock that take in the George Caleb Bingham Home (1837), the Saline County Courthouse (1839), the Sites Home (1875) and Gun Shop (1844), and the Print Shop (1868). Tours are conducted daily Memorial Day through Labor Day and weekends in spring and fall. Admission fee. The state site includes several picnic places, hiking trails, and a camping area on the limestone bluffs overlooking the Missouri River.

Arrow Rock Lyceum Theatre. 114 High St.; (660) 837-3311; lyceumtheatre.org. The Lyceum is Missouri's oldest professional regional theater and the only professional theater serving rural Missouri. Popular, professional summer theater is presented here in rotating repertory from May through Aug and into parts of Oct. Buy your tickets early because these shows do indeed sell out quickly. Admission fee.

Missouri River Bird Observatory. 406 Main; (660) 837-3888; mrbo.org. This organization is all about making central Missouri a great place for the birds and the bees and in so doing, getting humans outside more to appreciate the natural world. Sign up for classes and workshops in person or online. There are programs geared for children and adults to help with habitat restoration projects and more. Watch for festivals and other events sponsored by MRBO.

Sappington African American Cemetery State Historic Site. (660) 837-3330; mostateparks.com. Head south out of Arrow Rock on County Road TT for six miles. Turn left on County Road AA. Travel less than one mile. Look for signs. Added to Missouri's list of State Historic Sites in 2021, the Sappington African American Cemetery dates to 1856 when the enslaved people of Dr. John Sappington were buried here in unmarked graves. The cemetery continued to be used after emancipation by generations of Black Americans whose family had history in this area. Jazz musician James C. Van Buren was buried here in 2012. Take time to read the interpretive panels and reflect on the contributions these people made to Arrow Rock. Open 24/7. Free.

where to shop

Many Arrow Rock merchants and businesses operate seasonally with hours that are frequently subject to change. It's always best to call ahead to the Arrow Rock Area Merchants Association, (660) 837-3352; arrowrock.org.

Arrow Rock Antiques. Main Street; (660) 837-3333. This shop features period furniture and needlepoint. Open weekends or by appointment.

Arrow Rock Craft Shop. Main Street (in the Masonic Lodge Building); (660) 784-2441. Wood and fabric artwork, clothing, quilts, china, jewelry, and toys are offered here, plus breads, plants, confections, and seasonal produce. Open daily May through Oct and weekends only Dec and Apr.

Bucksnort Trading Company. (660) 837-3324. Those who participate in period reenactments know of Bucksnort, formerly located in Blackwater. Here you can find 19th-century clothing and patterns, as well as authentic Native American pottery, jewelry, and artifacts. Part museum, part mercantile, this place is an experience in itself. Open Thurs through Sat, June through Oct.

where to eat

Catalpa. 500 High St.; (660) 837-3324. Liz Huff has a history of creating a gourmet dining experience in other area restaurants, and she does it again here with steaks, seafood, and fowl. Catalpa is open only on weekends and nights the Lyceum performs, so call ahead. $$

J. Huston's Tavern. Main Street; (660) 837-3200; hustontavern.com. Built in 1834, this is believed to be the oldest continuously operating restaurant west of the Mississippi. The tavern continues to serve the public as it served those who drove their wagons over the Santa Fe Trail. The fare includes catfish, country ham, and fried chicken. Huston's is always open for lunch and dinner on weekends, but hours vary during the week and off-seasons, so call ahead. Reservations are recommended the nights the Lyceum Theatre is hosting a performance. $$

where to stay

Borgman's Bed & Breakfast. 706 Van Buren; (660) 837-3350. This 1850s-era home offers four rooms and three shared baths. A family-style breakfast is served in the kitchen and features the owner's home-baked items. You'll love the cinnamon rolls. Open year-round; no cards. $

Flint Creek Inn. 507 Seventh St.; (660) 837-3352; flintcreekinn.com. Located on the banks of the Flint Creek, this modern inn is filled with artwork from communities all along the Santa Fe Trail. It's also filled with wonderful aromas coming from the in-house bakery. Each of the five rooms has large windows, great for bird-watching along the creek. As a result, each room is named for a bird. $$

boonville, mo

Settled in 1810, Boonville is the oldest surviving town on the Missouri River. The town still exhibits the cultural mix of original Southern settlers along with the influx of German immigrants who settled here in the mid-19th century. Boonville's many restored historic buildings, restaurants, and bed-and-breakfasts make this a place worth visiting.

Boonville is also the county seat of Cooper County and the site of the first Civil War battle fought in Missouri (June 1861).

Boonville was a town that made the transition from being a major river port to a booming railroad town. Many remnants of this era can still be seen, including the restored MKT depot.

Named for Daniel Boone (as was the Boonslick region), Boonville prospered during the late 1820s. German immigrants arrived 10 years later, and the river trade and Santa Fe Trail activity were the economic forces that sustained the town. The advent of railroads and the resulting confusion from the Civil War engagements fought in and around Boonville slowed the city's growth. Boonville today remains an important local center for transportation, tourism, and agribusiness.

Boonville has more than 450 sites and structures listed on the National Register of Historic Places.

getting there

Boonville is the next exit, just three miles east on I-70 from Arrow Rock.

where to go

Boonville Area Chamber of Commerce. Katy Depot, 320 First St.; (660) 882-2721; boonvillemochamber.com. The restored 1912 depot houses the Katy Trail offices and the Boonville Chamber of Commerce. Katy Trail gift items are sold here.

Friends of Historic Boonville. 614 E. Morgan; (660) 882-7977; friendsofhistoricboonville .org. Pick up brochures for self-guided tours of the area and other information about the Boonslick region.

Boonville Visitors Center and Museum. 100 E. Spring St.; (660) 882-3967; goboonville. com. Located in a historic old warehouse, this museum includes a half-scale model of the Lewis and Clark keelboat that passed this way in 1804, as well as other exhibits about the river and railroad history that made Boonville what it is.

Cooper County Jail Museum, Jailers Residence, and Hanging Barn. Friends of Historic Boonville, 614 E. Morgan; (660) 882-7977. Built in 1848, this was the oldest continuously used county jail in Missouri until it closed in 1978. The last public hanging took place here in 1930, when a man named Lawrence Mabry was executed for a robbery and murder in Pettis County. This hanging was a factor in the elimination of capital punishment in Cooper County. The most famous prisoner held here was Frank James, brother of Jesse James. He was brought here on April 24, 1884, to answer a warrant for his arrest for a train robbery (what else?) that took place in 1876. Sympathetic citizens of Boonville raised his bond in a matter of hours, and the case was later dismissed for lack of evidence. Open daily. Admission fee.

Katy Trail State Park. Cooper County trailheads in Boonville, Clifton City, and Pilot Grove; (800) 334-6946; mostateparks.com. As the trail heads east from Boonville, travelers experience some of the prettiest country in Missouri and are on an official part of the Lewis and Clark National Historic Trail because of its close proximity to the Missouri River. Heading west from these trailheads, the trail begins to move through open prairie away from the river.

Mitchell Antique Motor Car Museum. 100 E. Spring St.; (660) 882-3967; mitchellcarcollection.com. Unless you are a motorhead, most people are not familiar with the line of stylish "touring cars" created by the Mitchell-Lewis Motor Company of Wisconsin. They were in business from 1900–1924 and made motorcycles, bicycles, and wagons. The owner of this museum, Lewis Mitchell, is a descendant of those founders. His collection is considered the largest in the country. Tours by appointment only.

Roslyn Heights. 821 Main St.; (660) 882-5320. This 1894 Queen Anne home features Romanesque Revival structures, towers, turrets, gable dormers, and a porte cochere with Moorish decorative elements. Paneled front doors open from the front porch into a reception hall, and the entrance hall's original tile floor is intact. The house is graced by a geometrically designed stairway with motifs that illustrate the use of machinery during the Industrial Revolution. The parlor features a hand-painted ceiling and mahogany fireplace mantel. Tours by appointment only. Admission fee.

Starr Pines Christmas Tree Farm. 21298 Pleasant Hill Rd.; (660) 882-6858; starpines. com. This 200-acre Christmas tree farm is open seasonally, beginning in November. It's a wonderful day trip to play with farm animals, pick out a tree and gifts in the barn, and sip some hot cider. A favorite in the gift shop is locally produced honey and fresh farm eggs, both a necessity for your holiday baking and gift giving.

Thespian Hall. Main and Vine Streets; (660) 882-7977; friendsofhistoricboonville.org. This restored Greek Revival opera house, built in 1857, is owned and managed by the Friends of Historic Boonville. It is the oldest theater still in use west of the Alleghenies and is on the National Register of Historic Places. If you can, time your visit to coincide with one of the music festivals held here. The Missouri River Festival of the Arts in August brings in fine performers, ranging from symphony orchestras and ballet companies to jazz, pop, and the-ater groups. The Big Muddy Folk Festival in April plays host to local and national musicians. Tours are available by appointment.

Warm Springs Ranch. 25270 MO 98; (888) 972-5933; warmspringsranch.com. This is a second home and breeding facility for the famous Anheuser Busch Clydesdales. About 100 horses enjoy the spacious pastures and rural living between Boonville and Rocheport. Tours are offered daily Apr through Oct except Wed and include the stables, pastures, fancy-schmancy trailers, and an up-close-and-personal photo op with those massive horses. Reservations are required. If you're looking for a memorable gift opportunity, check out the behind-the-scenes packages. Admission fee.

where to eat

Derailed Coffee Bar and Café. 104 W. Spring St.; (660) 672-1358; derailedcoffee.com. Just steps from the Katy Trail, the bright red building is more than just a coffee shop. It's an eclectic space that begs for you to sit and chat while enjoying rich coffee from around the world and yummy breakfast and lunch dishes. From granola to burritos for breakfast to pulled pork tacos and caprese salads for lunch, you'll enjoy your time here getting to know the Boonville community. $

The Fred. 501 High St., inside the Hotel Frederick; (660) 882-8282. The setting and the menu complement each other at The Fred. Your basic bacon cheeseburger and apple bacon sliders speak to the simplicity of this mid-Missouri location, but the goat cheese lasa-gna and portobello ravioli remind you that mid-Missouri takes a back seat to no one when it comes to good food. The wine list includes many local labels, but also an impressive selec-tion of those from around the world. Dinner only. Closed Sun through Mon. $–$$

where to stay

Boonville Luxury Lodging. 519 High St.; (660) 888-2425; boonvilleluxurylodging.com. Eight rooms in three adjoining historic buildings showcase the history and opulence of Boon-ville 150 years ago while providing a relaxing and refreshing getaway. Choose from a French cottage, a classic Victorian, or a Grand Victorian manor. A breakfast buffet and afternoon cocktail hour allow for opportunities to ask questions of the owners who have brought these spaces back to life. $$

Hotel Frederick. 501 High St.; (660) 882-2828; hotelfrederick.com. With a fabulous perch above the Missouri River, the Hotel Frederick has been welcoming guests since 1905. But after some less than glorious days, the hotel was renovated and reopened in glorious style in July 2007. The 30 guest rooms today are decorated as they would have been 100 years ago, but with modern and comfortable amenities such as towel warmers, freshly pressed bed linens, and complimentary wireless Internet. The designer soaps are by Indigo Wild in

Kansas City, and the classic bathroom dividers are by Kansas City glass artists Bill Drummond and Peregrine Honig. Many of the lobby antiques are original to the hotel. Ask the front desk about the bicycles on loan to explore the Katy Trail. A continental breakfast is included, but enjoy a full lunch or an evening meal at The Fred. $$–$$$

pilot grove, mo

As you head south from I-70 toward Pilot Grove, be alert to the lovely farmsteads and particularly the barns. Here you'll find a number of quilt barns that dot Cooper, Saltine, and Howard counties.

where to go

Cooper County Historical Society. 111 Roe St.; (660) 834-3582; coopercountyhistorical-society.org. Among the great stories told here is that of Hannah Cole, who in 1810, crossed the Missouri River with her nine children and built a cabin on the site of what is now Boonville. Learn about the Civilian Conservation Corps work camp in Pilot Grove during the Great Depression and the day Pilot Grove was nearly blown off the map. The historical society has an impressive collection of genealogy material if you think you have relatives from this region. Call ahead to determine open hours.

Katy Trail Trailhead. From Pilot Grove to Boonville is considered the toughest 11 miles on the statewide trail because of the uphill grade. But it's worth it here to ride across I-70, the only overhead crossing on the trail. And the vistas of the Missouri River and rolling countryside make the effort all worth it.

Pleasant Green. 7045 MO 135, Pilot Grove; (660) 834-3945. Located nine miles south of Pilot Grove, this Federal-style brick mansion is built of handmade bricks and native stone. It was begun as a one-room house, with additions added from the 1830s through the 1870s, and was once a plantation of 2,500 acres. Settled by Winston and Polly Walker of Virginia in 1818, it survived Civil War raids and years of neglect. Many original furnishings are part of the home, and the facade has been returned to its 1877 appearance. The home is listed on the National Register of Historic Places and includes outbuildings that feature an old hexagonal barn, a curing shed, and restored living space for enslaved people who worked this plantation. The 1870 Pleasant Green Post Office building was moved here to serve as a mini-gallery for local artists. The home is open to tour by appointment. Guides in antebellum dress serve coffee or tea in the dining room by advance request. Admission fee.

where to eat

Katarina's Homestyle Café. 208 College St.; (660) 834-4000. If you're traveling I-70 and it's near lunchtime, pull off at the Pilot Grove exit and head south to Pilot Grove. This little town has the best restaurant ever, known especially for its eclectic selection of homemade pies, cobblers, and cakes. Open for lunch only Mon through Sat. $

new franklin, mo

Like many communities that developed on the banks of a major waterway, New Franklin has flooded and moved to higher ground over the years as the mighty Missouri has changed its course. Although many people today consider Independence the beginning of the Santa Fe Trail, it was first New Franklin, before the town underwent many of its floods and relocations. Look for the Santa Fe Trail Monument where the Katy Trail crosses Route 5 and the kiosks on Broadway that tell the history of the Santa Fe Trail.

Today a sleepy little town on the north banks of the Missouri River, New Franklin has made some great contributions to state history and beyond. For example, the composer of *The Missouri Waltz*, the state's official song, Edgar Settles, was born in and is now buried in New Franklin. Of more modern interest, country music singer Sara Evans, also calls New Franklin home.

getting there

New Franklin is three miles north of Boonville on MO 5.

where to go

New Franklin City Hall. 130 E. Broadway; (660) 848-2288; newfranklinmo.org. Here you'll find brochures about the community.

Boone's Lick State Historic Site. Located eight miles northwest of New Franklin, near Boonesboro; (660) 837-3330; mostateparks.com. Take MO 87 west from the northern approach to the Missouri River Bridge on MO 5 to MO 187, about one mile north of Boonesboro. Continue two miles west to the site of the salt springs, worked by the sons of Daniel Boone beginning around 1805. The year before, Captains Meriwether Lewis and William Clark noted this area and its potential for development in their journals. The state of Missouri has a kiosk here with information about the Boonslick region and the salt springs. A trail with informational signs winds through the woods by the remnants of the saltworks, and there's a shelter house with picnic tables, as well as public restrooms. Free. Artifacts from the industry are displayed at the Arrow Rock State Historic Site.

where to stay

Katy Roundhouse. 1893 Katy Dr. (Katy Trail Mile Marker 189); (660) 848-2232; katyroundhousecamping.weebly.com/. Located on the grounds of a century-old, restored train depot, the Katy Roundhouse stands on the site of the former MKT Railroad switching yard. The area offers a full-service campground with spacious, secluded campsites for tent camping, including picnic tables, fire rings, and bike racks. In addition, there are full RV hookups, modern shower facilities, and public restrooms. For whatever reason, the GPS on most phones does not recognize the address. Find directions on the website instead. $

Rivercene Bed and Breakfast. 127 County Rd. 463; (660) 848-2497. Listed on the National Register of Historic Places, this 15-room mansion was built by Captain Joseph Kinney. The riverboat baron began construction in 1864 on the floodplain, leading locals to call the structure Kinney's Folly. Kinney was undaunted. Finding the highest flood point, he built the house one foot higher. Of course, he hadn't counted on the Great Flood of 1993, when four feet of water flooded the living room and Rivercene was accessible only by boat.

The home is a fully restored mansion, incorporating the splendor of Kinney's original architectural masterpiece. It has Italian marble for the nine fireplaces, black walnut for the front doors, and a hand-carved mahogany staircase. A few years after Kinney completed Rivercene, the architectural plan was duplicated for the present Governor's Mansion in Jefferson City. Each room has queen-size beds and private baths, or you can take your choice of a two-room suite or a room with a whirlpool. A delicious breakfast is served in the large dining room. $$–$$$

fayette, mo

Fayette is the seat of Howard County; thus the town is centered around the lovely 1900s-era courthouse. The delightful tradition of a town crier "crying" the results on election night still occurs on these courthouse stairs. The Fayette Cornet Band plays on the grounds most Thursday nights in the summer. Two city lakes with campgrounds and picnic areas make for a lovely stay.

getting there

From New Franklin, travel 11 miles north on MO 5 to Fayette, the home of Central Methodist University.

where to go

Fayette City Hall. 117 Main St.; (660) 248-5246; cityoffayettemo.com. Stop by City Hall for information on special events and other attractions in the area.

The Ashby-Hodge Gallery of American Art. On the campus of Central Methodist University, 411 Central Methodist Sq.; (660) 246-6324; centralmethodist.edu. Opened in 1993, the Ashby-Hodge Gallery holds a special collection of oil paintings, lithographs, watercolors, bronzes, graphite drawings, and acrylics representing the work of American regional artists. The gallery holds rare pieces by Swedish-born artist Birger Sandzén, lithographs by Jackson

Lee Nesbitt, an ink and wash by Thomas Hart Benton, a rare egg tempera on panel by Charles Banks Wilson, and many other interesting pieces. This little gem of a place also features special exhibits throughout the year, often bringing in the artists themselves to greet guests at gallery openings. Open Sun through Thurs afternoons. Free.

Morrison Observatory. Located on Park Road across from Fayette City Park; (660) 248-6383; centralmethodist.edu. Dating to 1875, this observatory still has its original lens and is the oldest observatory west of the Mississippi. Although it is now owned and operated by Central Methodist University, it was first built in nearby Glasgow for Pritchard College. The observatory is not open for regular hours, but opens to the public a few evenings each spring and fall or when some interesting astronomical occurrence is expected. Free.

where to eat

Emmet's Kitchen and Tap. 111 Main St.; (660) 248-3363; emmetskitchenandtap.com. People in these parts know that authentic Cajun food and a good time can be found at this hot spot on the square in Fayette. The shrimp po'boy and bourbon pecan pie are direct from Louisiana, but the Kansas City strip steak and double-smoked pork chop remind you that good food comes from the Midwest as well. The wine list is impressive. Check the Facebook page for the monthly "Chef's Table" special. Open daily for lunch, Mon through Sat for dinner. $$

Miknan's Main Street Pub. 107 N. Main St.; (660) 248-9911. Known for their burgers, Miknan's also pulls together a mean buffalo Philly steak sandwich and prime rib sandwich. Try them with fried spicy green beans. Open daily for lunch and dinner. $$

rocheport, mo

The town is a perfect romantic getaway close to home, yet it also offers Katy Trail access for family outings. Boutique shops, an art gallery, cafes, a winery and bistro with a panoramic river-bluff view, and superior bed-and-breakfasts are part of its charm. Each summer the town's population swells from 225 persons to as many as 30,000 visitors, many of whom are Katy Trail travelers.

Located on the Missouri River, Rocheport was founded in 1825 and grew rapidly as steamboat transportation brought business to town. In 1849, 57 steamboats made 500 landings at Rocheport. Nine years earlier the Whig Party held its convention in Rocheport and thousands of delegates arrived by carriage, wagon, steamboat, and horseback to support William Henry Harrison's presidential campaign.

Rocheport has survived disasters, including the Civil War and the Great Flood of 1993, when the 243-foot-long MKT Railroad tunnel, built in 1893, was filled with four feet of water.

Rocheport also affords one of the most beautiful views along the Katy Trail, parts of which wind along the river under the spectacular Moniteau Bluffs.

Rocheport is on the National Register of Historic Places, and many of its residents live and work in restored 19th-century homes and buildings.

For more information on Rocheport, visit rocheport-mo.com.

getting there

From Fayette, drop south on MO 240 just 12 miles into Rocheport. From New Franklin you can head east on US 40 to Route BB or head east from Boonville on I-70 to the Rocheport exit.

where to go

Rocheport General Store. 202 Central St.; (573) 698-2282; rocheportgeneralstore.com. More of a cafe and coffee shop than a true country store, this is the scene of a number of special events in Rocheport. From live music on weekends to a street bowling competition on St. Patrick's Day, the good times originate at the Rocheport General Store. But yes, you can buy sundries here along with souvenirs and a nice sandwich, ice cream, or coffee. There's live music on occasion. Closed Mon and Tues.

Meriwether's Cafe and Bike Shop. 700 First St.; (573) 698-1222; meriwethercafeandbikeshop.com. From Katy Trail mile marker 179, you can literally pedal into the parking lot of Meriwether's. This nice little operation began as a small sandwich shop and eventually expanded into a dining room with an adjacent bike shop. The cafe is noted for its excellent breakfasts and locally sourced foods, plus fresh homemade baked goods. Fresh fruit and grilled portobello mushroom sandwiches are on the healthy side of the menu. Named for Meriwether Lewis of Lewis and Clark Trail fame, this has a wonderful patio where many choose to enjoy ice cream or just a big bottle of water and trail mix. You can buy or rent bikes here, or if yours has a problem, get it repaired. Child carts, tandems, and mountain bikes can be rented by the hour or by the day. Closed Wed.

where to shop

Lookout Farm. 13601 W. Highway BB; (573) 821-6699; lavenderlookout.com. One of just a handful of lavender farms in Missouri, this one comes with five varieties of lavender. Operated by sisters Kelly and Kimi, they encourage you to plan your visit in June because that's when the lavender is in bloom. Located on a bluff overlooking the lavender fields, this is a spectacular setting for Mother Nature to show off her good stuff. In addition to great lavender products, it's a great place for family or engagement photos. Call ahead for permission. Open seasonally, but you can always order online or visit their stall at the Columbia Farmers Market.

Stockton Mercantile. 204 Central St.; (573) 698-4580; stocktonmercantile.com. This fun old building is all about creaky floors and tucked away spaces, all filled with interesting treasures for your home and for yourself. Oh, sure, buy something for a friend while you're here. You'll also find a few antiques tucked in among the modern treasures, as well as repurposed goodies. If you've been to Rocheport before, you may remember this as Granny's. It's still the same family. Diane Dunn is now the third generation of her family to own this store. Hours vary, but Stockton Mercantile is usually open seven days a week.

where to eat

Les Bourgeois Vineyards, Winery, and Bistro. 14020 W. Hwy. BB (one mile north of I-70 on Route BB); (573) 698-2300; missouriwine.com. This unique restaurant and winery makes a great place to unwind and enjoy a spectacular sunset from atop a river bluff. The land here offers rich soil and a microclimate that is ideal for grape production. Les Bourgeois produces red, white, and blush table wines from French hybrid grapes and native cultivars. The restaurant offers an outdoor wine garden and indoor dining featuring a variety of nicely prepared fish, chicken, and steak dinners, plus great desserts. $$–$$$

where to stay

Katy Trail Bed and Bikefest. 101 Lewis St.; (573) 698-2453; katytrailbb.com. This modest Victorian home was built in 1880 and is on the National Register of Historic Places. The Katy offers four rooms, including a converted railroad boxcar in the backyard that sleeps up to five and has a private bath, refrigerator, and cable television. The upstairs of the main house offers a family suite with a private bath, queen-size bed, and futon. There is a smaller bedroom downstairs with one double bed. Above the garage is a large rustic room with two beds and a sleeper sofa, which serves as a bunkhouse for cost-conscious travelers. $

Mount Nebo Inn. 801 First St.; (573) 881-6160; mountneboinn.com. This lovely inn has two large suites as well a large outdoor patio if you want to gather with friends staying in other parts of Rocheport. Would you like to get out on the Missouri River to feel the power of the mighty Mo? Ask Matthew about his guide services, which include bird-watching and sunset wine cruises. $$$

Schoolhouse Bed and Breakfast. Third and Clark Streets; (573) 698-2022; schoolhouse-bandb.com. Touted as one of the country's top 10 romantic inns, the Schoolhouse has been the subject of greeting cards and magazine articles. Large, framed prints of the famous Dick and Jane primer grace the walls of this former schoolhouse. Elegantly refurbished, it offers 10 bedrooms with private baths, two of which have a "sweetheart" Jacuzzi. Each of the guest rooms is decorated in beautiful antiques. An upstairs dining room offers a full breakfast of coffee, fresh fruit compote, baked bread or muffins, and egg strata. Two nearby properties are self-service lodging for larger groups. $$–$$$

columbia, mo

You don't have to be a college student to enjoy yourself in Columbia, though it is home to the University of Missouri, Stephens College, and Columbia College. On any given summer night, you can listen to live jazz and blues outdoors or catch a concert by noted artists at the Blue Note, one of the best live-entertainment venues in the state.

If you're looking for one-of-a-kind finds, visit downtown Columbia's shops, which sell everything from handmade Brazilian tables, regional art, and rare books to items that reflect social, political, and environmental issues. Several youthful restaurateurs have taken it upon themselves to impart fresh and vigorous menus that have boosted the city's image as a restaurant town. Competition has spurred the upgrading of menus and ambience to keep pace with demand.

Columbia is a very bike-friendly town with nearly 200 miles of bike paths, marked bike lanes, and abundant bike parking. And of course, it connects to the Katy Trail. Downtown Columbia has 44 electric car charging stations.

getting there

From Rocheport, return to I-70 and travel just 10 miles east to Columbia.

where to go

African American Heritage Trail. A two-mile walking tour of central Columbia showcases the "other Columbia," a 30-square-block area north of Broadway once known as Sharp's End. Completed in 2020, the trail includes 20 markers as well as the home of "Blind" Boone, the renowned musician and composer who called central Missouri home. Pick up a trail map at the Columbia Regional Economic Development offices at 500 E. Walnut. Free.

Columbia Convention and Visitors Bureau. 300 S. Providence Rd.; (573) 874-2489; visitcolumbiamo.com. The office is located just across the street from Flat Branch Park and the MKT Trailhead, so as you pick up your brochures and get your questions answered, you may study your options in a beautiful outdoor setting.

The Blue Note. 17 N. Ninth St.; (573) 874-1944; thebluenote.com. Since 1980, one of central Missouri's best live-entertainment venues has been located in this restored vaudeville theater that features renowned blues, reggae, rock, and folk artists. This is also the performance venue for the Como Comedy Club, as well as the True/False Film Festival and other events.

Columbia College. 1001 Rogers St.; (800) 231-2391; ccis.edu. This was the first institution of higher education for women chartered by a state legislature west of the Mississippi River. Founded in 1851, the coeducational school is located on 26 acres in the midst of the city.

Day trippers may enjoy checking out the student and local work featured in the Sid Larson Gallery.

MKT Trail. Fourth and Cherry Streets (downtown) to Scott Boulevard (Route TT); (573) 874-7460. Walk, jog, or bike on this 8.9-mile wheelchair-accessible trail, which varies from an urban walkway to a densely wooded passageway. Parking is available at Stadium, Forum, and Scott Boulevard accesses. The MKT is Columbia's spur connection to the Katy Trail. The Martin Luther King Jr. outdoor amphitheater is located at the Stadium access.

Rock Bridge Memorial State Park. 5901 S. MO 163; (573) 449-7402; mostateparks .com. This 2,273-acre park takes its name from the area where a stream flows beneath a natural rock bridge formation. The park offers hiking trails, picnic areas, and a wilderness discovery area in both wooded areas and restored prairies. But the park is best known for the Devil's Icebox Cave, the sixth-longest cave in Missouri, with more than six miles of passages.

You'll get to stoop, squat, crawl, and climb through teeny, tiny passages that can be rather confining, paddle and portage canoes, and hang out with a colony of gray bats. Call the park office to arrange a tour. The park is free; fee for cave tour. Open daily.

Shelter Gardens. 1817 W. Broadway; (573) 214-4715; shelterinsurance.com. This company has an award-winning, five-acre garden in the heart of town, with more than 300 varieties of trees and shrubs, as well as 15,000 annuals and perennials. Particularly impressive is the outstanding architectural landscaping that fills the entire garden with sweeping color and beauty. Take your lunch on the lawn or enjoy a quiet walk through the tree-shaded paths. Public concerts are held on designated Sunday evenings in June and July.

The grounds also include a one-room schoolhouse relocated from Brunswick, Missouri. There is also a rose garden, with more than 60 varieties of grandifloras, floribundas, and standard tea roses, along with a massive sundial. In addition, there are a shaded pool and a stream featuring a waterfall—the sound alone is enough to calm you after a rough day. Free.

Stephens College. 1200 E. Broadway; (800) 876-7207; stephens.edu. Founded in 1833, Stephens College is the second-oldest women's college in the nation. It offers programs in the arts, business, professional studies, and liberal arts and sciences. The performing arts department is well respected for its productions and summer stock throughout the Midwest. The Firestone Baars Chapel features a unique four-foyer design created by Eero Saarinen, who also designed the St. Louis Gateway Arch. Also on campus in Lena Raney Wood Hall (6 N. College St.; [573] 876-7220) is the Historic Costume Museum, a collection of more than 13,000 pieces of clothing by designers from around the world. Each semester, students create new exhibits that interpret how the clothes we wear reflect our culture.

Twin Lakes Recreation Area. 2500 Chapel Hill Rd.; (573) 874-7460. This family-oriented facility offers swimming, boating, fishing, hiking, and nature study. The six-acre swimming lake has a deck, a diving platform, water slides, and a large sand beach. There's a water playground separate from the lake for small children and paddleboats available for rent. Bring your best friend to the dog park.

University of Missouri-Columbia. Eighth and Elm Streets; (573) 882-2121; mizzou.edu. The first public university west of the Mississippi River, "Mizzou" was founded in 1839. The 1,265-acre campus has an enrollment of nearly 30,000 students. UMC is one of the few institutions in the country that houses journalism, law, medicine, agriculture, engineering, and veterinary medicine on a single campus. The Mizzou journalism school was the first such school in the world and remains the respected leader in training professional journalists.

The center of the campus is the historic Francis Quadrangle, at the entrance of Eighth and Elm Streets. Its 18 surrounding buildings are on the National Register of Historic Places. The row of six Ionic columns that adorn the center of the Francis Quadrangle once supported the portico of Academic Hall, the first building erected on campus. The open area around the columns is the center of the cluster of redbrick buildings known as the Red Campus. It is modeled after Thomas Jefferson's design for the University of Virginia. Walking through those columns into the quad is a freshman class orientation rite, and passing through the columns, back into the world, is a treasured memory at graduation.

UMC houses the first monument erected for the grave of Thomas Jefferson. When Virginia decided to erect a new monument for Jefferson's grave and give the original away, UMC was first in line to grab the valuable castoff. Since President Jefferson was instrumental in acquiring UMC as the first state university in the Louisiana Purchase Territory, Mizzou was the logical choice to house the prized stone slab. The entire campus is considered a botanical garden with nine individual gardens identified on campus. Thomas Jefferson would have liked that.

If you are not interested in the academics and just want a tour of the campus, call (800) 856-2181.

Museum of Anthropology. Lower level of Ellis Library; (573) 882-3764; anthromuseum.missouri.edu. The Museum of Anthropology is one of those tucked-away-and-taken-for-granted places that doesn't get much fanfare. As early as 1885 UMC began accepting gifts of ethnographic materials, finally organizing them into a cohesive collection in 1902. The only anthropology museum in the state and one of the few in the Midwest, its archaeological collection is the largest holding of prehistoric Missouri artifacts in the world, including those dating from 9,000 BC to modern times.

The Grayson Archery Collection housed here is one of the largest and most comprehensive collections of its kind in the world. Unusual thumb rings of carved jade used by Chinese archers represent only a fraction of the materials that are showcased in the museum's exhibit hall.

There are a number of Native American exhibits, dating from 11,000 years ago to the present. Works by Hopi artist Iris Nampeyo, plus Santa Clara pottery and authentic Hopi kachinas, are showcased. There is also a prehistoric section of Native American work that features Hohokam and Anasazi pottery. Open Mon through Fri. Free.

The Museum of Art and Archaeology. Ellis Library; (573) 882-3591. One of the best-kept secrets in the Midwest, this gem of a museum houses 13,000 pieces of art and artifacts from six continents and is the third-largest collection of its kind in Missouri. The Saul and Gladys Weinberg Gallery of Ancient Art is one of the most comprehensive in the state and features exhibits from ancient Egypt, Palestine, the Near East, Greece, Italy, and the Roman world. Particularly noteworthy is the oldest piece in the museum, a 250,000-year-old ax handle, as well as a 4,000-year-old cuneiform tablet and case that afford a glimpse into an early form of human communication before computers and texting. A Cypro-Archaic vessel, thrown before 600 BC, is a reminder that the venerable craft of pottery is blessed with longevity, while coins and gaming pieces from Egypt, Alexandria, and Rome tell the story of leisure-time spending sprees long before riverboat casinos. Closed Mon, open late on Thurs. Free.

Boone County History and Culture Center. 3801 Ponderosa St.; (573) 443-8936; boonehistory.org. Located three miles south of the junction of MO 63 and I-70, the visitor center is housed in a traditional family farmhouse. The museum contains the history of the area from prehistoric to present day in its 16,000 square feet of exhibition space. The Montminy Art Gallery located on-site showcases the talents of mid-Missouri artists as well as the outstanding collection of half a million photographic images that are part of the Boone County Historical Society Photo Archives, which date from the late 1800s to the mid-20th century.

Just north of the museum is the Maplewood Home, a historic Victorian residence built in 1877 that is listed on the National Register of Historic Places. Boone Junction Village, a historic town, consists of an 1820s-era log cabin, a Victorian home, and a 1920s-era general store, one-room schoolhouse, and other buildings. Open Wed through Sat, 10 a.m. to 5 p.m. The museum is free, but a charge is necessary for guided tours of the historic village.

where to shop

Central Columbia Association Special Business District. 11 S. 10th St.; (573) 442-6816; discoverthedistrict.com. Columbia's downtown district is filled with fine restaurants, shops, galleries, bookstores, museums, and one-of-a-kind specialty stores that cover 50 square blocks surrounding Broadway. Below are just a few noteworthy places:

Bluestem Missouri Crafts. 13 S. Ninth St.; (573) 442-0211; bluestemcrafts.com. This unusual store is actually a partnership of craftspeople who feature their own ceramic jewelry, weaving, pottery, and batik work. In addition, Bluestem is a showcase for an extensive collection of handmade functional and decorative work by other artists. Pottery, glass, wood, metal, and fiber art are represented here. Baskets, wooden boxes, toys, cards, and clothing made in Missouri are part of the colorful displays. The Neighboring States Gallery features the work of equally talented artisans from the states that border Missouri and includes a large selection of pieces by Decorah, Iowa, artist Brian Andreas. Open daily.

Calhoun's. 911 E. Broadway; (573) 443-3614. This pleasant gift shop reminds those who forget it that Columbia is home to more than college students. It's a fun place to browse, where you may find some unusual jewelry, a fresh scent for candles, a raucous birthday gift for an adult friend, or maybe something for newborn babies. Gift wrapping is free and creative.

The Candy Factory. 701 E. Cherry St.; (573) 443-8222; thecandyfactory.biz. This bright and cheery candy store is renowned for its delicious handmade chocolates, including choc-olate-covered strawberries and scrumptious truffles. For real chocoholics, there's always the Ultimate Pizza, a gourmet treat featuring 1.5 pounds of deep-dish chocolate topped with fresh pecans, cashews, walnuts, cherries, and marshmallows and drizzled with white chocolate. Closed Sun.

Columbia Art League Gallery. 207 S. Ninth St.; (573) 443-8838; columbiaartleague.org. Art lovers will find an eclectic collection of paintings, ceramics, jewelry, photography, and works in wood, metal, and fiber at this bright and contemporary gallery, which has been showing work by local and regional artists for more than 50 years. A changing schedule of exhibits in the main gallery is testament to the myriad forms of creativity in this mid-Missouri art colony. Closed Sun and Mon.

Poppy. 920 E. Broadway; (573) 442-3223; poppymadebyhand.com. Easily one of the best places in the country to find authentic American crafts, this store has been a fixture in down-town Columbia since the early 1980s. Poppy's offers an excellent collection of contemporary artwork in clay, fiber, metal, wood, glass, and jewelry, as well as two-dimensional art. If you're looking for something different, this is the place to come. Open daily.

Orchids and Art. 98 Corporate Lake Dr.; (573) 875-5989. Displays by local and regional artists are surrounded by flowering orchids, which are also for sale. The gallery collection rotates often and includes prints, mixed media, paintings, drawings, and photography. Closed Sun.

Skylark Bookshop. 22 S. Ninth St.; (573) 777-6990; skylarkbookshop.com. Local author Alex George (*A Good American*, *Setting Free the Kites*, *The Paris Hours*) is the creative genius behind this beloved independent bookshop. He is also the founder of the Unbound Book Festival each April. Skylark is a bright and cheery place with knowledgeable staff who love nothing more than to talk to you about their favorite works. Follow Skylark's social media for the latest on author visits and other special events. Open daily.

where to eat

Barred Owl Butcher and Table. 47 E. Broadway; (573) 442-9323; barredowlbutcher. com. This is an old-fashioned butcher shop, like was once popular in every community. However, it's also one of Columbia's most popular restaurants for a romantic or celebratory dinner. Ben Parks creates craft charcuterie after working with local farmers to source most products served at the restaurant and butchery. The restaurant is open for dinner only, Wed through Sat. $$

Broadway Diner. 22 S. Fourth St.; (573) 875-1173. This working-class establishment opened in 1949 and is the only remaining diner of its style in Missouri. It features breakfast anytime and daily lunch specials for under $5. Come here for real hash browns and freshly mashed potatoes. Open Wed through Sun for breakfast and lunch. $

Buck's Ice Cream Place. Eckles Hall, East Rollins and College Streets (on the UMC Campus); (573) 882-1088. Under the supervision of UMC's Department of Food Science and College of Agriculture, Buck's is a student-run research, teaching, and service operation. It's also a gathering spot for aficionados of good ice cream. Mizzou's "Truman the Tiger" mascot is the inspiration for Buck's Tiger Stripe ice cream, a mixture of vanilla and chocolate, with some orange coloring thrown in to account for the tigerlike hue. All ice cream is freshly made, is available in dipped and packaged forms, and weighs about 30 percent more per serving than most commercial products. Closed weekends. $

C.C.'s City Broiler. 1401 Forum Blvd.; (573) 445-7772; ccscitybroiler.com. This excellent steakhouse is renowned for its corn-fed Black Angus beef, hand-cut daily on the premises and cooked exactly as you like it. The signature item is a bone-in filet mignon, accented with a special seasoning that makes the flavor sing. All steaks come with the restaurant's famous jalapeño twice-baked potato, burgundy mushrooms, salad or soup, and fresh, hot sourdough bread. On the lighter side, the chargrilled seafood is always fresh, and you can mix and match a meal of steak and shrimp, steak and oysters, or steak and lobster tail. There's a wall-to-wall wait on weekends, so come early. Dinner is served seven nights a week. $$–$$$

Ernie's. 1005 Walnut St.; (573) 874-7804. This venerable art deco storefront establishment has been in business since 1934. Hearty breakfasts, classic sandwiches, and luncheon specials are offered, as are espresso, cappuccino, and lattes. One of the best things about Ernie's is the ambience. The eclectic assortment of patrons ranges from babies to bearded octogenarians. Blue-collar workers elbow in side by side at the counters with college students and faculty. Open daily until 2 p.m. $

Lakota Coffee Company. 24 S. Ninth St.; (573) 874-2852. This popular coffee roastery, located in the heart of downtown, roasts its own beans daily. The owner named the place for the Lakota Sioux, who loved the taste and smell of hot, strong coffee and who would, in their caffeine quest, raid wagon trains and steal the beans for their own coffee klatches.

Today, the company gives back to several Native American causes. The establishment's lattes and cappuccinos are served in enormous *Alice in Wonderland*–size cups. You have your choice of scones, croissants, biscotti, lox and bagels, and other edibles for dipping and sipping. Open daily. $

The Main Squeeze. 28 S. Ninth St.; (573) 817-5616; main-squeeze.com. Start your morning with a 16-ounce Elvis Parsley—a mixture made with beets, spinach, parsley, celery, carrots, and garlic—which provides the equivalent of five servings of vegetables. Have a smoothie or go for the homemade soups, hearty sandwiches, salads, or fresh baked goods. There are no preservatives or artificial colors or flavors in anything you'll eat here. Breakfast can be free-range organic eggs, whole-grain pancakes, organic roasted potatoes, scrambled tofu, breakfast burritos, or biscuits with soy sausage gravy. There are also wheat-free nondairy entrees for vegans. Open Wed through Sun 9 a.m. to 6 p.m. $

Sophia's. 3915 S. Providence Rd.; (573) 874-8009. This popular restaurant has a laid-back, cosmopolitan ambience that goes well with its southern European fare that includes tapas, pastas, fresh seafood, steaks, and more. For after-dinner sport, there's always the bocce ball court located next to the outdoor patio. There is usually a 30- to 40-minute wait to get in, but early birds could luck out. For late-night owls, Sophia's stays open until 11 p.m. during the week and until midnight on weekends for the restaurant and until 1 a.m. for the bar. $$–$$$

Sycamore. 800 E. Broadway; (573) 874-8090; sycamorerestaurant.com. Focusing on local suppliers and seasonal ingredients, Sycamore is an excellent choice for a lunch with soups and salads or dinner with large plates of steak, duck, and trout. Unexpected offerings like a swordfish club or carrot cashew soup on this ever-changing menu keep local foodies returning regularly. With more than 50 beers and as many wines on the menu, Sycamore has become known as a diverse dining destination. Check out the local art for sale on the walls. $$

Uprise Bakery. 10 Hitt St.; (573) 256-2265. Located in the former Coca-Cola distribution center in Columbia, the bakery is a part of the Rag Tag independent film building. Come here for coffee and scones on Sunday morning before first-time screenings next door. Everything is made on-site, including the alcohol, the corned beef, the bread, and the butter, and most ingredients are supplied locally. The cookies and cupcakes are worth the drive all the way from Kansas City. $

worth more time:
fulton, mo

Located east of Columbia on US Highway 54 within the "Kingdom of Callaway," Fulton is farther from Kansas City than a typical day trip. But the extraordinary history and unique experience offered in this little community is certainly worthy of attention and a paragraph or two for your consideration for a weekend getaway.

One of two highly rated private colleges in Fulton, Westminster College holds an endowment that regularly brings speakers of "international significance" to campus. On March 5, 1946, Winston Churchill, invited by his good friend and Missouri resident Harry Truman, came to central Missouri and delivered a speech formally called "The Sinews of Peace" speech. We know it today as the Iron Curtain Speech.

As a result of Churchill's historic address here, a phenomenal museum has developed called America's National Churchill Museum. It includes sections of the Berlin Wall sculpted by Churchill's granddaughter, a Christopher Wren–designed church from London that dates to the 1600s and other experiences one would never expect in a tiny little town in central Missouri. World leaders have visited this community. You should too. For more information, visit visitfulton.com or call (573) 642-7692.

day trip 03

east

ragtime and capitol highlights:
sedalia, mo; tipton, mo; california, mo;
jefferson city, mo

getting there

From downtown Kansas City, take Highway 71 to I-470 to US 50 E about 60 miles to reach Sedalia.

sedalia, mo

Sedalia's history dates to 1857, when General George R. Smith founded a town amid the prairie grasses. He envisioned a prosperous railroad city and named it Sedville, after his daughter's nickname. Friends eventually persuaded him to use the more mellifluous "Sedalia" to commemorate his progeny.

When the Civil War erupted, Sedalia was in the thick of the fighting. Missouri, though a state where slavery was legal, did not secede from the Union. Sedalia was captured and held by the Confederates and later, was made the seat of Pettis County.

The railroad, as Smith foresaw, did indeed play an important role in the town's growth. Sedalia flourished and drew people with talent, such as Scott Joplin, who became known as the King of Ragtime. His sound spread across the country with compositions like the "Maple Leaf Rag," one of the finest pieces of ragtime music ever written. A historical monument was built at the Maple Leaf Club site in the 100 block of East Main Street, where Joplin lived and worked.

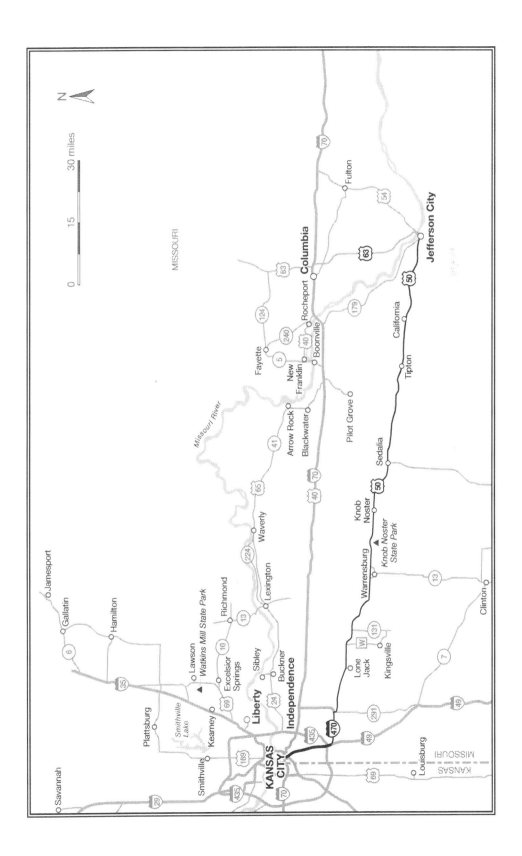

Each June, Sedalia hosts the Scott Joplin Ragtime Festival, the only classical ragtime festival in the world and commemorates the noted composer's work. Musicians and fans from around the globe come to the birthplace of ragtime.

Aside from its musical past, beautiful architecture can also be found in Sedalia. The old homes that line Broadway (US 50), the buildings on the State Fairgrounds, and the downtown area are all of interest. A free walking tour brochure that highlights 57 historic buildings in Sedalia is available at the chamber of commerce.

where to go

Sedalia Chamber of Commerce. 600 E. Third St., Katy Depot Historic Site; (800) 827-5295; visitsedaliamo.com. The MKT Depot was built in 1896. In addition to housing the chamber offices, there's a remarkably interesting exhibit about the history of Sedalia and train travel. A children's area allows kids to dress up as an engineer and manually operate a wooden train along its tracks. Katy Trail souvenirs and Missouri gift items are for sale in a well-stocked gift shop. The Katy Trail passes directly in front of the depot. Here you can pick up all sorts of brochures about things to do in the city. Sedalia has 24 car charging stations.

Art Impressions. 412 S. Ohio St.; (660) 826-4343; artimpressions.net. More than 30 local and regional artists are represented in the light and airy gallery in the historic district. Glassworks, fiber art, and oil and acrylic paintings are for sale along with soaps, jewelry, and decorative note cards. On occasion an artist will demonstrate his or her technique, such as a glass-blowing demonstration on the street in front of the gallery. Matting and framing services are also available. Open Tues through Sat or by appointment.

Bothwell Lodge Historic Site. 19349 Bothwell Park Rd.; (660) 827-0510; mostateparks .com. Located six miles north of Sedalia on US 65, this 180-acre park offers visitors scenic bluffs and wooded trails, including three miles of mountain-biking trails. It features picnic areas and Bothwell Lodge, a century-old lodge built atop two caves open for tours year-round. Admission fee to enter the lodge.

Daum Contemporary Art Museum. 3201 W. 16th St.; (660) 530-5888; daummuseum .org. Located on the campus of State Fair Community College, these nine galleries exhibit paintings, drawings, prints, photographs, and sculptures by Midwestern artists. A focal point is a chandelier in the atrium created by glass artist Dale Chihuly. The museum rotates exhibits four times a year. Free. Closed Mon.

Liberty Center Association for the Arts. 111 W. Fifth St.; (660) 827-3228; libertycentersedalia.com. This renovated 1920s theater in downtown serves as the center for performing and cultural arts in the area. Franklin and Eleanor Roosevelt once stopped here on a nationwide tour to thank World War I veterans. Visual artists display their work at Gallery 111, and the Sedalia Community Theatre's all-volunteer troupe stages three productions a year. Check the website for a schedule of classes and workshops and other art events.

Missouri State Fair. State Fairgrounds, 2503 W. 16th St.; (800) 422-FAIR or (660) 530-5600; mostatefair.com. The 397-acre showplace for agriculture and industry comes alive with color and excitement in late August for 10 days of shows, exhibits, and competitions, drawing nearly 400,000 people every year. Admission fee.

Nostalgia Vintage Apparel and Marketplace. 219 S. Ohio St.; (660) 851-2749. Carolyn Miller has built a home for her love of vintage fashion in the former C.W. Flower Department Store. Carolyn's part museum, part lecture hall, and part resale shop provides a fascinating look at how fashion has shaped our culture, and vice versa. For groups of at least 20 or more, Carolyn will provide a lunch, dessert, or treats as the program dictates. Open Tues through Sat, 10 a.m. to 5 p.m.

Paint Brush Prairie Conservation Area. Located nine miles south of Sedalia, off US 65 (watch for signs); (660) 530-5500. This 300-plus-acre natural area captures the historic atmosphere at the time of homesteading. Unique plant species have been restored to the area, encouraging the return of native animals like prairie chickens, upland sandpipers, and Henslow's sparrows. Missouri Audubon has designated it an important bird area. Hiking trails wind throughout the area.

Scott Joplin Store. 103 E. Fourth St. (inside the Hotel Bothwell); (660) 816-2217; scottjoplin.org. This is the home of the Scott Joplin Foundation, which coordinates the annual festival each June. You can buy tickets here but also find out just about anything you want to know about the musician who called Sedalia home. His music is for sale here along with lots of other memorabilia. Open Mon through Fri.

where to eat

Clara's North 65 Café. 22938 N. 65 Hwy.; (660) 829-3322; clarasnorth65cafe.com. How often do you get a chance to eat authentic Colombian cuisine in small-town Missouri? You can do so, starting with breakfast, at Clara's Café. A native of rural Colombia, South America (as opposed to Columbia, Missouri), Clara was raised in her grandmother's restaurant, where she loved to make cornmeal cakes known as "arepas" and empanadas. Clara also serves Colombia barbeque, which is basically skewered meats cooked over an open flame. Open Mon through Sat, 6 a.m. to 2 p.m. $

Kedhe's Barbeque. 1915 S. Limit Ave.; (660) 951-3444; kehdesbbqsedalia.com. The Kehde family has been serving up good food in one form or another for four generations in Sedalia, but this is our favorite—a barbeque joint inside a beautifully lit and refurbished train car. In addition to good barbeque, you'll find daily specials that include catfish, fried chicken, and pork tenderloin, among other treats. Open Wed through Sun, 11 a.m. to 8 p.m. $

where to stay

Hotel Bothwell. 103 E. Fourth St.; (660) 826-5588; hotelbothwell.com. This National Historic Landmark hotel originally opened in June 1927 and over the years hosted such names as Harry S. Truman, Bette Davis, and Clint Eastwood. The Hotel Bothwell, now an Ascend Hotel Collection, preserves much of the original class and charm that drew thousands through its doors for more than 75 years. Original telephone booths in one corner of the lobby and a six-story mail chute contribute to the feeling of yesteryear, as do original marble floors, walnut woodwork, and a lower-level "speakeasy." The hotel has 48 rooms, each unique in its furnishings and décor. Some of the rooms have been renovated into suites and long-term apartments, and six have been remodeled to their exact appearance in 1927. A coffee shop, restaurant, and gift shop add plenty of pizzazz to this familiar face in downtown Sedalia. $$

tipton, mo

This town of 3,000 or so is known for the eight ball that serves as the water tower. Once upon a time, Fischer Manufacturing made billiards tables and the accompanying balls, and they contributed to the city's water tower. The company no longer has a plant here, but the eight ball remains.

where to go

Dutch Bakery & Bulk Food Store. 709 US Highway 50; (660) 433-2865; dutchbakery-andbulkfoodstorellc.business.site. For more than 45 years, this has been the place to find everything you need in the kitchen and beyond. And the whole time, it's been owned and operated by the Hoover family. Homemade breads, cakes, pies, and cookies fill the air with a wonderful aroma as you stroll the clean-as-a-whistle aisles filled with bulk food ranging from dried beans and coffee to nuts and candies to pastas and noodles. The deli showcases local meats and cheeses. You'll also find a nice selection of kitchen utensils and small appliances, pots and pans, and everything you need to turn that bulk food into a fabulous meal at home. Open Mon through Sat, 7 a.m. to 6 p.m.

McCall's Candles Factory Shoppe. 809 US Highway 50; (660) 433-2380; mccallscandles.com. Started in her home by a local woman in 1994, McCall's Candles now has more than 60 fragrances created in a massive factory in Tipton. The cute canning jar look is part of the appeal. But if you don't like open flames, the company also creates a line of flameless candles and smell goods. Although McCall's Candles are carried in shops across North America, you get a 20 percent discount by shopping here in Tipton. Open Mon through Sat, 9 a.m. to 5 p.m.

california, mo

For most people, California is just a zip-through spot on US 50, but if you take time to turn into the little village, you will find the heart of America. California is just one of those places with lots of hardworking, middle-class citizens who take pride in maintaining their homes and their communities. They are awfully proud of the Veterans Memorial Park, dedicated in 2022. Many will remember Burgers' Smokehouse, a fixture in these parts since 1927. The family-owned business still exists supplying area restaurants and filling online orders, but the retail business and little museum on smoking meats did not reopen after Covid. You can still order their smoked turkeys, chickens, and other meats at smokehouse.com.

getting there

From Jefferson City, head west on US 50 about 20 miles to the hamlet of California.

where to go

Grind Coffee & Bistro. 314 S. Oak St.; (573) 205-7779; grindcalimo.com. One of the most comfortable places in mid-Missouri is this little coffee shop in downtown California. Operated by Chelsea McGill, one of the community's biggest supporters, Grind offers dozens of specialty drinks and an inviting menu of breakfast and lunch items. The bakery alone is worth the drive. And this is one of the retail locations where you can still purchase freshly sliced Burgers' Smokehouse meats and cheeses. Open Mon through Sat., 6 a.m. to 6 p.m. $

Finke Opera House. 315 High St.; (573) 690-9363; finketheatre.com. Built in 1885, the Finke is one of several such buildings in Missouri designed by J.B. Legg, a well-known St. Louis architect of the time. Like most old buildings in small towns, it went from elaborate opera and vaudeville performances to movie theater and then decay as it was boarded up in the early 1980s. But a group of locals banded together to save many of California's old buildings. Now the 275-seat theater is once again filled with an enthusiastic audience for community theater, musical performances, and special events.

The Milkbarn. 517 N. High St.; (573) 230-4462. This fun shop is filled with great, refurbished finds and antiques from auctions around the Midwest and other home décor items. You'll find handcrafted jewelry by local artisans and yes, you can buy gift packages of Burgers' Smokehouse products as well. Stop in for some inspiration to make your home a bit more interesting. Open Thurs through Sat.

The Winding Road. 324 S. Oak St.; (573) 415-6395; windingstore.com. Find some of the most beautiful work by Missouri craft artisans in this store. Tables made from reclaimed barnwood, soy candles, pottery, and locally made soaps are among the selections. But you'll also find a nice collection of rugs, linens, kitchenware, and florals. It's just a fun place to make your home a little more inviting. Open Tues through Sat.

jefferson city, mo

Like two sides of a coin, Columbia and Jefferson City are separated by less than 30 miles, yet there's a world of difference between them. Located south of Columbia on US 63, Jefferson City is exactly the opposite of Columbia in atmosphere and ambience. Columbia is a liberal and laid-back college town with a high degree of tolerance for unconventional appearances and beliefs. Jefferson City is an old, conservative city that thrives on influence, politics, and power lunches, most likely taken at acceptable restaurants with acquaintances grouped according to social behavior and dress code. In Jefferson City, moderate nonconformists fit in as long as no boats are seriously rocked.

Jefferson City's unique art and architecture are worth the day trip. Jefferson City is home to the magnificent State Capitol Building, where the Missouri legislature convenes. The Governor's Mansion and Governor's Garden, Jefferson Landing State Historic Site, Cole County Museum, and other historic points of interest are also worth visiting. Travelers on the Lewis and Clark Trail will find several points of interest here.

If you decide to spend the night, you'll find accommodations that cater to business and leisure travelers alike, as well as a smattering of good restaurants. Leave time for a visit to the Runge Nature Center and Missouri's most delicious secret, the Central Dairy.

getting there

From Columbia you have a couple of ways to reach Jefferson City. Heading back west on I-70 to MO 179, the road takes you through some pretty countryside that passes the Runge Nature Center on the way to Jefferson City. US 63 South is faster and connects with US 54, the mid-Missouri gateway to the Lake of the Ozarks region.

where to go

Jefferson City Convention and Visitors Bureau. 700 E. Capitol St.; (800) 769-4183 or (573) 632-2820; visitjeffersoncity.com. Visit this downtown office for answers to lots of questions and pick up discount coupons at area businesses. More importantly, get your picture made in a replica jail cell from the old state penitentiary.

Clark's Hill/Norton State Historic Site. Osage Hickory Street, Osage City; (573) 449-7402; mostateparks.com. This unit of the Missouri State Park System is near Osage City just east of Jefferson City. This 13-acre property, donated to the state by William and Carol Norton of Jefferson City, is believed to be where William Clark camped on June 1, 1804, at the mouth of the Osage River. A half-mile trail leads you up to the bluff and includes interpretive signs. Be alert for ticks in all Missouri state parks.

Cole County Historical Museum. 109 Madison St.; (573) 635-1850. Located across from the Governor's Mansion, the museum is housed in an 1871 building that features a collection of inaugural ball gowns of the former First Ladies of the state, along with other vintage cloth-ing and Victorian furnishings. One floor of the four-story building is devoted to the Civil War in Missouri. Open Tues through Sat, or by appointment. Free.

Governor's Mansion. 100 Madison St.; (573) 751-7929. Built in 1871, the official residence of Missouri's First Family has an interior that is authentically restored to the Renaissance Revival period and includes a winding stairway, marble fireplaces, elaborate ceiling stencil-ing, and period furnishings. Portraits of Missouri's First Ladies are showcased on the walls. Docents in period costumes conduct tours of the first floor Tues through Thurs except during Aug and Dec. The grounds also hold the Carnahan Memorial Garden, dedicated to Gover-nor Carnahan, his son, and an aide who were killed in a plane crash. It is filled with flowers, pools, and walkways. Christmas Candlelight Tours are held at the mansion two evenings in Dec. Free.

Jefferson Landing State Historic Site (Lohman Building and Union Hotel). Jefferson and Water Streets; (573) 751-2854; mostateparks.com/jeffersonland.com. The three-story Lohman Building, constructed of limestone in 1839, is thought to be the oldest structure in Jefferson City. It served steamboat passengers during the city's heyday as a busy river town. Charles Lohman, a native of Germany, operated an inn here at that time. A small museum on the premises depicts the history of the area. Adjacent to the Lohman Building is the Union Hotel. It was built in the 1850s, when the community was a busy center for rail and river traffic; it operated as a hotel following the Civil War and continued to do business until the decline of steamboating. The Elizabeth Rozier Gallery in the building features Missouri's arts, artists, and cultures. An Amtrak station is located on the first floor of the Union Hotel. Both buildings are open Tues through Sat. Free.

Lincoln University. 820 Chestnut St.; (573) 681-5599; lincoln.edu. Established in 1866, the university is situated on 52 rolling acres and is a source for cultural events, sports activities, and continuing education. The Soldiers Memorial at the center of campus is an impressive bronze sculpture that pays homage to the 62nd US Colored Infantry of the Civil War, which established Lincoln University. Free tours are available.

Missouri State Capitol Building. 201 W. Capitol Ave.; (573) 751-4127; visitjeffersoncity .com. Recognized among the nation's capitol buildings for its art and architecture, the Mis-souri State Capitol sits on three acres of ground and rises 262 feet to the top of its dome. Completed in 1918, the Renaissance-style building is where Missouri's state senators and representatives meet from Jan through May to enact laws that govern the state. On Tues, Wed, or Thurs morning, you can watch the political process unfold from the visitors' gallery. The Missouri Museum, located on the first floor, features exhibits of historical significance, including portraits of Meriwether Lewis and William Clark. The large state seal in the center of the first-floor rotunda is wrought in bronze and can be viewed from a higher location during a tour of the building. Daily guided tours take in the legislators' chambers, architecture and design, and the Thomas Hart Benton Mural. The Gallery of Famous Missourians is located on the third floor.

The Benton Mural. House Lounge, on the third floor, west wing of the Missouri State Capitol. One of the most important and best reasons to visit the Missouri State Capitol is for the Thomas Hart Benton Mural, an expansive, stunning masterpiece that reflects the enormous genius behind it. Painted in 1936, the work covers four walls with a breadth and scope that reflect the legends, history, landmarks, industry, and people of Missouri. Entitled *A Social History of the State of Missouri*, the mural offended many people because of its "lack of refinement." Refined, Benton was not, since he wanted to portray "activities that did not require being polite." His mural, in addition to its niceties, also depicts racist actions, hangings, and other messy and corrupt things that human beings—even Missourians—did in their zeal to build a state.

So enraged were the legislators by Benton's masterpiece that they deliberately defaced the mural, dashing out lighted cigars on it. They were about to whitewash it altogether when Benton's famous temper erupted. He took his case to the media and to the Missouri people, who backed him. The politicians relented and the painting stayed. There is no charge to see the restored work. Benton would have liked that.

Missouri State Highway Patrol Museum. 1510 E. Elm St.; (573) 526-6149. Part education/safety center and part museum, this museum includes patrol cars, uniforms, weapons, and other equipment dating to the department's inception in 1931. Interactive exhibits test a driver's speed and reflexes as items appear on the screen. There's a train safety quiz for children three to six years old and an interactive train crossing exhibit in which kids can drive the train. Kids will also love Otto, the talking car. Open Mon through Fri, 8 a.m. to 5 p.m. Free.

Missouri State Penitentiary Tours. 115 Lafayette St.; (866) 998-6998; missouripentours .com. This is certainly one of the most memorable tours you'll ever take, and no matter how creepy it sounds at first, you really should tour the old state pen. Built in 1836, the Missouri State Penitentiary operated until 2004—the longest operating penitentiary west of the Mississippi. At one point it held 5,200 inmates, making it the largest prison in the world. It accepted its first prisoner the week the Alamo was under siege. It was open and holding prisoners 100 years before Alcatraz became a prison. In the 1950s and 1960s, it was called the bloodiest 47 acres in America because of the violence inside.

It's one of only three state penitentiaries open for tours in the US: Alcatraz, Eastern Pennsylvania, and now Missouri. Sonny Liston learned to box here, and a mural of him painted by another inmate can still be seen on the exercise field wall. James Earl Ray escaped here in November 1967 in a bread truck with the intent of assassinating Martin Luther King. Blanche Barrow of the Bonnie and Clyde gang did time here, as did Pretty Boy Floyd and a number of minor gangsters of the period.

The two-hour tours, often led by former prison guards, begin in dungeons in the oldest parts of the prison and end at the execution chamber. In between, you learn a surprising amount about the evolution of American culture and its philosophy of incarceration and punishment. The buildings have no lighting, no heating or air conditioning, and no working plumbing. If you have mobility issues, this may not be the tour for you because there are many stairs and uneven surfaces, and no place to sit and rest.

A few tips: Bring a flashlight to see better in some buildings. Don't be cute by pulling a cell door closed behind you. There are few remaining keys to most cells. You could stay for a long, long time. And be respectful in the execution chamber. Human beings died here.

The pen coordinates paranormal tours, photography tours, and a fun "prison break" run. Across the street in the former warden's home, a museum provides additional insight to prison industries and life behind the walls. Admission fee.

Runge Nature Center. MO 179; (573) 526-5544; mdc.mo.gov/areas/cnc/runge. This 3,000-square-foot facility west of downtown is the Department of Conservation's show-piece. Missouri's habitats are explored in a variety of exhibits and dioramas that feature the state's wetlands, agricultural lands, rivers and streams, ponds and lakes, prairies, glades, forests, and caves. Hiking trails, outdoor demonstrations, and naturalist-guided programs are offered over 112 acres, seven days a week. Indoors is a lovely bird and wildlife viewing area with lots of seating. Free.

where to eat

Arris Pizza. 117 W. High St.; (573) 635-9225, arrispizzapalace.com. A favorite since 1961 in Jefferson City, Arris Pizza is known for its Greek-style pizza, which is baked in a shallow pan, and some fabulous sandwiches. Sun-dried tomato mozzarella paninis with fresh cia-batta and an Aegean sandwich, which is grilled eggplant, pepper, zucchini, and mozzarella cheese, are highlights of the menu. $

Central Dairy. 610 Madison St.; (573) 635-6148; centraldairy.biz. In Jefferson City, the milkman still makes deliveries to your door twice a week, courtesy of Central Dairy, a mid-Missouri operation that sells products made in its plant from locally produced milk. The owner keeps his prices low at the ice cream store as a goodwill gesture to the community, so everybody can afford to come here. Prices are minuscule for colossal blockbuster sundaes and splits so top heavy with triple dips of ice cream, marshmallow, and hot fudge toppings and nuts that you'll need several napkins just to clean up. Hand-packed pints and quarts are so affordable that serious aficionados will want to bring a cooler and plenty of dry ice to take some home. $

Das Stein Haus Restaurant and Lounge. 1436 Southridge Dr. (off US 54, behind the Conoco station); (573) 634-3869; dassteinhaus.com. This is an authentic German restau-rant operated by Helmut Stein, a native of Berlin. He came to this country in 1968 and first cooked in New Orleans at Brennan's. He moved to Jefferson City in the 1970s. German specialties here include Rouladen, Wiener schnitzel, smoked pork chops with sauerkraut, sauerbraten, and bratwurst. Dinners also feature chateaubriand for two, veal medallions, frog legs, and Long Island Duckling Flambé, topped with orange sauce and served with spiced rice and red cabbage. The lounge features karaoke on Fri and Sat. Closed Sun and Mon. $$

Ecco Lounge. 703 Jefferson St.; (573) 636-8751. In 1838, the land on the corner of Jefferson and Dunklin was purchased for $32; in 1840 the back parking lot was bought for $26 more. The building was erected in 1858, making this the second oldest bar in Missouri, and served as a "beer saloon." *Lounge* has replaced the word *saloon,* but beer is beer, and Ecco serves it up along with giant beer-battered onion rings and hefty burgers made from ground chuck and topped with blue cheese. Specialties are hot spiced shrimp, prime rib, and steak. $

Prison Brews. 305 Ash St.; (573) 635-0678; prisonbrews.com. Building on the popularity of the state penitentiary tours just a few blocks away, this dilapidated old building was saved in 2008 to become Jefferson City's craft brewery. Actual cell doors from the old penitentiary separate booths, and pictures from the prison's notorious past line the walls. The bar area itself is located in a cell, and if you're looking for the restrooms, follow the signs to the gas chambers. A bocce ball court is located outside, and league play is an exciting event in town. Wood-fired pizza, salads, and Reubens fill the menu, and they are all really good. $–$$

where to stay

Parker's Place. 624 E. Capitol; (573) 301-5987; parkersplacejc.com. This beautiful home was built with prison labor in the early 1900s. Lester Parker made his money operating a shoe factory inside the prison, also using prison labor. It's something to think about as you enjoy the lovely space, just across the street from the old state pen. $$

day trip 04

east

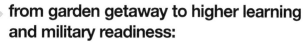

from garden getaway to higher learning and military readiness:
lone jack, mo; kingsville, mo; warrensburg, mo; knob noster, mo

lone jack, mo

A historic Civil War battlefield, one of the largest botanical gardens between Kansas City and Denver, a first-class bed-and-breakfast, and a dog that made national history back in 1870 are part of this unusual day trip that will acquaint you with this fascinating yet relatively undiscovered region.

getting there

From downtown, take US 71 (Bruce Watkins Parkway) south to US 50 East about 35 miles to reach Lone Jack.

where to go

Lone Jack Civil War Museum and Cemetery. 301 S. Bynum Rd. (one block south of US 50); (816) 697-8833; historiclonejack.org. This is the site of the August 16, 1862, Battle of Lone Jack, where five hours of bloody, hand-to-hand fighting ensued. The event is depicted in dioramas, artifacts, and other displays that showcase what happened on this Civil War battleground. An annual commemoration is held the weekend closest to the original battle date. Open daily Apr through Oct; weekends Nov through Mar (donations suggested).

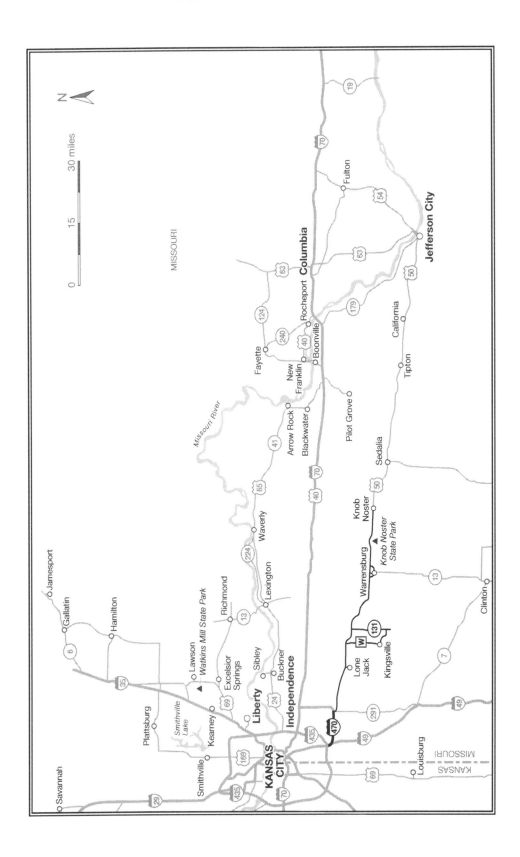

The Pumpkin Pad. 35100 E. Outerbelt Rd.; (816) 874-2527; thepumpkinpad.net. This wonderful seasonal attraction has so much more than pumpkins. Harvest your own sunflowers, get lost in one of three corn mazes, and enjoy a bonfire and roast marshmallows. There are dozens of games, such as corn hole and spider swings, as well as food trucks and live music. The pad opens in early Sept.

kingsville, mo

Kingsville is a rather low-key community where most activities center around the high school sports teams and Little League baseball. Its residents, for the most part, live on a bit of acreage where they enjoy their horses and other outdoor pursuits. The village was put on the map when the state's largest botanical garden opened here in the 1980s.

getting there

Continue east on US 50 another 20 miles to reach Kingsville and Powell Gardens.

where to go

Powell Gardens. 1609 NW US 50; (816) 697-2600; powellgardens.org. Powell Gardens is a not-for-profit, 915-acre botanical garden dedicated to beautifying and preserving the natural environment. Established in 1984 through a generous gift from the Powell Family Foundation, Powell Gardens is an outdoor paradise for gardeners and nature lovers, offering a changing palette of colorful flowers and plants throughout the year.

Powell Gardens utilizes horticultural displays, education, and research to serve the Kansas City community and surrounding areas. Gardens of annuals, perennials, native plants, ornamental grasses, and other seasonal plantings make up this spectacular facility.

Visitors may enjoy strolling through the Perennial Garden, Rock and Waterfall Garden, Island Garden, and Terrace Garden at the Visitor Education Center. Other highlights include the magnificent structures designed by architects Fay Jones and Maurice Jennings. These include the Marjorie Powell Allen Chapel, the Visitor Education Center, and the Wildflower Pavilion.

Powell Gardens offers year-round special events, educational classes, and environmental programs for children and adults; a lovely gift shop; and an excellent cafe where you can refresh and relax before or after your visit. Open daily. Admission fee.

In 2019, Powell Gardens received a donation of a 40-acre prairie in southwest Pettis County. Called Ona's Prairie in honor of Ona Gieschen, the land had been in her family since the mid-1800s. The prairie is not open to the public on a daily basis, but can be accessed with permission from Powell Gardens for research purposes and limited tours.

warrensburg, mo

Warrensburg has plenty of antique stores, specialty shops, restaurants, and cafes to visit. The town is the home of the University of Central Missouri, known for its outstanding technology and aviation programs. If you have a dog or have ever used the phrase "Dog is a man's best friend," then you will enjoy your exploration of Warrensburg. Learn about Old Drum and pose for selfies with the dog statues around town.

Amtrak has two stops daily from Kansas City in Warrensburg. Consider taking the train for the day or carrying on to Sedalia or Jefferson City for this day trip (see East Day Trip 03, p. 62).

getting there

From Kingsville, continue east along US 50 for 35 miles to Warrensburg.

where to go

Warrensburg Chamber of Commerce. 100 S. Holden St.; (660) 747-3168; warrensburg .org. Here you can learn what treasures this community has tucked away from the spotlight's glare on the university. The chamber offices are located in the former Missouri Pacific Railroad Depot, which also serves as an Amtrak station.

Blind Boone Park. 402 W. Pine St.; (660) 747-7178; blindboonepark.org. Once representative of segregation in Warrensburg, this long-forgotten park has been restored and is now the pride of the city. The park is named for former Warrensburg resident Willie Boone, the son of a former enslaved person, who lost his eyesight at six months but grew to be an accomplished concert pianist. Today's park includes a statue of Boone along with other sculptures, a gazebo, and a sensory garden, all designed around the needs of the visually impaired. There's also a shuffleboard court, horseshoe pits, and a great picnic area. The park is the location for a music festival each June.

Old Drum Monument. Market and Holden Streets (on the grounds of the Johnson County Courthouse); (660) 747-3168. In 1870 Senator George Graham Vest won a court battle and the hearts of dog lovers when he paid his famous tribute to the dog during the *Burden v. Hornsby* court case in 1870. That eulogy won the case for Charles Burden, whose favorite hound, Drum, was shot by Leonidas Hornsby, a neighbor. Burden sued for damages, and the trial became the focus of national attention. After several appeals the case reached the Missouri Supreme Court. Vest's eulogy, which he made in his final appeal to the jury, became a classic speech that reached the hearts of dog lovers around the world. He said, "The one absolutely unselfish friend that a man can have in this selfish world, the one that never deserts him, the one that never proves ungrateful or treacherous, is his dog." Who could resist a speech like that? Burden was subsequently awarded $50 in damages for the loss of this favorite dog. Old Drum remains a prominent figure in many Warrensburg activities, including an Old Drum Festival and dog show each June..

University of Central Missouri. Office of Admissions, Administration Building 104; (660) 543-4111; ucmo.edu. Founded in 1871, UCM, still commonly referred to as Central Missouri State University, despite legislative efforts otherwise, offers a wide range of academic programs in applied sciences and technology, arts and sciences, business and economics, and education and human services. The 1,050-acre campus offers opportunities to attend events and exhibitions of fine and performing arts, including those featuring celebrities in the entertainment and musical fields. The James L. Highlander Theater offers two main-stage or dinner-theater productions each semester. The UCM Archives and Museum, located in the James C. Kirkpatrick Library, houses a diverse display of artifacts that changes themes monthly. The Gallery of Art and Design, located in the Art Building at 217 Clark St. ([660] 543-4481), has exhibits of student work and visiting artists. Open Mon through Fri. Free.

where to eat

Fitters Pub. 131 W. Pine St.; (660) 429-3500; myfitters.com. The upstairs patio at Fitters is the place to enjoy a glass of wine or a beer and a burger. Indoors, you won't miss a game because of the dozens of big screen TVs. Known for its pizza and wraps, Fitters has some killer sandwiches and a great selection of local beers. Open Mon through Sat, 11 a.m. to 1:30 a.m.; Sun, 11 a.m. to midnight. $

Heroes Restaurant and Pub. 107 Pine St.; (660) 747-3162; heroeswarrensburg.com. Popular with college students and local businesspeople for lunch, this spacious pub in the downtown district is famous for its huge helpings of onion rings and cheese fries. Other than that, you might catch a Mules or Jennies sporting event on TV while enjoying your choice of salads, burgers, steaks, and pastas. The homemade desserts, such as carrot cake, are the best! $

where to shop

Meyer's Market. 202 N. Holden St.; (660) 362-0779; meyersmarket.com. Part general store for your healthy groceries, part deli and ice cream parlor, Meyer's Market is shopping the old-fashioned way. You'll find lots of gift items as well, and a fun sassy experience with the staff on hand. Grab a deli sandwich and head to Knob Noster State Park. Open daily.

MKT Clothing Co. 219 N. Holden St.; (660) 624-7069. This women's clothing store is fun and friendly, like a shopping date with your best friend. Owners Rachel and Karen are best friends and strive to bring that warmth to every customer who walks in the door. Check out their products to support medical research for ALS and the clothing line that supports caregivers. Open Tues through Sat, 10 a.m. to 5 p.m.

Primitive Stiches Quilt Shop. 34 SW 365th Rd.; (660) 747-7787. Your creative itch will get a good scratch at this fabric shop. You'll find patterns, rug kits, stocking ideas, and much more. Melissa Towne is the creative force behind this store. Ask for help on any project. She's been there, done that and learned from her mistakes. Open Tues through Sat., 10 a.m. to 5 p.m.

Tranquility Shop. 128 N. Holden St.; (660) 362-0788; tranquilityshop.com. Calm down. That's what this shop is all about. From candles and tea and aromatherapy, your bases are covered. The bath products are made from all natural ingredients. If you're up for a Tarot card reading, Marie will help you with that and other metaphysical tools. Home décor items and jewelry contribute to the goal of tranquility in all parts of our lives. Open Tues through Sat., 10 a.m. to 5 p.m.

knob noster, mo

Ten miles east on US 50 brings you to Knob Noster. The funny sounding name actually means "Our Hills." It's a pleasant little farming community dominated by Whiteman Air Force Base and high school sports. You'll find a number of antique and consignment shops in town as well as several gift shops.

where to go

Knob Noster State Park. 873 SE 10 Road.; (660) 563-2463; mostateparks.com. Put your kayak or canoe on your roof, grab a rod and reel, and head out for a lovely day in this Missouri State Park. Many of the trails, campgrounds, and buildings were constructed by the Civilian Conservation Corps in the Great Depression. But Missouri has added to it over the years with a nature center and swimming pool at one of the group campgrounds. The park has about 17 miles of trails and two orienteering courses. Be alert for ticks in Missouri state parks. Open year-round. Free.

Montserrat Vineyards. 104 NE 641 Hwy., Knob Noster; (660) 747-9463; monserratvineyardsandfarms. There was once a little town in this area called Montserrat, thus the name of this lovely vineyard and winery. The traditional Missouri Norton is one of the bronze medal winners here, but while you're tasting, take a sip of the chocolate wine. Yum.

Whiteman Air Force Base. (660) 687-6560; whiteman.af.mil. Often in television or movies with a military or political theme, you may hear passing reference to "those bombers from Missouri." They're talking about Whiteman Air Force Base, the home of the Stealth Bombers and the 509th Bomb Wing Mission. During the Cold War, from 1964 to 1993, this base was also home to Minuteman Missiles. It's a serious place where reaction times are measured in split seconds and mistakes cannot be made. Tours are available Mon through Fri and must be scheduled in advance. Free.

where to eat

Panther Steakhouse. 506 W. McPherson St.; (660) 563-3930. You'll find basic comfort food here in the family-friendly location that's low on frills but high on friendly service and community spirit. Go for a chicken cheeseburger or a chicken fried steak with mashed potatoes and gravy. Open daily, 10 a.m. to 8 p.m.

Williams & Williams Thai Carry-Out. 1505 S. State St.; (660) 563-3209. There's no seating at this delicious little spot, so grab an order to enjoy at Knob Noster State Park or elsewhere. All of your Thai favorites and more are on the menu, including Phad Thai, Quet Thew Gai, and Bame. Mon through Fri, 11 a.m. to 7 p.m.

where to stay

The Silos at Prairie Vale Farm Stay. 29300 MO 127; (573) 280-3947; thesilosatprairievale.com. Located just a little south of and halfway between Knob Noster and Sedalia is an opportunity to spend the night in a grain silo. Wendy and Doug Needy own Prairie Vale Farm, which is home to a wide variety of farm animals; eight grain silos; and four teenage daughters, one of which was frustrated because she didn't have her own room. So they turned one of the grain silos into a bedroom for her, complete with kitchen, bath, and air conditioning. It was a huge hit, and after the daughters went to college, Doug and Wendy converted another grain silo to a somewhat ritzier experience by adding fire rings, yard games, and a hammock outside and opening this unusual bed and breakfast. $$

southeast

day trip 01

southeast

>>>> **water, water everywhere:**
clinton, mo; warsaw, mo; lowry city, mo

clinton, mo

Located approximately halfway between Kansas City and Springfield at the intersection of MO 13 and US 7, Clinton is popular for boaters and anglers who enjoy the quiet pace of Truman Lake's 55,000 acres. Hunting is popular in the area as well. It is also the westernmost trailhead of the Katy Trail.

Day trippers will appreciate more than 100 shops, restaurants, and businesses thriving in the four blocks of Main Street, including seven antique shops. Look for the unusual murals painted on downtown buildings, including the one with all the baby chicks. Clinton claims to have once been the Baby Chick Capital of the World. If you're looking for unusual collectibles from Missouri communities, a miniature village consisting of the courthouse, the Katy Trail Depot, and the other buildings is for sale at area businesses. The downtown square comes alive for Olde Glory Days, a four-day festival surrounding Independence Day and the second Saturday of each warm-weather month for Cruise Nights.

Get around downtown on Bird scooters, those environmentally friendly electric modes of transportation.

getting there

From downtown Kansas City, Clinton is a straight shot on US 71 (Bruce Watkins Parkway). Rush-hour traffic will slow you considerably, but otherwise, plan on about an hour and 20

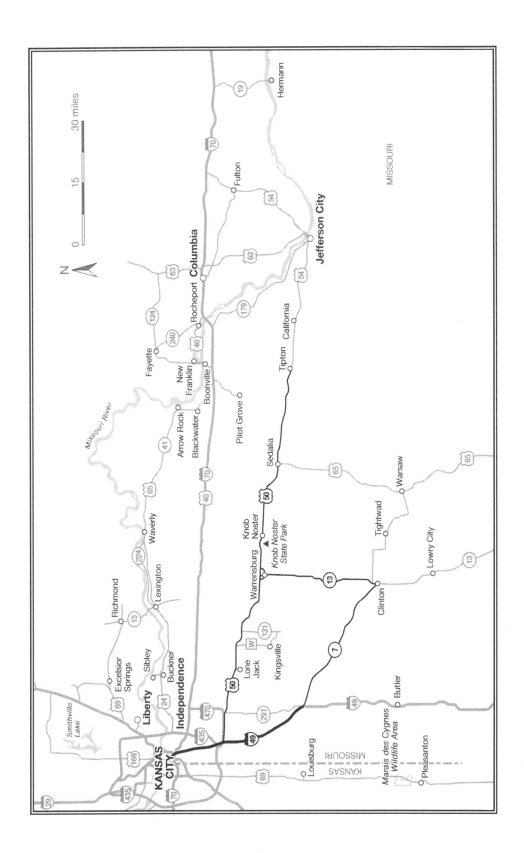

minutes to make the 75-mile drive. If you're traveling from Warrensburg, drive 28 miles south out of Warrensburg on MO 13.

where to go

Bluebird Mercantile. 104 S. Main St.; (660) 383-1818; thebluebirdmerc.com. We love this general store setting because of its emphasis on Missouri-made products. The Bluebird is one of the many retail outlets now carrying Burgers' Smokehouse products. But you'll also find T-shirts that celebrate the Katy Trail, wine cork maps, and Missouri-scented candles. What does Missouri smell like? You'll just have to light one and see. Open Mon through Sat, 10 a.m. to 5 p.m.

Clinton Chamber of Commerce. 200 S. Main St.; (660) 885-8166; clintonmo.com. Located in a storefront building that dates to the 1880s, like much of downtown Clinton, the chamber of commerce will have information for all that there is to do and see in the little community. There are 14 electric car charging stations in Clinton.

Heartland Community Theatre. 108 N. Washington St.; (660) 351-5288. The talented people of the Clinton area coordinate three or four productions a year in this historic space downtown. Check the theater's Facebook page for the latest show.

Henry County Museum and Cultural Arts Center. 203 W. Franklin St.; (660) 885-8414; henrycountymomuseum.org. A fully restored Anheuser-Busch distribution center (built in 1886) serves as the main building of the museum. The annex features building facades that would have been found here in the late 1800s. The museum includes the former Henry County Bank, built in 1887, which now serves as a performing arts center.

Simple Pleasures. 107 S. Washington St.; (660) 383-1810; simplepleasuresgifts.com. Find adorable goodies for new babies and newlyweds here, along with a fun collection of games, toys, puzzles, books, and something special for your furry friends at home. This is just a pleasant little boutique filled with "simple pleasures" in life. Open Mon through Fri, 10 a.m. to 5 p.m.; Sat 10 a.m. to 4 p.m.

clinton's checkered past

In 1923, Lawrence Brown opened a manufacturing company in Clinton that many credit with inventing the game of Chinese checkers. In reality, the game was invented in Germany in the 1830s, but Brown was the first to create the colored, star-patterned board that we associate with Chinese checkers. The boards were handmade and painted by the thousands from the 1920s to the 1950s in Clinton. Today, they are highly collectible and sell for up to $50 a board, living up to Lawrence Brown's trademark that it is "a game for all ages."

White Flower Quilt Shop. 150 W. Jefferson St.; (660) 492-5379; whiteflowerquiltshop. com. Best friends Mary Cupp and Cheryl Craig opened this comprehensive quilt shop. They are fans of floral patterns by Kaffe Fassett and the bright colors of Kimberbell Basics. But recognizing their location near Truman Lake, Mary and Cheryl stock fabric for the anglers and hunters in your family. You don't know how to quilt and don't even have a sewing machine? No worries. The White Flower Quilt Shop includes a community sewing room where you can practice your skills and ask questions of the region's most talented quilters. Open Mon through Sat, 9 a.m. Closed Sun.

Wagoner Park. Sedalia Avenue and 52 Highway. Depending on how you look at it, Missouri's magnificent Katy Trail begins or ends in Clinton at this 19-acre park. There's plenty of parking if you want to hike or bike a few miles of the trail from here. Or stop by the baseball complex and check out some of the fine Little League action in town.

where to eat

Ben Franklin Bistro. 106 Main St.; (660) 890-2021; benfranklinbistro.com. Once a Ben Franklin five and dime store, this coffee shop rivals anything that Starbucks can brew. In addition to whole-bean or ground coffee that you can take home with you or any whipped-up latte or mocha combination you could ask for, the fruit smoothies are wonderful on a hot summer day. Come in early for Belgian waffles with nuts and whipped cream or lunch sandwiches named after Ben Franklin and his contemporaries. Enjoy your treats and free wireless Internet access at one of the many antique tables, which are for sale along with other primitive antiques. Closed Sun. $

Serrano's. 114 W. Jefferson St.; (660) 383-1730; serranosmexicanmo.com. This longtime local favorite is all about authentic Mexican cuisine for breakfast, lunch, or dinner. Try the yummy Choripollo, which is chicken and chorizo sausage, or the burrito tapatio. Without a doubt, they have the best margaritas and fried ice cream in town. Open Tues through Sun, 10:30 a.m. to 9 p.m. Closed Mon. $

Square 109. 109 S. Washington St.; (660) 890-2552. This family-friendly restaurant serves good old Midwestern comfort food. Fried chicken and real mashed potatoes compete with the meatloaf special as the most popular menu items. But you'll also find a wholesome spaghetti and meat sauce, lasagna, and chicken alfredo. Open for breakfast, lunch, and dinner, Mon through Sat, 5 a.m. to 8 p.m.

where to stay

Bucksaw Resort and Marina. 670 SE 803 Rd.; (660) 477-3900; bucksaw.com. This casual, family-friendly resort has a bit of everything to satisfy your weekend getaway needs. Guest rooms, although sparsely furnished, are clean and comfortable. The outdoor pool and deck are as inviting as a day on a pontoon boat, available for rent at the marina. Fishing boats are also available, along with all the trappings for a day on the lake. For campers and RVers, the campground is equally clean and comprehensive. Enjoy lunch or dinner at the restaurant in-season. $

warsaw, mo

From Clinton, travel east on State Highway 7 about 28 miles, crossing several branches of Truman Lake, to Warsaw. This route will take you through the hysterically named village of Tightwad. There was once a bank in Tightwad that had accounts from all 50 states and multiple countries. Everyone wanted a checking account from the Tightwad National Bank. Unfortunately, the bank closed a few years back, a disappointment to frugal investors everywhere.

Honoring a Polish officer who fought in the American Revolution, Warsaw is named for the capital of Poland. It is the county seat of Benton County.

where to go

Benton County Chamber of Commerce. 181 Harrison St.; (660) 438-5922 or (660) 438-2090; welcometowarsaw.com. Stop by to get a map of the Warsaw Historic tour, which includes information on the Butterfield Overland Stagecoach route through this area and more. Ask about the Benton County Quilt Barn Trail.

Benton County Historical Museum. 1660 Hilltop Dr.; (660) 438-2304; bencomo.org. A fun exhibit on steamboats that once plied the Osage River is a fun reason to visit this well done county museum. In addition to historic fishing equipment used on the lakes and a special room on children's history, this museum has an extensive collection of arrowheads and other artifacts from the Native Americans who first called Benton County home. Open Fri through Sun, Apr through Oct. Admission fee.

Benton Ridge Winery, Bistro, and Campground. 25518 Fitzpatrick Ave.; (660) 776-9463; bentonridgewineryandcampground.com. So much more than a lovely winery, Benton Ridge includes a restaurant, a performance space for live bands, multiple hiking trails, and two fishing ponds. With 75 acres, there are woodlots for RVs, tents, and everything in between, as well as a few cabins for rent. Oh, and they make some pretty good wine.

Joe Dice Swinging Bridge. Located on Highway 7 just east of Warsaw; (660) 438-2090. It may give you pause to realize this bridge that's been in use since 1924 was designed by an architect who didn't go further than fourth grade in his formal education. But Joe Dice built 31 suspension bridges, including this one across the Osage River that is on the National Register. Since 1979, it's been closed to automobile traffic, so it's perfectly safe and a lot of fun for bicyclists, walkers, and others. The bridge is wheelchair-accessible.

Truman Lake. 15968 Truman Rd.; (660) 438-2836. Named for our 33rd president, Truman Lake is fed by four rivers and covers more than 56,000 acres in Benton, Henry, St. Clair, and Hickory counties. It's known primarily as a great fishing lake, specifically if you fish for crappie, white and striped bass, channel cat, and walleye. There are five marinas on the lake, dozens of camp sites, hiking trails, and off-road vehicle trails. The visitors center is worthy of a stop. It shares the history of the Osage River valley, including information on area wildlife, the construction of the dam, and archeological artifacts found in the area that is now covered by water. The upper deck offers a great view of the reservoir. Take time to walk the three-quarter-mile nature trail and to visit the log cabins and other buildings that represent life in this region before the dam was built. Free.

Truman Lake Opry. 11022 Highway 7; (660)723-2181; trumanlakeopry.com. This live entertainment venue hosts local bands, comedy shows, and a Wild West dinner show on weekends. Fee.

where to eat

Cosmic Café. 504 W. Main St.; (660) 438-6171. Shannon Noland and her team welcome you to their special little place, which has been voted among the top coffee shops in Missouri multiple times. In addition to a great selection of drinks, the Cosmic Café offers a nice selection of paninis, salads, wraps, and burgers. But the desserts are the real reason to stop by. Chocolate blackberry buttercream cake, lemon blueberry cheesecake cake, and malted milk coconut cake—they are all too pretty to eat. Open Mon through Sat, 7 a.m. to 3 p.m. or later. $

My Secret Garden Tea Room. 420 Commercial St; (660) 438-2848. A part of the Warsaw Flower shop, this comfortable space Is renowned for soups, quiches, and homemade cobbler. Open for lunch only Tues through Fri. $

lowry city, mo

This is an interesting part of Missouri, geographically speaking. It's where the rolling hills of the Ozarks begin to flatten out and become the Great Plains. And Lowry City, with just about 600 residents, takes advantage of the rural opportunities Mother Nature provides here. Fans of country music may know the name Teea Goans. She grew up here, has performed regularly on the Grand Ole Opry since 2010 and recorded five albums.

osceola cheese store—look for the purple mouse

The Osceola Cheese Store has been a fixture in these parts since 1944 when W.K. and Ruth Scott decided they wanted to tinker in the cheese-making business. They called it Riverview Cheese then, and nearly 1,000 dairy farms in the area supplied milk for the cheese.

Business grew nicely for nearly 25 years until the Army Corps of Engineers began flooding 260 square miles of west-central Missouri to form Truman Lake. Osceola Cheese had to move up the hill to its current, very visible location on Highway 13.

Fortunately for Osceola, there are some serious cheese lovers in Missouri. The store carries more than 200 kinds of domestic cheeses. Wisconsin string cheese is their best seller. On an average day, the Osceola Cheese Store sells about 1,000 pounds of cheese, along with crackers, sauces, jams, and other goodies. Some say it is the largest cheese store in the US.

The Osceola Cheese Store no longer relies on local dairy cows to make these many varieties of cheese. Instead, "happy cows" in Wisconsin and a few in Ohio contribute to the goodies found on Missouri Highway 13, exactly halfway between Springfield and Kansas City.

For your own taste of Osceola Cheese, visit osceolacheese.com, or call (417) 646-8131, or stop in any day of the year except for Thanksgiving and Christmas.

It's tempting to just zoom on past Lowry City along Highway 13 in your rush to get elsewhere, but take a moment, turning west into town, to explore this little village. You might find a home décor store with something you need or a restaurant that surprises you with its creativity out here "where the Ozarks meets the Plains."

getting there

From Clinton, drive south on MO 13 for 17 miles.

what to do

American Revolutionary War Flag Way. 6120 SE US 54, Collins. Here along the gravel roadway that leads to Ken Molzahn's farmhouse, you'll see hundreds of replica flags from the Revolutionary War in the US. These include American, French, Spanish, British, Loyalist, Hessian, and Native American flags. Ken is a retired history teacher who had used some of the flags as teaching tools in his classroom. Now that he is retired, he has devoted hundreds of hours of researching more flags that would have flown during the Revolution. They include flags of protest to British taxation and tyranny and various military units from different countries and colonies. He adds a few more flags each spring, complete with flagpoles and descriptive plates for each banner. At last count, there were more than 320 flags, each flown at some time during America's eight-year battle for independence. Ken keeps the flags flying only April to October to protect them from the worst of winter weather.

Gordan's Orchard. (417) 646-8889. The actual street address does not play well with Siri. Instead, head south on MO 13 out of Osceola for 4.5 miles. Look on your right for a big sign. That's it. Bring a cooler, a big basket, and lots of room in your vehicle for a visit to the family-owned orchard. Grown right on their property are 34 varieties of peaches and 15 varieties of apples. But St. Clair County is home to a large Amish community, so you'll always find fresh produce from those local gardens as well as Amish-made jellies, jams, sauces, and more. Grab some packages of dried soup mix and a jar of homemade horseradish mustard, and don't leave without enjoying a cider slushie. Yum! Open daily, May through Nov, 8 a.m. to 6 p.m.

St. Clair County Quilt Block Journey. (417) 309-1786; stclairbusiness.com/tourism. This growing community asset brightens the public-facing sides of barns and businesses throughout St. Clair County. With about 16 quilt blocks and more on the way, the effort highlights a uniquely American art form. Quilter or not, it's a pleasant afternoon driving around the county looking for the next colorful quilt block. For printed maps and other information, stop by the Economic Development Office at 501 Second St. in Osceola.

Sugarfoot BBQ. 5440 NE Highway 82; (417) 646-5800; sugarfootbbq.com. This fun place has a bit of a Caribbean vibe to its décor with some fake palm trees, a patio, and colorful lights, but it's all Missouri serious when it comes to barbeque. Choose from seven rubs and hickory-smoked meats. The beans are good; the coleslaw is horseradish based. And it's served like good barbeque should be served—on butcher-block paper. But the best part is the fresh homemade pie. Each day, Nancy and Meredith are back in the kitchen, creating dough from scratch, and as often as possible, using fresh, local fruit. Blackberry and apple are most common, but sometimes they shake it up a bit. And in strawberry season, you'll have the option of a fresh strawberry shortcake to finish off that meal. Open daily, 10:30 a.m. until late. $

worth more time:
springfield, mo

While it is possible to drive to Springfield and back in a day, it's not a true day trip. Springfield is a community that deserves a few days of your time. This is the birthplace of Route 66. As a result, Springfield is the home of the first drive-through restaurant in the country and a funky motel that dates to 1938. Springfield is also the birthplace of a unique culinary treasure called Springfield Style Cashew Chicken, which should only be experienced at Leong's Asian Diner.

But not all is so quirky. The Springfield Art Museum is a treasure, as is the botanical gardens and a magnificently restored theater called the Gillioz. The childhood home of Brad Pitt, whose family still lives here, Springfield is also home to an artisan chocolatier renowned worldwide.

Find out more at springfieldmo.com or (417) 881-5300.

south

day trip 01

south

>>>> **precious moments:**
butler, mo; carthage, mo

butler, mo

Fans of nice courthouse squares will enjoy a walk around downtown Butler and the court-house. The streets still boast their original brick pavement, and the courthouse lawn, complete with gazebo, is a pleasant place to sit on a park bench and take it all in. Butler is quite proud of its history as the first community west of the Mississippi to have electricity—several months before lightbulbs burned in St. Louis or Kansas City. Butler and Bates County are a part of the Freedom's Frontier National Heritage Area.

getting there

Take US 71/I-49 south out of Kansas City 65 miles into Butler.

where to go

Bates County Museum. 802 Elks Dr.; (660) 679-0134; batescountymuseum.org. Once the county poor farm, today this historic building contains the riches of Bates County's past. The Bates County Historical Society has its offices and research materials here. The second floor of the museum is devoted to eight theme rooms, including opportunities to learn more about the talents of former Butler residents Robert Heinlein, a renowned science fiction writer, and Charles Fisk, a big band leader. The former dormitory wing is a timeline room that begins with the history of the Osage Indians and the Harmony Indian Mission, which opened in

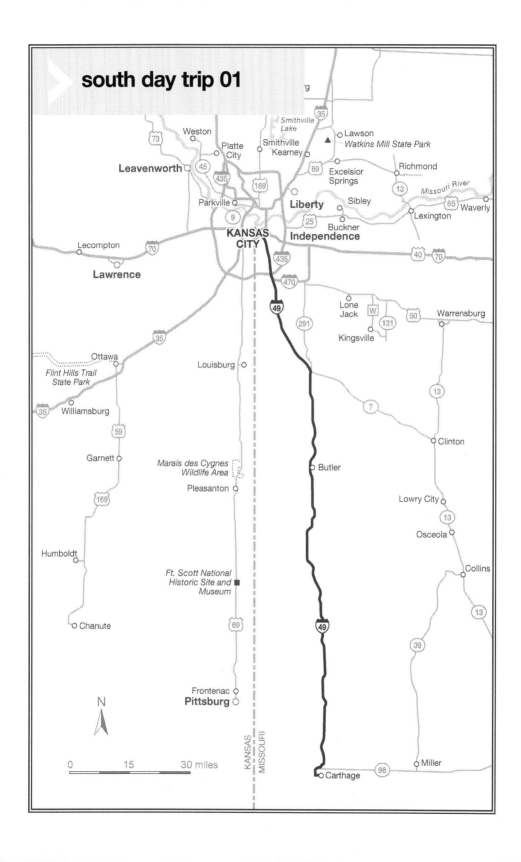

south day trip 01

1821. Two former one-room schoolhouses from Bates County have also been moved to the site. A priceless Steinway grand piano, Model B, from 1876, is a part of the collection and the focal point of recitals and other events at the museum. Open Apr through Oct, Tues through Sat. Admission fee.

Poplar Heights Living History Farm. 5250 NE County Rd. 5004; (990) 200-5620 or (660) 679-0764; poplarheightsfarmorg. After years of community efforts to restore this historic home and farmstead, the Poplar Heights Farm now showcases life in the 1890s in Bates County. The 640 acres includes a home, a broom factory, a corn barn, farm animals, and hiking trails. Throughout the year, the farm hosts special events like cooking classes, tea parties, and holiday celebrations. Hours vary throughout the year. Admission.

carthage, mo

Founded in 1842, Carthage was the site of the first major land battle of the Civil War after the US Congress formally declared war against the South on July 5, 1861. Events of the battle are highlighted at the Battle of Carthage State Historic Site. The town was destroyed by guerrilla warfare in 1864. After the Civil War, Carthage drew investors and entrepreneurs, and by the end of the 19th century, it is reported to have had more millionaires per capita than any other US city. Much of the wealth came from mining the region's rich deposits of lead, zinc, and gray marble. Elaborate Victorian architecture still stands to mark the heyday when the town had unlimited prosperity. A driving tour of several of the Victorian homes in the area or a walking tour of the Courthouse Square Historic District is a lovely afternoon in this community. The streets are lined with hundreds of mature maple trees that make the autumn months here spectacular.

Route 66 continues to bring travelers from around the world through Carthage, while getting their kicks on the Mother Road.

getting there

From Butler, continue down US 71/I-49 for 70 miles straight into Carthage.

where to go

Carthage Convention and Visitors Bureau. 116 W. Third St.; (417) 359-8181; visitcarthage.com. Pick up brochures of area attractions and walking tours here, and find answers to many of your questions.

"Battle of Carthage" Civil War Museum. 205 N. Grant St.; (417) 237-7060 or (417) 682-2279. The museum features authentic artifacts and information about the battle at Carthage, as well as other skirmishes around southwest Missouri. An elaborate, detailed mural of the event, painted by local artist Andy Thomas, and a diorama depicting the battle are showcased here. There's also an entertaining exhibit on Carthage native Belle Star, the notorious female outlaw who rode with the Jesse James gang. Open Tues through Sat, 9 a.m. to 5 p.m.; Sun, 1 to 5 p.m. Free.

Battle of Carthage State Historic Site. Near East Chestnut and River Streets, east of downtown Carthage; mostateparks.com/carthage.htm. This small park, less than eight acres, remains relatively untouched since the battle here in 1861. A simple walking tour takes you over the grounds where both Union and Confederate troops camped, fought, and died. Open daily. Free.

Jasper County Courthouse. Between Third and Fourth Streets, two blocks east of Garrison Street; (417) 358-0421 or (800) 404-0421; visitcarthage.com. Designed in 1894 by Maximilian Orlopp of New Orleans, the Romanesque Revival structure was constructed of native stone quarried by the Carthage Stone Company. It was completed in 1895 at a cost of $100,000 and is on the National Register of Historic Places. Inside, visitors can see several displays of Civil War artifacts and a mural by local artist Lowell Davis entitled "Forged by Fire."

Precious Moments Chapel and Gardens. 480 Chapel Rd.; (800) 543-7975; preciousmomentschapel.com. This is Samuel J. Butcher's "gift of thanksgiving to the Lord." Murals covering 5,000 square feet depict scenes from the Old and New Testaments. The Precious Moments Art Gallery showcases the history behind Precious Moments, original pieces of art by local artists, and personal family memorabilia. The visitor center is patterned after a European village. Cottage- and castle-like structures within the village house several shops. Gospel and bluegrass music shows are presented several times daily. The Fountain of Angels show is a water display choreographed to music and light. The Precious Moments Collectors Christmas Weekend, held the first weekend in December, features a candlelight service, dinner, classes, and tours of the Butcher home. Open daily. Free to tour chapel.

where to stay

Boots Court Motel. 107 S. Garrison Ave.; (417) 310-2989; bootscourt66.com. A fixture on Route 66 since 1939, the Boots Court Motel had deteriorated and closed in the 21st century. However, a community foundation was developed to restore the motel to its original glory while adding modern conveniences, and it is now open for business again. It is said that Clark Cable spent a night here. The Boots today boasts "a radio in every room," as it did in 1939, but more modern conveniences as well. It's a charming little place with just 13 rooms, original glass door knobs, neon sign, and a vintage Carthage police car sitting out front. $

fly with santa, the easter bunny, and more

Old Route 66 is also known as State Highway 96 in these parts. About 20 miles east of Carthage, Old Route 66 intersects with State Highway 97. Head north just miles and you come to the most interesting, entertaining little enterprise. Kiman Kingsley is a crop duster and built a runway and hangar on his 4,000-acre family farm to accommodate his passion for aviation. Over the years, it just got bigger and bigger until he housed 20 airplanes and multiple pilots coming and going from around the world.

So he built a little restaurant for them to eat at called The Hangar Kafe and decorated it with all sorts of model airplanes hanging from the ceiling. Kiman is also a hot air balloon pilot, so he has lots of that stuff hanging around. This is one of the best restaurants anywhere for roast beef or chicken fried steak with home-made mashed potatoes, rolls, pies and ice cream, and really friendly service. People started coming from all over.

Then the Ozark Sky Diving Club began using the airfield, and guests at the restaurant started pulling their chairs outside to watch people jump out of airplanes. So they built a patio with lots of picnic tables and occasionally invited bands to play on the weekends. And more people started coming. Despite all that, things are slow on the farm and in the crop dusting/sky diving business in December, so Rachael, the restaurant manager, thought it would be fun to dress her boss (a rather rotund individual) like Santa Claus and have him take people for a ride in his bright red Cessna 180 (for a fee, of course). That went so well, the Easter Bunny had to get involved and he throws colorful eggs from the sky.

The point is, there's always something going on at the Kingsley Air Field and Hangar Kafe. Be sure to check the website to see what's happening before you drive down (hangarkafe.com), but you can be sure, whatever it is will be fun. Seriously, there's no other place like this in the Midwest.

southwest

day trip 01

southwest

>>>>> **apple cider, wildlife & history:**
louisburg, ks; pleasanton, ks;
fort scott, ks; pittsburg, ks

Southeast Kansas is filled with stores that tout themselves as antique shops but in actuality are crammed wall to wall with flea-market "junque." Just as long as you know what to expect, it's fun to browse and you might discover an occasional treasure, but don't expect a Sotheby-style find.

Southeast Kansas does have unexpected charm. In small towns, such as Chanute, tree-lined cobblestone streets, gorgeous old homes, and whole city blocks have been preserved. Southeast Kansans take pride in their historic heritage, and the area holds many architecturally significant structures—including one of singularly weighty importance called Big Brutus.

louisburg, ks

If you ask most Kansas Citians about Louisburg, there's a good chance they'll think of apples. That's because of the Louisburg Cider Mill, which is a huge reason many people journey to the little community. Many of the residents here are active in the equine business. A drive along the back roads reveals spacious homes and barns, with show horses of several breeds grazing in pastures outlined by white fences. If you ever want to take riding lessons, you'll find several farms in this area where they are offered.

getting there

Follow US 69 south out of downtown about 40 miles to the Louisburg exit.

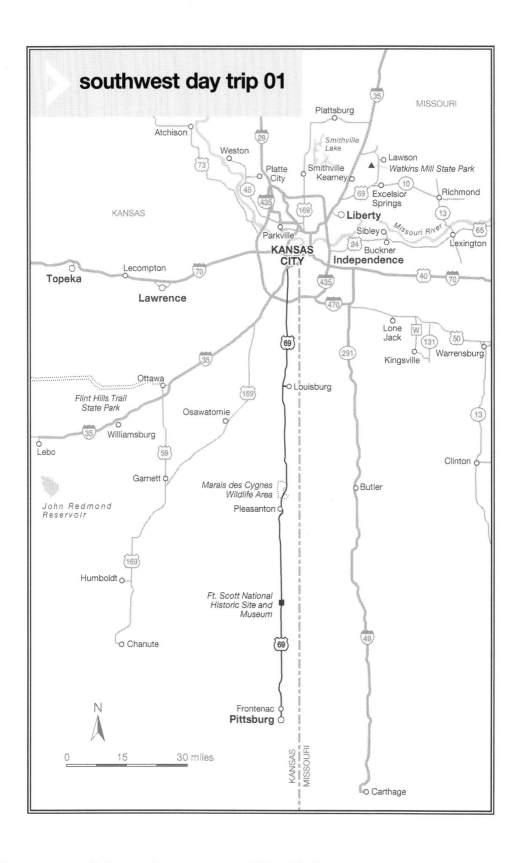

southwest day trip 01

where to go

Louisburg Cider Mill. 14730 KS 68; (913) 837-5202; louisburgcidermill.com. If the idea of cold apple cider, fresh-baked bread, and homemade cider doughnuts intrigues you, this is the place to go for a quick getaway. This family-owned business has been a fixture since the 1970s and has become a prime destination in October for the CiderFest, which includes a corn maze and pumpkin patch. The store, which is open year-round, offers cider products and natural foods in old-time barrels and cases to give the feeling of a country emporium. While you're there, don't forget to sample the doughnuts. These cakelike goodies, made with cider, have a marvelous texture. You can watch the doughnuts being made and then take home the results.

The cider mill is also the home of the **Lost Trail Root Beer Company.** This special root-beer brew is refined in eastern Kansas from a family recipe passed down through generations to the present owners. Apples are pressed every day except Fri and Sun from Sept through Nov. The store is open seven days a week except Thanksgiving and Christmas.

Powell Observatory. 26500 Melrose St. (three miles northwest of Louisburg); (913) 438-3825; askc.org. Run by the Astronomical Society of Kansas City, Powell Observatory houses a 30-inch computer-controlled telescope for public viewing of the night skies from May to Oct. Located in Lewis-Young Park, the facility has a heated classroom (with restrooms) attached to the 20-foot domed observatory, where star-observing parties are held twice a month. Children must be at least 12 years old to attend. If you can't make it to Louisburg, programs are live-streamed the second Saturday of each month. Free, but donations appreciated.

Somerset Ridge Vineyard & Winery. 29725 Somerset Rd.; (913) 491-0038; somersetridge.com. Located six miles west of Louisburg, this boutique winery has about 10 labels produced from the 5,000 vines that the Reynolds family planted in 1998. They invite guests to their tasting room Wed through Sun all year-round, but especially during Oktoberfest weekends. You'll enjoy live music, food trucks, and charcuterie boards as well as wines.

where to shop

Louisburg Market Street. 1220 W. Amity St.; (913) 837-3434; louisburgmarketstreet.com. This store boasts 26,000 square feet of antiques and architectural salvage as well as handcrafted items and home goods. Nearly 75 vendors and artisans have space here. Check the website for the variety of fun events to make shopping here a true outing. Tues through Sat, 10 a.m. to 5 p.m.; Sun, noon to 5 p.m.

Simply Selah. Five Peoria St.; (913) 837-3110. This lovely vintage clothing and antique store, combined with home décor boutique, spills over into multiple rooms of the former Louisburg High School. It's possible to spend hours wandering from room to room where independent craft artisans showcase their talents. Other rooms are filled with antiques or fun clothing items. Open Wed through Sat, 10 a.m. to 5 p.m.; Sun, 1 to 5 p.m.

where to eat

Miss B's Café. 1006 S. Metcalf Rd.; (913) 837-5974; missbscafelouisburg.com. Get out of bed early for this day trip to Louisburg and breakfast at Miss B's. The cinnamon rolls are to die for, but the homemade biscuits and gravy are worth the drive as well. Do a bit of shopping in downtown Louisburg, then come back for lunch. You'll find fabulous homemade lasagna, homemade potato chips with your sandwiches, and homemade pies. Before you head home, get a bucket of fried chicken and sides to go. Open Tues through Sun, 7 a.m. to 2 p.m. $

pleasanton, ks

Despite its pleasant name, the entire region around Pleasanton experienced a great deal of bloodshed in Kansas' fight for statehood prior to the Civil War and is a part of the Freedom's Frontier National Heritage Area. But today, it is a very pleasant place indeed, surrounded by protected areas for wildlife and migrating birds.

getting there

Continue south out of Louisburg on US 69 another 30 miles to reach Pleasanton.

where to go

Isinglass Estate Winery. 16241 W. 381 St., La Cygne; (913) 259-9411; isinglass-estate. com. This is so much more than a winery, although the Vore family makes some nice wines. Spread out across 600 acres, the estate offers horseback riding, vineyard tours, yoga classes, opportunities to cuddle with baby pigs, a Tibetan yak, and English Baby Doll sheep. If you want to learn about polo, that's possible, too, while enjoying a flatbread pizza in the Gastropub. Spend the night in a covered wagon or one of three little cottages on the property. The tasting room is open Mar through Dec. Fri, 2 to 7 p.m.; Sat and Sun, noon to 6 p.m.

Marais des Cygnes Wildlife Area. Managed by the Kansas Department of Wildlife and Parks, 16382 US 69, Pleasanton; (913) 352-8941. Those who have an eye for the unexpected can find wonder in the beauty of the Marais des Cygnes Wildlife Area. Located outside La Cygne in the picturesque floodplain of eastern Kansas, the refuge occupies more than 7,000 acres of man-made marshes rippling with natural lakes and laced with miles of rivers and creeks.

The area is a resting place for migratory waterfowl and other birds. Primitive camping is available, as well as hunting and fishing with the proper license.

The refuge takes its name from the Marais des Cygnes River, meaning "marsh of the swans," a title bestowed by early French trappers. Ironically, there is a good chance that what the trappers saw were not swans, but white pelicans that migrate through the area each spring. Flocks of these graceful, long-billed creatures can be seen floating in the water in early May. Their presence in the marsh pool, tinted a rosy amber by the setting sun, creates a surrealistic splendor.

Ducks, geese, herons, egrets, and birds of prey can also be spotted in the marshy area. During spring and fall migration, the temporary population of migrating ducks may reach 150,000. So far, 300 species of birds have been sighted at Marais des Cygnes, and about 115 species, including mallards, blue- and green-winged teal, and Canada geese, nest here.

As for fishing, it's plentiful in spring when crappies and catfish abound.

The fishing draws people who stand along the marsh banks for much of the day, hoping to catch their evening meal. Those driving campers park alongside the water and sit in lawn chairs, casting in their lines at twilight.

Marais des Cygnes National Wildlife Refuge. (913) 352-8956; fws.gov/maraisdescygnes. Located just across Highway 69 from the state property, these 7,500 acres, managed by the US Fish and Wildlife Service, are unique for their abundance of large tracts of bottomland hardwood forest. Common species are pin and burr oak, pecan, walnut, and hickory. Six hiking trails, including one concrete ADA-accessible trail, allows for opportunities to explore that habitat for wild turkey, deer, and lots of birds. Because this is predominantly woodland, there is not the abundance of waterfowl seen here as on the state-managed property nearby. More than 35 species of warblers have been documented during the spring migration. The best viewing is usually in May in forested areas. A new visitor interpretive center opened in 2022.

Marais des Cygnes State Historic Site. 26426 E. 1700th Rd.; (913) 352-8890. The days leading up to the Civil War were extremely violent on the border between Missouri and Kansas, and this 43-acre park documents one of the many tragedies. In May 1858, 11 unarmed and innocent abolitionist free-staters were captured, and 10 were shot, resulting in 5 fatalities in what is now called the Marais des Cygnes Massacre. Open daily. Free.

Trading Post Museum. 15710 N. Fourth St.; (913) 352-6441. There was once a little town here called Trading Post, and this little museum is all that is left to tell the story. You may explore a genealogy library, one-room schoolhouse, log cabin, and a few other outbuildings. This tiny spot played an important role as a rendezvous for a pro-slavery gang in the 1850s. Here the pro- and antislavery forces fought over whether the territory should enter the Union as a free or slave state. Open Apr through Nov.

where to stay

Cedar Crest Lodge. 25939 E. 1000 Rd.; (913) 352-6533; cedarcrestlodge.com. If you can't get enough of the natural beauty of the great outdoors of this region, spend the night with Matt and Laura Cunningham at Cedar Crest Lodge. Their 7,000-square-foot home is situated on 113 acres of rolling hills, trees, and ponds. Their 11 guest rooms reflect their love of travel. Laura is a great cook, preparing a breakfast you will long remember using produce and herbs she grows right out her back door. If you like to paint and decorate, ask them about their painting seminars. Or if you need a massage or other spa treatment, they can make arrangements for that as well. Go for a hike on the trails through their property and follow up with some stargazing in the night sky. $–$$

fort scott, ks

All along the Overland Trails, US Cavalry forts, such as Fort Scott, sprang up to defend western settlements. Between 1838 and 1845 a military road was constructed through the Indian Territory to connect Fort Leavenworth in Kansas and Fort Gibson in Oklahoma. Throughout the years the road was traveled by soldiers, immigrants, Native Americans, outlaws, and traders.

Today the old military road no longer exists, but modern US 69 and other connecting pathways located near its original route have been designated the Frontier Military Scenic Byway. Fort Leavenworth and Fort Scott, two of the remaining historic Kansas forts that lie along that route, are open to tour today.

From Apr to Dec, the restored military fort hosts a series of special events featuring activities that portray a vivid picture of life on a frontier post during the 19th century.

One of Fort Scott's most famous residents was internationally acclaimed photographer, filmmaker, and poet Gordon Parks, born here in 1912. Not until 2003 did the city of Fort Scott finally pay tribute to this accomplished Black man, first with a permanent exhibit in the gallery space of Mercy Health Center and more recently with the Gordon Parks Center for Cultural Diversity at Fort Scott Community College. An annual celebration in October honors his contribution to the city of Fort Scott and the world.

And someday another celebration may take place for comedic genius Jason Sudeikis, a former *Saturday Night Live* cast member, star of several movies, and Academy award winner for *Ted Lasso*. Sudeikis attended Fort Scott Community College on a basketball scholarship.

Visitors may enjoy taking advantage of the bike share program to explore the town.

getting there

From Pleasanton, continue south on US 69 another 25 miles to Fort Scott.

where to go

Fort Scott Tourism Information Center. 231 E. Wall St.; (620) 670-2750; visitfortscott .com. Find a complimentary cup of lemonade or coffee waiting for you here, along with information about theme weekends, special living history programs, and seasonal celebrations. This is also where Dolly the Trolley tours start each day at 10 a.m., which take visitors through the historic city, including Fort Scott National Cemetery. The tours are completely narrated and leave hourly from the center. Fee for trolley tours.

Fort Scott National Historic Site. Old Fort Boulevard; (620) 223-0310; nps.gov/fosc. The restored 1842 Frontier Military Fort was built to keep peace between Native Americans and the settlers. The troops wound up policing the plains, supplying Union armies during the Civil War, and protecting railroad workers in the 1870s. A major tourist attraction that brings visitors from around the world, Fort Scott is the only completely restored frontier fort of the pre–Civil War period in the United States. Now designated a National Historic Site, the fort is located right in the center of the city, within walking distance of many shops and dining establishments.

Fort Scott's 18 structures, including a hospital, a guardhouse, a bakery, and barracks, tell the story of the mounted Dragoons, "bleeding Kansas," and the Civil War. Open for self-guided tours year-round; closed Thanksgiving, Christmas, and New Year's Day. Admission fee.

Gordon Parks Center for Culture and Diversity. Fort Scott Community College, 2108 S. Horton; (620) 223-2700, ext 5850; gordonparkscenter.org. Honoring one of the city's most accomplished residents and one of the world's leading photographers, writers, and filmmakers, this facility on the campus of Fort Scott Community College is a resource for those who wish to explore social issues such as racism and poverty and understand how those issues influence the arts. The collection includes 30 of his photographs, his cameras, a number of books, and other personal items. Programs throughout the year delve into these subjects, and exhibits include the results of an annual photo contest and materials from Parks's private collection. Open Mon through Fri during the academic year. Free.

The Lavender Patch. 2376 Locust Rd.; (620) 223-1364; thelavenderpatchfarm.com. Who doesn't love the smell of lavender? So imagine how great more than 1,000 lavender plants smell when they are in bloom at Betsy and Davin Reichard's little farm. That's usually in late June, when the Reichard's host a little festival, but throughout the year, Betsy is creating lotions, soaps, sachets, and baking kits using dried lavender. The hours vary greatly due to the season and weather, so call before you visit.

Lowell Milken Center for Unsung Heroes. 1 S. Main; (620) 223-1312; lowellmilkencenter.org. Few places in the Midwest will move you or challenge you like the Lowell Milken Center. Inspired by a teacher who changed his life, Lowell Milken opened this facility to celebrate unsung heroes and encourage others to ask themselves "What do you stand for?" From a

Catholic woman who saved Jewish children from the Warsaw ghetto to a photographer who helped expose human rights abuses in the Congo, this museum celebrates people who have made a difference in the most trying of situations. Learn about opportunities to create your own project to help others, funded through this center. "You, too, can make a difference." Mon through Sat, 10 a.m. to 5 p.m.

National Cemetery. 900 E. National Ave.; (620) 223-2840. The National Cemetery is older than Arlington and just as historically important. Native American scouts buried here include many with memorable names and histories. Soldiers interred on these grounds include Black infantrymen from the country's first Colored Volunteer Infantry. Free.

Victorian Downtown. From Old Fort Boulevard to Sixth Street. The six-block downtown area is on the National Register of Historic Places. Buildings from the period 1860 to 1919 have been restored and are the architectural showpiece of the city. Many homes feature ornate woodwork designs of gingerbread, stained and leaded glass, turrets, hitching posts, and stepping-stones for carriages. Walking-tour information is available from the Fort Scott Tourist Information Center.

where to eat

Aunt Toadies. 1411 E. Wall St.; (620) 223-5007. This local hot spot has earned its reputation for absolutely everything being made from scratch. Fried chicken, meatloaf, and roast beef sandwiches are among the daily specials. Friday-night steaks are locally sourced from a farm in nearby Sheldon, Missouri. Open Mon through Fri, 11 a.m. to 8 p.m.; Sat, 4 to 8 p.m. Closed Sun. $

Crooners. 117 S. Main St.; (620) 224-9787; fscrooners.com. The best Sunday brunch in southeast Kansas is among the offerings at this downtown establishment, complete with bakery, patio, and lounge. If a special occasion brings you to Fort Scott or if you're craving something a little high end, consider this fine-dining restaurant known for its steaks, seafood ravioli, and grilled swordfish. A large group may enjoy a family-style dinner of pasta or Cajun chicken. Open Wed through Sat, 5 to 9 p.m. Sun brunch, 10:30 a.m. to 1:30 p.m. $$

Nu Grille. 24 N. National Ave.; (620) 223-9949. A local favorite since 1946, the Nu Grille is famous for homemade onion rings, cheap but decent hamburgers, and a sense of nostalgia. Homemade chili and chili dogs are also popular. If you want to know what's going on in Fort Scott, stop in for coffee midmorning at the Nu Grille and eavesdrop on the locals. Open seven days a week, 7 a.m. until late. $

where to stay

Courtland Hotel and Spa. 121 E. First St.; (620) 223-0098; courtlandhotel.com. Originally built in 1906 to accommodate the railroad workers and travelers through Fort Scott, the

Courtland and its 15 rooms have been renovated numerous times and continue to serve modern travelers. The tin ceilings are original as are many of the fixtures, but combined with elegant amenities from the 21st century. Frank and Cheryl Adamson are the owners, who are on-site every day to help your stay be comfortable. Breakfast is included in the room rate. The Aveda Spa contributes to the relaxing getaway here. $

Twin Mansions Bed and Breakfast. 742 and 750 S. National Ave.; drywoodcreek.com/bed-and-breakfast. These two identical mansions were built by a wealthy banker for his two daughters in the 1880s. Today the homes become one with the gracious hospitality of Carrie and Marty Elton. One inn is home to the Dry Wood Creek Café, which is where guests enjoy breakfast. The other inn is home to five spacious guest rooms, recently remodeled with modern amenities. Breakfast and lunch are also open to the public here. $$–$$$

bee the change

About halfway between Fort Scott and Pittsburg on Highway 69, turn east on Deer Road and head toward the Missouri border. Here you'll see a sign for Black Dogs Farm, a heartfelt destination trying to save the honeybees and other critters as well. Bryan and Barbara Ritter were your basic Kansas City suburbanites when they became increasingly aware of the impacts of the diminishing population of honeybees in our world. So they decided to do their part.

In 2010, they bought 80 acres and planted fruit trees, wildflowers, and such that make bees happy, and they built a bunch of hives. But then Bryan learned the hard way that he is extremely allergic to bee stings. They passed their beehives on to other caring keepers. They are still glad to talk to you about what they learned about bee keeping.

They also bought a bunch of sheep because they like the wool. Barbara spins yarn, which she has for sale, along with scarves, hats, and shawls that she knits. They also sell eggs and jellies from the fresh fruit on the farm, and walnuts from those massive trees.

Despite the bees that initially led to this farm, their real passion is rescue dogs, particularly black dogs, which are the least likely to be adopted and most likely to be abused. They care for these dogs and, if possible, will adopt them out to good families.

Bryan and Barbara are always looking for help on the farm because saving the world is a lot of work for just two people. They host firewood-cutting parties and sheep-shearing parties and nut-harvesting events. If you want to stay a while, there's a camper you can rent just to sit and watch the fireflies at night. The website is blackdogsfarm.net. Or call at (620) 223-2702.

pittsburg, ks

The "Fried Chicken Capital of Southeast Kansas," Pittsburg has several chicken emporiums from which to choose. It is also famous for being the jumping-off point for the attraction known as Big Brutus, a 16-story-high, one-of-a-kind mining shovel located just southwest of Pittsburg near West Mineral, Kansas.

At first glance you might not know that this town has a lot of Old World drama behind it. Pittsburg was actually an early-20th-century settlement of Europeans who came to work in the coal mines. Those who live here today are the descendants of people who traveled to this part of Crawford County from Sicily, Austria, and Bohemia.

Pittsburg, along with the tiny town of Frontenac, which borders it to the north, was a Crawford County mining community that appealed to those who wanted to escape poverty, oppression, and political injustice. Lured by the promise of work, the immigrants who toiled in the mines brought an unusual mix of cultural and ethnic backgrounds to southeast Kansas. Between 1880 and 1940, more than 31,000 people from 52 countries flocked here to begin deep-shaft mining, the most dangerous method of digging coal out of the earth.

Eventually the area became known as the Little Balkans region because of the number of Europeans who settled here.

Crawford County's colorful past is celebrated with a number of festivals. Little Balkans Days, held on Labor Day weekend, features bocce ball, a parade, polka music, arts-and-crafts booths, and ethnic foods. Like many communities, Pittsburg has invested in colorful murals and many of them showcase the miners and spirit of the people who dug these mines and built a community.

getting there

From Fort Scott, continue south on US 69 another 30 miles to reach Pittsburg.

where to go

Crawford County Convention and Visitors Bureau. 117 W. Fourth St.; (620) 231-1212; explorecrawfordcounty.com. Stop in for answers to any questions you may have and a hardy welcome to the community.

Crawford State Park. 1 Lake Rd., Farlington; (620) 362-3671. Located about halfway between Fort Scott and Pittsburg, this 500-acre state park is worthy of a bit of exploration. There's plenty of camping, a nice swimming beach, boat ramps, and other amenities, but also something that most other state parks don't have: Crawford Lake and the entire park were built by the Civilian Conservation Corps in the 1930s. They actually dug this lake by hand. An on-site memorial tells the entire history of the CCC, the Great Depression, how the men of the CCC learned to read and write, and how a camp in a community really helped lift that particular community out of the Depression ahead of other regions. On special holidays, the Avenue of Flags, featuring 50 state flags and 50 US flags, crosses the dam in honor of the men who built the lake and others who have donated to its upkeep.

Big Brutus. Located six miles west of the junction of KS 7 and KS 102, West Mineral; (620) 827-6177; bigbrutus.org. He's formally known as the Bucyrus Erie 1850 B, but his friends just call him Big Brutus. This 11-million-pound mining shovel is 16 stories high—something you see from a distance as you drive across the Kansas prairie. The Pittsburg & Midway Coal Mining Company purchased Big Brutus at a cost of $6.5 million—not to dig coal but to remove the dirt and rocks covering the coal seams. From 1962 to 1974, more than 9 million tons of coal were gouged out of the dirt, laying bare the land and leaving hundreds of "strip pits" behind. In 1974, when it was no longer cost-effective to operate Big Brutus, the steam shovel was shut down.

The legacy of Big Brutus could have been an environmental disaster; instead, it is a rare instance of a mined land reclamation success story. The Pittsburg & Midway Coal Mining Company donated the area surrounding Big Brutus to the Kansas Department of Wildlife and Parks, which, in turn, has reclaimed the 14,250 acres of land as a haven for hunting and fishing.

The Big Brutus Visitors Center tells the colorful history and heritage of the region. You can take a self-guided tour or climb up Big Brutus's boom, but you have to be at least 13 years old. There are primitive camping facilities and RV hookups on-site, plus picnic tables and hot showers to meet the needs of campers and visitors. Open daily. Admission fee.

Crawford County Historical Museum. 651 S. US 69; (620) 231-1440. The colorful history of Crawford County is featured in interesting exhibits that include vintage clothing, coal-mining and farming artifacts, photographs, and horse-drawn vehicles. Miss America 1968 was from this area, and her handmade dress with 30 pounds of sequins is also on display. Outdoor displays include a one-room schoolhouse, an authentic neighborhood grocery store, and a coal-mining steam shovel. Open Thurs through Sun afternoons or by appointment. Free.

Hotel Stilwell. 707 Broadway; (620) 235-1997. Built in 1880, the historic hotel has hosted guests who have included William Jennings Bryan, Eugene Debs, Susan B. Anthony, and Theodore Roosevelt. The building was restored in 1997 and is on the National Register of Historic Places. The architectural design features a grand stone entry flanked by brick columns on the first floor, wide bay windows, a circular leaded skylight, generous ornate plasterwork, and stained-glass windows. The upper floors have been converted to apartments for senior citizens, while the first-floor historic common areas are open to the public to tour. There are a few businesses operating inside, including Otto's Cafe, so it's certainly appropriate for you to come in and look around. You'll be impressed.

Mined Land Wildlife Area. Between Pittsburg and West Mineral; (620) 231-3173; kdwp .state.ks.us. Several hundred water-filled former strip pits dot the Mined Land Wildlife Area, a 14,000-acre region with about 1,500 acres of public waters near the communities of West Mineral and Pittsburg. More than 200 lakes in the area are managed for fishing. Sport fish are abundant here, with largemouth bass, spotted bass, channel catfish, walleye, and a specially stocked lake trout being favorites of anglers.

Native grasses have been reintroduced here, along with a variety of wildlife. Several marshes have been constructed to attract ducks and geese.

With its diversity of terrain and animal life, the Mined Land Wildlife Area is popular with photographers and wildlife observers, as well as hunters. Quail, white-tailed deer, and wild turkey are found in abundance, as are raccoons, muskrats, bobcats, coyotes, and a herd of rather photogenic buffalo. As the wildlife area covers parts of three counties, directions and addresses are impossible, but call the wildlife and parks office for input on the aspects in which you are most interested.

Pittsburg State University. 1701 S. Broadway; (620) 235-4122; pittstate.edu. This campus of 5,200 students on the south end of town has extensive landscaping, outdoor sculptures, a hike/bike trail, and other impressive features. The campus is home to three art galleries with quality exhibitions rotating throughout the year, and a quality student theater program. Another popular attraction on campus is the Veterans Memorial Amphitheatre, which features patriotic bronzes, a half-scale replica of the Vietnam Veterans Memorial in Washington, D.C., and seating for 250. The university sponsors a Visiting Writers Series, a Performing Arts and Lecture Series, and a Solo and Chamber Music Series. Pitt is the only university in the country with a gorilla as a mascot, thus the large number of gorilla sightings around town.

where to shop

Frontenac Bakery. 211 N. Crawford St., Frontenac; (620) 231-7908. Established in 1900, this bakery has had only five owners in more than 100 years. That list now includes Mike and Jayme Mjelde. In addition to providing bread to all of the chicken restaurants, this bakery has a nice selection of breadsticks and hard-crust Italian breads for you to enjoy at home. But check out the cinnamon rolls. During the worst of the pandemic, the Mjeldes and their team provided cinnamon rolls to health-care workers throughout southeast Kansas. Open daily, 8 a.m.

Pallucca & Son. 207 E. McKay St., Frontenac; (620) 231-7700. This off-the-beaten-path find is a fun place to stop and shop. Opened in 1912, Pallucca's is family owned and oper-ated and specializes in imported Italian foods. The meat department carries everything you need for making a great Italian sandwich, from large imported Italian hams to handmade

Italian sausage. Fine pasta, dessert items, candies, and sauces from Italy line the shelves, along with American-made products. Open Mon through Sat, 9 a.m. to 6 p.m.

where to eat

As the "Fried Chicken Capital of Southeast Kansas," Pittsburg is home to ethnic-influenced restaurants that serve fried chicken with German potato salad, coleslaw with garlic dressing, and peppers, tomatoes, and bread. This custom began in 1934, when Anne Pichler's husband was injured in the mines. Born near Budapest, the woman best known as Chicken Annie had a family to raise; therefore she started selling fried chicken out of her home to make a living. Eventually Chicken Annie opened her restaurant, which became so famous that it began to draw competitors. In 1943 Mary Zerngast opened her fried chicken restaurant down the road from Chicken Annie's. Chicken Mary and Chicken Annie went head to head as the famous southeast Kansas chicken wars heated up. Today, these and other family-owned restaurants still compete for business as the fowl play continues. The chicken places open at 4 p.m. for dinner only on weekdays; those open on Sun offer dinner from 11 a.m. to 8 p.m. They include the following:

Barto's Idle Hour. 201 S. Santa Fe, Frontenac; (620) 232-9834. Closed Sun and Mon. $$

Chicken Annie's of Girard. KS 5 east of Girard. (620) 724-4090. Closed Mon and Tues. $$

Chicken Annie's Original. 1143 E. 600th Ave., Pittsburg; (620) 231-9460. Closed Mon. $$

Chicken Mary's. 1133 E. 600th Ave., Pittsburg; (620) 231-9510. Closed Mon. $$

Gebhardt Chicken Dinners. 124 N. 260th St., Mulberry; (620) 764-3451. Open Fri through Mon. $$

Pichler's Chicken Annie's®. 1271 S. 220th St., Pittsburg; (620) 232-9260. Closed Mon. $$

other restaurants of interest

Jim's Steak and Chop House. 1912 N. Broadway; (620) 231-5770. Established in 1938, this third-generation family-owned and -operated restaurant has been in the same location for 80-plus years. Renowned in the area for its juicy steaks, the restaurant also offers chicken and seafood specialties. Jim's serves dinner only, starting at 4 p.m. Closed Sun. $$–$$$

The Jolly Fox Brewery. 301 S. Broadway; (620) 670-5999; jollyfoxbrew.com. The first craft brewery to open in Pittsburg, the Jolly Fox has a great Sunday brunch, great burgers, and great pizza. Oh, and the craft beer is pretty good as well. Open Tues through Thurs, 3 to 9 p.m.; Fri and Sat, 11 a.m. to 11 p.m.; Sun, 10 a.m. to 3 p.m. $

Otto's Cafe. 711 N. Broadway; (620) 231-6110. Built in 1945 as an annex to old Hotel Stilwell, this dining establishment is a throwback to the days when coffee shops were plentiful. Simple food, prepared well, is what you'll find here. Breakfast features everything from omelets and waffles to French toast and biscuits and gravy. If you're in the mood for Otto's excellent version of fried chicken, make plans for your lunch here. Leave room for homemade dessert. Open for breakfast and lunch. Closed Sun. $–$$ (no cards)

day trip 02

southwest

civil war & safaris:
osawatomie, ks; garnett, ks; humboldt, ks; chanute, ks

Don't head out on this trip expecting blockbuster attractions, but it's those unexpected little surprises that make this journey worthwhile. The towns listed here all have shady, tree-lined streets and historic old homes and buildings that have been lovingly preserved. It's a part of the world where people take pride in their homes and expect their neighbors to do the same, and where folks will greet you on the street and welcome you wholeheartedly into their communities. But with your first stop in Osawatomie, you'll find that has not always been the case.

osawatomie, ks

This pleasant community of less than 5,000 people is and always will be associated with the cause of freedom in the United States and around the world because of one resident who lived here for just about nine months in 1855–1856. His name was John Brown. He committed brutal murders while living here, yet probably did more than any single individual to assure that Kansas became a free state and that slavery would eventually be abolished in the United States.

getting there

From downtown, head south on I-35 about 20 miles to exit 215, which is US 169. Follow US 169 another 30 miles straight into Osawatomie.

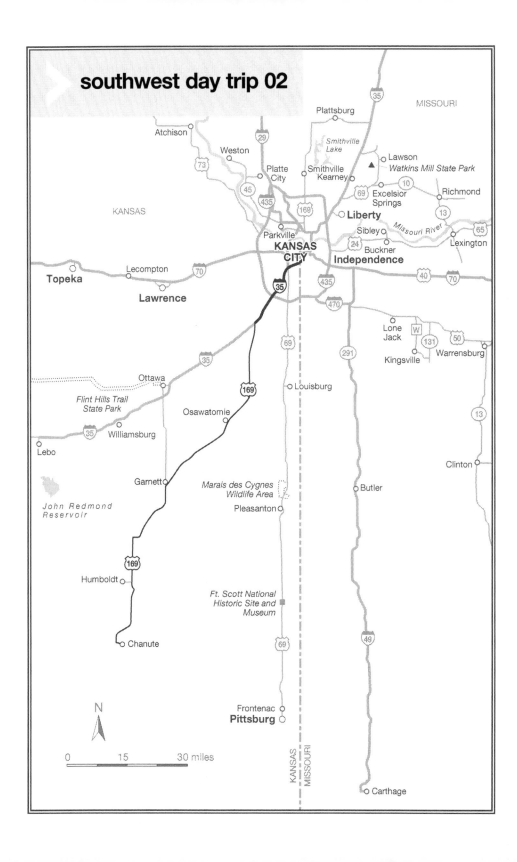

where to go

Osawatomie Chamber of Commerce. 509 Fifth St.; (913) 755-4114; osawatomiechamber.org. The chamber office is located inside a replica of the Union Pacific Railroad depot that served this city for generations. When the railroad unceremoniously demolished the original depot, city leaders got together and recreated it in an empty lot on Main Street. The chamber offices are located here with all sorts of information about the community. A small museum and gift shop are also on the premises. Open daily.

Flint Hills Trail State Park. 1400 South St. This 117-mile-long trails-to-trails project passes through five counties in central Kansas with Osawatomie being the eastern terminus or as the locals call it, Mile Zero. It's a particularly attractive trailhead with an archway over the trail, perfect for photos, a pedestrian bridge, an information kiosk, and most important, clean, modern restrooms with flush toilets.

John Brown State Historic Site. 10th and Main Streets; (913) 755-4384. This little cabin in the John Brown Memorial Park actually belonged to the Reverend Samuel Adair and his wife, Florella. It was a stop on the Underground Railroad and survived the Battle of Osawatomie in August of 1856. John Brown was a frequent visitor to this home, and the story of his role in Kansas and US history makes the museum a valuable day trip. Open Tues through Sat.

Miami County Trolley. (913) 306-3388; miamicountytrolley.com. Enjoy a leisurely ride through rural Miami County to visit four of the county's wineries. This is a fun activity to celebrate a birthday, an anniversary, or just another great day to be alive.

where to stay

Netherfield Natural Farm. 24126 KS Highway 7; (202) 487-6742; netherfieldnaturalfarm.com. This fabulous farm getaway offers much more than a place to escape for a few days. In addition to a hot tub, a swimming pool, and a bar in the barn, you'll be able to partake in cooking classes on how to make the best biscuits ever or pasta or any variety of recipes. The five guest rooms are named after the original owners of the house. Get to know Jesse and Rhoda because that room has a balcony. $$

garnett, ks

This small community features three lakes, more than 1,000 acres of parks, a hiking/biking trail, an unusual bed-and-breakfast, and a small but interesting museum that displays works of regional artists and more. For more information: Garnett Area Chamber of Commerce, 131 W. 5th St.; (785) 448-6767; simplygarnett.com.

getting there

From Osawatomie head southwest on US 169 just another 30 miles to Garnett.

where to go

Anderson County Courthouse. Garnett Town Square; (785) 448-6767. Designed by prominent architect George P. Washburn, the courthouse was dedicated in 1902 and is listed on the National Register of Historic Places. A classic example of Romanesque architecture, it features a restored courtroom with stained-glass windows. Open weekdays. Free.

Cedar Valley Reservoir. Located 7.5 miles west of Garnett on Kentucky Road; (785) 448-5496. The beautiful scenery here provides the perfect getaway, with floating docks, boat loading ramps, picnic areas, and wilderness and RV camping facilities. Free. Boating, fishing, and camping permits required.

Lake Garnett. North Lake Road; (785) 448-5496. The 55-acre lake offers recreational facilities that include a golf course, campsites, sporting clay range, swimming pool, and much more. Free. Boating, fishing, and camping permits required.

Prairie Spirit Rail Trail. Kansas Department of Wildlife and Parks, 419 S. Oak St.; (785) 448-6767; bikeprairiespirit.org. This 52-mile trail from Ottawa to Iola passes through Garnett on what was once the Santa Fe Railroad right-of-way. It provides a picturesque hiking and biking excursion in and around the city. Motorized wheelchairs are welcome. Trail permits are not required inside city limits but are needed for youngsters under 16 who venture outside town. Open daily during daylight hours. Free.

Santa Fe Depot. Main Street and Eighth Avenue. Built during the Depression years, this depot saw the passage of many trains until its closing in 1974. Beautifully restored in 1996, it now serves as a trailhead for users of the Prairie Spirit Rail Trail. The depot visitor center provides tourism information and has exhibits of railroad memorabilia on display, along with a wildflower garden. Free.

Thelma Moore Community Playhouse. 140 W. Fifth Ave.; (785) 304-1683; chamber-playerstheatre.org. The former Garnett United Presbyterian Church is now the home of this charming and energetic group of local thespians. Usually one or two shows a year are all they manage with a team of dedicated volunteers, but oh, how good the shows are. The community players are raising funds to build an actual theater. Check the website for the next production, then head to Garnett to help these fine actors achieve their goals.

Valley View Elk Farm. 27640 NW Jewel Rd.; (785) 448-3085. Rodney and Rachelle Miller operate this elk farm and sell the very healthy meat at area farmers' markets or from their farm, where tours are offered. Tram rides to the pastures get you up close to the majestic animals, but completely protected by fencing. Products for sale include dropped elk antlers, velvet products, and a variety of meat products. Appointments are necessary, so call in advance. Fee.

Walker Art Gallery. 125 W. Fourth Ave.; (785) 448-3388. A rare collection of paintings, sculptures, prints, and drawings donated to Garnett by Maynard Walker features works by John Steuart Curry, Edouard Manet, and Jean Baptiste Corot. The conservators from Kansas City's Nelson-Atkins Museum of Art have restored many of the paintings. Docent tours are available by reservation. Free. Closed Sun.

where to eat

Toddy's Back Porch. 26192 NE Neosho Rd.; (785) 448-9800. It's difficult to decide what is best about this place: the wood-fired pizza or the live music that is a part of many evening gatherings. And the bar has a surprisingly diverse selection of mixings for a fine cocktail hour. Corn hole tournaments and Chiefs football create some serious sports anxiety here, but come on down. They are always celebrating something at Toddy's. FYI, Toddy is Jim Todd, whom we are told is quite a fan of Scotch. Open evenings only, Wed through Sat, about 4 p.m. until midnight or later. $

Troyer's 1883. 101 W. Fourth Ave.; (785) 443-1339. Housed in an 1883 building that was once a bank, this space offers an eclectic experience in dining and shopping. Come early for a cup of coffee and something fresh from the bakery, then enjoy watching various artists at work in the studio space and maybe find a goodie for yourself from the craft artisans whose work is for sale here. Have a yummy lunch in a lovely setting that features high ceilings and oak furniture. Open daily, 7 a.m. to 8 p.m. $

humboldt, ks

It's not often that a tiny little town on the Kansas prairie gets a write-up in the *New York Times* travel section as a great place to visit. But in January 2022, the newspaper showcased Humboldt right along with seemingly more exotic places through Europe, Africa, and Asia. The excitement comes from a grassroots effort to revitalize the little town that has resulted in a number of shops, gardens, and events in the town of 2,000. Among the reasons to visit Humboldt is Friday-night movies on the square and a community-wide water fight each August.

getting there

Follow US 169 south out of Garnett, 330 miles to KS-224, otherwise known as Hawaii Road. Turn right, or west. Go two miles to Humboldt.

where to go

Humboldt Chamber of Commerce. 725 Bridge St.; (620) 473-3232; humboldtkansas. com.

Southwind Bike Trail. (620) 36-8128. This is a 6.5-mile crushed-rock trail that connects to the larger Prairie Spirit Trail in Iola. In all, you can walk or bike for nearly 60 miles. You'll ride over bridges, past historic railroad signs and plenty of Kansas scenery.

where to shop

Bijou Confectionary. 810 Bridge St.; (620) 228-2653; bijouconfectionary.com. This is worth the drive to Humboldt. More than 125 kinds of bulk candies, homemade macaroons, lots of fudge, and so many other goodies. With a definitive French flair and elegant presentation, this little confectionery would be right at home in some of the world's most cosmopolitan cities. Open Tues through Sat, 11 a.m. to 6 p.m.

Bison Woodworking. 1216 Hawaii Rd.; (844) 558-1527; bisonwoodworking.com. If you are looking for something unique for your kitchen, patio, or game room, this is the place. Using locally sourced oak, walnut, hickory, and alder, Craig and Dirk and their staff create beautiful tables, wine carts, and butcher blocks. Choose a lazy Susan with a message for your household or find a poker table for the game room that can't be found anywhere else. Most of all, find inspiration from local woodworkers who take pride in their finished product. Open Mon through Fri, 8 a.m. to 3 p.m.

Humboldt Mercantile. 102 S. Ninth St.; (620) 473-7009; humboldtmercantile.com. You'll find the community's best cup of coffee at Octagon City, one of many treats inside two adjoined storefronts downtown. You'll find the best of local growers and makers in a casual setting where the smell of great coffee keeps the conversation lively. Open daily.

chanute, ks

When you drive through downtown Chanute, you'll see a massive sculpture and memorial to the Wright Brothers, Wilbur and Orville, who conquered human flight. And you surely wonder why here in small-town Kansas? Well, we all know great accomplishments don't happen in a vacuum. There was a civil engineer named Octave Chanute who was a mentor to the brothers, teaching them many of the principles they would need to build an aircraft. The city of Chanute is named for this engineer, who helped build railroads throughout Kansas. He also designed the Kansas City Stockyards and the first bridge to cross the Missouri River in Kansas City.

getting there

Follow US 169 south out of Garnett for about 45 miles to Chanute.

where to go

Chanute Chamber of Commerce. 21 N. Lincoln St.; (620) 431-3350; chanutechamber .com. Here you can pick up brochures of driving tours past many of the community's fabulous Victorian homes. Another brochure highlights downtown businesses.

Chanute Art Gallery. 17 N. Lincoln St.; (620) 431-7807. The gallery provides a showcase for local area artists and Kansas Prairie Printmakers, such as Birger Sandzen and Charles Capps. Recent acquisitions include etchings by Luigi Kasimir. Unique for a small town, the gallery has more than 1,000 square feet of exhibit space and includes a gift shop featuring handcrafted items and original art. Special exhibits change monthly. Open Tues through Sat, noon to 4 p.m. Closed in Jan.

Chanute Historical Society Museum. 101 S. Lincoln St.; (620) 431-1814; chanutehistory. org. Sports fans will enjoy the exhibits on former KU and NBA star Ralph Miller and on Paul Lindblad, who played for the Texas Rangers, Oakland Athletics, and New York Yankees. Both are from Chanute. Other exhibits focus on the railroad history of the area. The museum is located in the historic Flat-Iron Building, constructed in 1907. The unique wedge-shaped building has been home to the Western Union Telegraph, a drugstore, a tavern, and a confectionery. Open weekends or by appointment.

Howard's Toys for Big Boys. 216 E. Main; (620) 902-5100. Howard Alger loves classic cars and has 27, so he opened this space on Main Street to share his collection. The collection includes a couple of Model As, a 1922 Buick, and a 1937 Packard. For those who have never seen the gas top fuel pumps that were the norm at gas stations 80 years ago, you can see those as well. Children will love the collection of pedal cars. Howard also displays his late wife's collection of 172 cookie jars. Open Mon through Thurs, 9 a.m. to 4 p.m.; Fri, 1 to 4 p.m. Tours by appt.

The Martin and Osa Johnson Safari Museum. 111 N. Lincoln St.; (620) 431-2730; safarimuseum.com. The early work of Martin and Osa Johnson captured the first photographic records of remote and little-known regions of the world in the early decades of the 20th century. This museum, located inside the historic Santa Fe Train Depot, offers a look at Africa in the early part of the 20th century, when it was still a mysterious, dark continent. At that time the American impression of Africa was confined to the machinations of movie moguls, who plied the public with yarns about Tarzan the Ape Man and mega-monkeys like King Kong. At one time the cannibals of Borneo and game-choked savannas of Africa represented an overwhelming diversity of life on this planet. Yet deep in the heart of Kansas, in the little town of Chanute, there is the ultimate documentation of wilderness and cultures that have long since vanished from the earth.

Dioramas portray African art and artifacts from Mali, horned crocodile headdresses and woodcarvings from Nigeria, carved masks from Guinea, 14-foot-high Sirige masks held in place by mouthpieces worn by warriors, and much more, plus a 10,000-volume natural history library and research facility that is open to the public to enjoy. Open Tues through Sat, 10 a.m. to 5 p.m. Fee.

Summit Hill Gardens. 2605 160th Rd.; (620) 212-3878; summithillgardens.com. Summit Hill was the location of the first school in Neosho County. Patsy Smead and her family have restored the school and a historic home, both of which have been moved to the site that serves as an event center, gift shop, and Airbnb. Many people come for the magnificent flower and herb gardens that surround the property or to pick blackberries in season. Patsy makes about 85 kinds of soap that are for sale in the gift shop and will offer demonstrations or lessons if you plan ahead. Open Sat only or by appointment.

where to eat

Cardinal Drug Store. 103 E. Main St.; (620) 431-9150; cardinaldrugstore.com. This old-fashioned drugstore is actually a drugstore with a pharmacist and other resources serving the community. However, the real attraction is the soda fountain that dates to 1914. It has a solid oak back bar complete with stained glass and enormous mirror, plus a 1937 marble fountain and equipment. Four high-seated chairs with arms and a 1908 solid brass cash register complete the illusion that you've just entered another era. Coca-Cola is made the old-fashioned way, using syrup and carbonated water. You can also get everything from sodas and sundaes to limeades and phosphates. The soda fountain is flanked by cabinets displaying old patent medicines, such as Lydia Pinkham's Blood Medicine, still in the original box. Dr. Miles' Heart Tonic and Regulator and a bottle of Scarless Liniment dating back to 1910 are among the curiosities. Closed Sun.

The Grain Bin. 314 E. Main St.; (620) 431-7373. Sharon Barnhardt is the proprietor of this friendly place where everyone seems to know everyone else and welcomes visitors like family. The Grain Bin is known for its open menu, which means you can order a cheeseburger or meatloaf for breakfast if you like or pancakes and scrambled eggs for lunch. On cool days, there's nothing better than Sharon's ham and bean soup. Open daily, 6 a.m. to 2 p.m.

Great Western Dining. Student Union, 800 W. 14th St.; 620-431-2820 Ext. 248. The best Sunday brunch in southeast Kansas is on campus at Neosho Community College. Throughout the week, the dining room is primarily for students, faculty, and staff, but on Sundays, the brunch buffet transforms the simple college atmosphere into an exciting dining opportunity. Prime rib, brisket, fried chicken, and salmon often accompany the big breakfast and salad buffet. And you can't beat the price. Open Sept through May; Sun, 11 a.m. to 1:30 p.m.

day trip 03

southwest

front porch to the flint hills:
ottawa, ks; williamsburg, ks;
lebo, ks; emporia, ks

This interesting day trip is one that hard-core foodies will like. It takes you to a truck stop, a barbecue joint, and an old-fashioned soda fountain where you can actually get a decent limeade.

Don't worry if you can't find the actual town of Lebo. You're basically looking for a big plateful of chicken fried steak, and it can be found at a sprawling truckers' paradise called Beto Junction—which is designated as being in Lebo but is actually off US 75 at exit 155.

There's nothing much to do in Williamsburg but eat spicy pork ribs, play pool, and listen to the jukebox at Guy and Mae's Tavern. These are the simple things that make life so good.

ottawa, ks

Ottawa University, established in 1883, boasts architectural assets, as does the Franklin County Courthouse and the restored 200 block of the central business district, listed on the National Register of Historic Places.

Ottawa has plenty of shops that specialize in furniture, collectibles, primitives, and "junque." You may want to time your visit with Skunk Run Days, the second weekend in June.

But come Election Day, you may want to brag that you have visited this part of Franklin County for no other reason than to tell the story of the "Naked Voters."

119

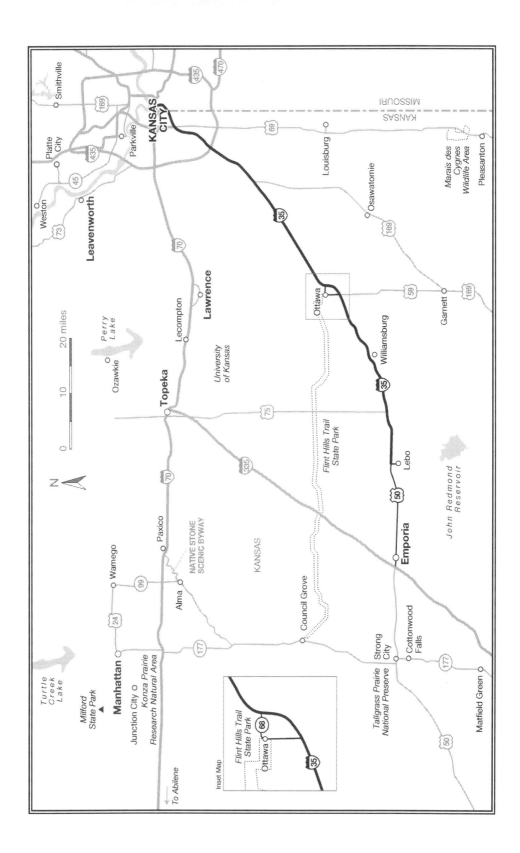

This is a stop along the way on the Franklin County Historical Society's Northeast Tour through Peoria, Wellsville, and other areas around Ottawa. This site commemorates 43 free-state men who were so desperate to cast their ballots against slavery in 1858 that they skinny-dipped their way to the polls.

Granted, there's not much to see there now, but just imagine 43 zealous voters fording three turbulent creeks to vote. Ponder, if you will, whether Americans today would go to such lengths. Would they strip off all their clothing, drop it on the bank, and plunge into a creek—just to enact a new law? Would they show up naked at the polls, letting their birthday suits drip dry in the open air? Of course not; they'd be arrested. Yet in 1858, the free-staters who made it to the polls defeated the pro-slavery issue by a "bare" minimum. A kind neighbor, who did not require that they dress for dinner, fed them before they returned home.

getting there

From downtown Kansas City, take I-35 south for 53 miles to exit 187. Turn west on KS 68 and travel less than two miles into Ottawa.

where to go

Franklin County Convention and Tourism Bureau. 2011 E. Logan St.; (785) 242-1411; franklincountyks.com. Located in what appears to be a Victorian home, the visitor center reflects the style of many homes in Franklin County. In addition to maps, brochures, and answers to your questions, you'll also find a nice gift shop of locally made products inside.

Elizabeth "Grandma" Layton Exhibit. Wellsville City Library, 115 W. Sixth St., Wellsville; (785) 883-2870. Elizabeth Layton was a remarkable artist whose work gained recognition in her later years. Having been through years of therapy, shock treatment, and drugs to find relief from depression, she tried drawing self-portraits to lift her emotional spirits. So effective was the relief that "Grandma" Layton went on to become a painter. Her work has been represented in numerous galleries and museums around the country, including the Smithsonian's American Art Museum in Washington, D.C. Through her artwork Grandma Layton spoke out against racism, commercialism, and nuclear war. Free. Closed Sun.

Franklin County Courthouse. Third and Main Streets; (785) 242-1232. Built in 1893 by noted architect George P. Washburn, the courthouse features a complex, steep-pitched hip roof with intersecting gables and four square corner towers. It has a four-sided clock, bell tower, and a statue of Justice that stands over the west gable. Tours are available from the Franklin County Historical Society. Free.

Franklin County Quilt Block Tour. frankcountyks.com/quilt-block-tour. If you're looking for just a nice drive in the country, pick up or download a copy of the Franklin County Quilt Block Tour brochure. There are more than 35 really complex quilt blocks painted on barns and the sides of buildings around the region. Be respectful of the private property on which they are located.

Kansas Belle Dinner Train. 1515 W. High St., Baldwin City; (785) 594-8505; kansasbelle. com. The Kansas Belle is located just north of Ottawa on US 59. It operates an authentic recreation of an American local passenger train and makes a seven-mile round trip through scenic farmland and woods, using early-20th-century vintage coaches. Open mid-May through Nov. Weekend runs only. Admission fee.

Old Depot Museum. Located one block west of Main Street on Tecumseh Street; (785) 242-1250. Operated by the Franklin County Historical Society, the two-story limestone building was constructed in 1888 as a depot for the Kansas City, Lawrence, and Southern Kansas Railway. Exhibits here include a model railroad and displays highlighting a number of Franklin County historical events. Open Tues through Sat, 10 a.m. to 4 p.m. Admission fee.

where to shop

Country Living and Boutique. 123 Main St.; (785) 242-1465; countrylivingandboutique. com. This well-loved boutique has been a local favorite since the 1980s, providing stylish clothing and accessories for women and a number of primitive home décor items. You'll find gifts and outdoor décor as well as some kitchen accessories. Open Tues through Fri, 10 a.m. to 5 p.m.; Sat, 10 a.m. to 2 p.m.

The Pink Suitcase. 312 S. Main St.; (785) 242-1884; shoppinksuitcase.com. Lots of fun wardrobe items and accessories for girls and young women. Open Tues through Sat, 10 a.m. to 4 p.m.

where to eat

Not Lost Brewing Co. 229 S. Main St.; (785) 214-4259; notlostbrewing.com. Stop in for a local IPA along with a German pretzel and mustard, a selection of paninis, or a charcuterie board, along with some philosophical conversation about those who wander, not being lost. Open Wed through Sat, 4 to 9 p.m.

williamsburg, ks

South of Ottawa is the dot-on-the-map town of Williamsburg. Its primary claim to fame is Guy and Mae's Tavern, which is worth a trip if you like hearty ribs and tasty sandwiches of beef and ham. But then you can also find some fresh fruits and veggies.

getting there

Williamsburg is 16 miles south of Ottawa on 1-35.

where to go

Pome on the Range. 2050 Idaho Rd.; (785) 746-5492; pomeontherange.com. This wonderful 80 acres is a cornucopia of fruits and vegetables and the good things that come from the Kansas soil. Hundreds of apple, peach, cherry, and pear trees make this a destination during you pick season, but you can also pick out a perfect pumpkin in October, choose some fresh vegetables in the market, and taste wine all year-round. Open seven days a week.

where to eat

Guy and Mae's Tavern. 119 W. William St.; (785) 746-8830. It sits among some timeworn buildings on what appears to be the town's largest street. Inside you'll find thick sandwiches of lean beef and ham, plus hearty slabs of pork ribs served on butcher paper. The sweet and spicy sauce is served on the side; other side dishes include baked beans, coleslaw, and potato salad. Written up in regional and national magazines, the place offers an unusual ambience that features a jukebox, a pool table, and good food served at yesterday's prices. Closed Sun and Mon as well as the last week in July and first week of Aug. $–$$ (no cards)

lebo, ks

You've had ribs, beef, and ham in Williamsburg. Still hungry? Head to the truck stop in Lebo to fill up on some country fried steak and other classic plates.

getting there

Continue another 23 miles down I-35 to exit 155 to reach Lebo.

where to go

Beto Junction. I-35 and US 75; (620) 256-6311. This sprawling truck stop takes its name from the first letters of four nearby cities: Burlington, Emporia, Topeka, and Ottawa. Food fans may want to make the trip just to chow down on trailblazer breakfasts that feature eggs with such meaty items as pork chops, chopped sirloin steak, ham, and Polish sausage. You might choose Beto Junction's fabulous chicken fried steak with eggs, or order it for dinner.

Indeed, it is worth the drive just to savor the huge portions of this spectacular tenderized steak—dipped in a light, flaky batter and fried just right—nestled atop buttery, made-from-scratch mashed potatoes and crowned with country gravy. More than a meal, this is an all-you-can-eat experience. Catering to anybody on two wheels or more, the entire facility also includes a travel store that is great fun to browse through. If you're looking for a combination hair dryer/vacuum, you'll find it here, along with a wide range of Kansas gifts, greeting cards, and more. Open daily. $$

emporia, ks

Emporia touts itself as the "Front Porch to the Flint Hills," an area that makes up the largest unbroken tract of tallgrass prairie in the county.

Founded in 1857, Emporia has made a name for itself by being the home of the National Teachers Hall of Fame and birthplace of Pulitzer Prize–winning journalist William Allen White. White died in 1944, having achieved success and fame. President Franklin Delano Roosevelt eulogized him, saying that he "ennobled the profession of journalism." White's birthplace in Emporia is now a state historic site.

However, in recent years, Emporia has proclaimed itself the Disc Golf Capital of the World. Dynamic Discs, started in Jeremy Rusco's basement while he was a bored college kid, is now the second-largest distributor of disc golf equipment in the country. The city has about two dozen disc golf courses and several businesses that sell collectable disc golfs. The Dynamic Discs Open each spring draws thousands of people from across the US and multiple countries.

Emporia has 10 electric car charging stations.

getting there

Continue driving south on I-35 out of Lebo for 20 miles for the three exits to Emporia.

where to go

Emporia Convention and Visitors Bureau. 719 Commercial St.; (620) 342-1600; visitemporia.com. Find out about the latest developments in the community and pick up discount coupons here for some of the sites.

All Veterans Memorial Park. 933 S. Commercial St.; (620) 342-1803. In a continuing effort to pay tribute to military veterans and Emporia's heritage of recognizing the service of veterans, this park, dedicated in 1991, features a World War II–era Sherman tank and a Vietnam-era Huey helicopter. The Kansas Purple Heart Monument is here, as is a monument to a local Medal of Honor recipient who gave his life for his country. The easily accessible park is located on the banks of the Cottonwood River, where lovely walking trails offer an opportunity for reflection. Open daily, dawn to dusk.

David Traylor Zoo of Emporia. 75 Soden Rd.; (620) 342-6558; emporiazoo.org. This is one of the five smallest accredited zoos in the country at just eight acres. The mountain lion and Nelson's elk are among the more popular exhibits. The zoo also has a nice assortment of birds, mammals, and reptiles housed in natural habitats. The zoo also features exceptional botanical displays and spectacular holiday lights. Open daily, with extended hours in the summer. Free.

Dynamic Discs. 612 Commercial St.; (620) 208-3472; dynamicdiscs.com. A little business started in Jeremy Rusco's parents' basement is now the largest distributor of disc golf equipment in the country. This is the retail outlet and where you can see the colorful trophy awarded for the Glass Blown Open, a tournament coordinated by Dynamic Discs in Emporia. Ask about warehouse tours. Open seven days a week.

Emporia State University. 1200 Commercial St.; (620) 341-5037; emporia.edu. Founded in 1863, the university was the state's first school for training teachers. Located on 200 acres, the campus offers special attractions of interest to tourists, such as the William Allen White Library. Manuscripts, correspondence, photographs, and other materials about the life and times of William Allen White can be found here. The student union has a Veteran's Wall of Honor that pays tribute to students and alumni who served in the armed forces. The Johnston Geology Museum and the Peterson Planetarium are worthy of your time. Free admission to all campus-related exhibits.

Flint Hills National Wildlife Refuge. Located 15 miles southeast of Emporia, near Hartford; (620) 392-5553; flinthills.fws.gov. One of a system of 400 refuges administered by the US Fish and Wildlife Service, the area is dedicated to the preservation and conservation of wildlife, primarily migratory waterfowl and bald eagles. Hiking, photography, boating, picnicking, camping, fishing, wild-food gathering, and hunting are allowed. Open daily. Free.

National Teachers Hall of Fame. 1320 Commercial Dr.; (620) 341-5660; nthf.org. One of the city's premier attractions, the hall of fame recognizes five teachers annually who have demonstrated a commitment to educating children from prekindergarten through high school. The walls hold tributes to some of the best teachers in America. There are galleries with cultural and artistic exhibits of general interest. In recent years, a memorial has been added to fallen educators who lost their lives in the line of duty. Closed Sun. Free.

Prairie Passage. Lyon County Fairgrounds, West US 50 and Industrial Road; (620) 342-1803. Eight massive limestone sculptures celebrating Emporia's origins and history were designed by artist Richard Stauffer and produced by the 1992 Kansas Sculptors Association. The sculptures present a variety of images about the land, its forces, and its people. Open daily. Free.

honoring our nation's veterans

For a generation of Americans, November 11 was first known as Armistice Day—the 11th day of the 11th month at which 11 a.m. tribute was paid to those who had fought and died in World War I.

It was to have been the war to end all wars, but as Americans lost their lives in World War II and then in Korea, Alvin King of Emporia realized that wars would keep coming and that there was an ongoing need to recognize the veterans who fought in them.

In 1953, King approached his congressional representative, Ed Rees of Emporia, and suggested the day be changed to Veterans Day to honor veterans of all military conflicts. Rees took King's proposal to Washington and to President Dwight Eisenhower, another Kansan and veteran of World War II.

The first nationwide observance of Veterans Day was on November 11, 1954. And each year, Emporia continues its recognition of veterans with a weeklong tribute that includes reenactments, lectures, parades, and other opportunities to learn about the contributions of military veterans. An All Veterans Park, at the intersection of Commercial Street and Soden Road, is a must-see while visiting Emporia. Many other parks and memorials around the community honor the contributions of veterans, including an exhibit at Emporia Service Area on the Kansas Turnpike honoring veteran Ken Bradstreet, who coordinated the work of many memorials and programs to Emporia veterans.

William Allen White State Historic Site. 927 Exchange St.; (620) 342-2800; kshs.org/places/white. William Allen White, born in Emporia in 1868, is the man for whom the University of Kansas School of Journalism is named. A prolific journalist who shaped public discussion on political and social matters nationwide for more than half a century, White won a Pulitzer Prize for editorials in his paper, the *Emporia Gazette*, and came to be respected around the world. His home is one of many sites in Emporia that explore the wit and wisdom that are studied today by journalists and educators around the world. Open Wed through Sat, Mar through Nov; weekends only, Dec through Feb. Admission fee.

where to eat

Radius Brewing Co. 610 Merchant St.; (620) 208-4677; radiusbrewing.com. Emporia's only craft brewery is also a place to throw some disc golf and get a great meal at the same time. The wood-fired pizza is most popular, and the open kitchen allows you to watch yours bake. But you can also find Cornish game hen on the menu, lobster ravioli, and other unexpected items on occasion. Open Tues through Sun, 11 a.m. to 10 p.m. $

where to stay

Gufler Mansion Bed and Breakfast. 612 W. 12th Ave.; (620) 983-6642; guflermansion. com. One of the most elegant homes to ever be built in Kansas is now a lovely bed-and-breakfast inn and event center. It took two years, from 1915 to 1917, for the 10,000-square-foot neoclassical-style home to be built for the family of Albert Gufler, a wholesale grocer. Today, each of the 12 guest rooms takes you far from Kansas with décor reflecting the owner's travels in Spain, France, Africa, China, and Thailand. A rooftop suite with three bedrooms would be great fun for a girlfriends' getaway or a small family reunion. $–$$

worth more time: wichita, ks

The largest city in Kansas is slightly more than three hours southwest of Kansas City on I-35, so more than a day trip. But if you've not been recently, plan a weekend getaway. The Wichita Wind Surge, a minor league farm team for the Minnesota Twins, provides some great baseball. The city provides great history, art, and a few really great restaurants. It's a nice couple of days, and one worth more of your time.

where to go

Wichita Convention and Visitors Bureau. 515 S. Main St.; (316) 265-2800; visitwichita .com. Stop by for a visitors' guide and a coupon book for reduced admission to many of the museums. And stand by for some cuddles from Gemma, a golden doodle who is the official visitor welcome dog.

Kansas Aviation Museum. 3350 S. George Washington Blvd.; (316) 683-9242; kansas-saviationmuseum.org. At one point, more than 70 percent of all private aircraft in the world were made right here in Wichita, and this museum is located at the terminal of the former municipal airport. Check out the Kansas Aviation Hall of Fame, test your skills in a flight simulator, or test your strength with an old hand-crank inertia engine. But the best thing is to watch volunteers lovingly restore old planes and talk with them about their work and their love of aviation. Open daily. $

Old Cowtown Museum. 1865 W. Museum Blvd.; (316) 219-1871; oldcowtown.org. This living history center is located on about 27 acres right off the Chisholm Trail. It contains a number of authentic buildings, including the first home building in Wichita in 1865. A chuckwagon supper on Fri, Sat, and Sun nights includes music and a comedy routine. Reservations required for the supper. Closed Mon and Tues. $

Wichita Art Museum. 1400 W. Museum Blvd.; (316) 268-4921; wichitaartmuseum.org. This little gem has been a part of the Wichita landscape for more than 75 years, highlighting the works of American artists, such as Charles Russell, Winslow Homer, and the Wyeth family. The Muse Cafe is a nice bright spot for a light lunch. Closed Mon. $

where to stay

Hotel at Old Town. 830 E. First St.; (316) 267-4800; hotelatoldtown.com. Exhibits of Wichita history fill the lobby of this hotel that dates to 1900. Rooms are all generous in size, many with balconies, hot tubs, and numerous amenities. Each room has a kitchenette, and a cupboard downstairs provides all you'll need to prepare a nice breakfast. It's a great place to stay if you plan on visiting the Saturday farmers' market. $$

west

day trip 01

west

history, culture jayhawks:
lawrence, ks

lawrence, ks

In 1863, when William Quantrill and his raiders burned Lawrence to the ground in the name of pro-slavery, who could know that the town would bounce back and become the destination that it is today?

It started when the University of Kansas was founded in1865. With a long tradition of supporting the arts, KU offers one of the finest art museums in the Midwest, a theater that features 12 productions annually and a School of Fine Arts that produces more than 400 events each year.

The university's diverse student mix has brought innovation and energy to the unusually stable local economy. On a hill where pioneers once paused along the Oregon Trail, KU's limestone buildings play host to scholars who come to study and learn on the beautiful, user-friendly campus. And, of course, KU sports and its connection to basketball history are legendary.

Lawrence today offers plenty of attractions and a downtown filled with boutiques, galleries, and gourmet restaurants, yet it also has a history behind it worth learning.

Kansas was a territory opened for European settlement in 1854. During this time, the issue of slavery in the soon-to-be-state dominated all aspects of life. A bitter struggle ensued for territorial control. Lawrence had Yankee blood, and pro-slavery neighbors in Missouri found that hard to bear. When the town became a center for free-state activity, trouble soon

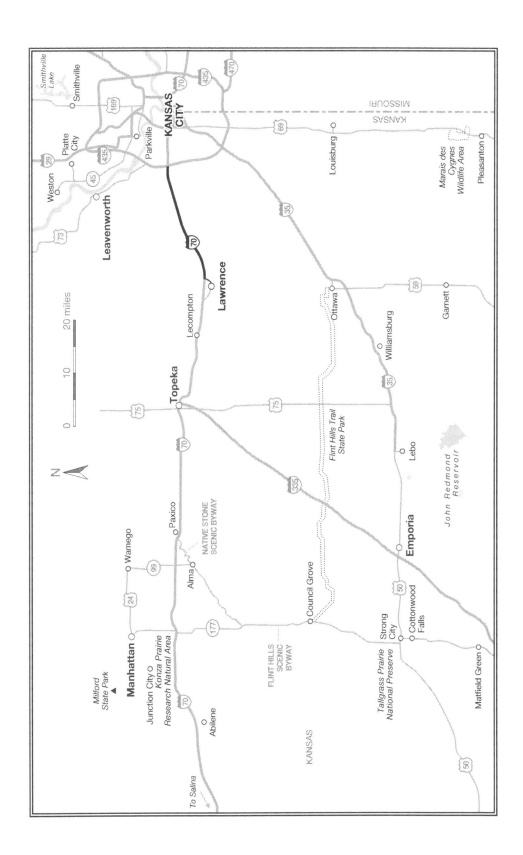

brewed between the abolitionists and the pro-slavers. Quantrill's morning raid on August 21, 1863, left Lawrence a shambles, with hundreds reported dead or missing and homes and businesses destroyed.

And as much as officials at the University of Kansas and University of Missouri would like the term "border wars" to disappear from local parlance, each time the two rival basketball teams meet in competition, the days of the Civil War in this region are remembered in a healthy sporting event.

When the Civil War ended, Lawrence's economy grew. The Kansas Pacific Railroad reached Lawrence in 1864, bringing new businesses and industry. In 1866 KU held its first session; Haskell Indian Nations University, now a registered National Historic Landmark, opened in 1884.

Today Lawrence, with its 19th-century Victorian homes and ornate downtown landmarks, has an identity all its own. You'll find 10 electric car charging stations in town.

getting there

Travel west 40 miles on I-70, remembering to have change for the toll booths.

where to go

Lawrence Visitors' Center. 812 Massachusetts St.; (785) 856-3040; explorelawrence. com. This visitor center includes a film on Quantrill's Raid, as well as exhibits on other parts of Lawrence history. Open Tues through Sat, 10 a.m. to 5 p.m.

Clinton Lake State Park. 798 N. 1415 Rd.; (785) 842-8562; ksoutdoors.com. Located three miles southwest of Lawrence, off Clinton Parkway (West 23rd Street), this 7,000-acre lake was developed and managed by the US Army Corps of Engineers, but the state of Kansas sublets some of the area for a state park. The federal government also offers services including camping. It's rather confusing for those making camping reservations, so double check your directions. Overall, the area provides 7,000 surface acres for boating, fishing, and swimming. Excellent opportunities for bicycling and for viewing wildlife abound. Between the state and federal areas, there are more than 70 miles of hiking trails, plus camping and picnicking areas, as well as a disc golf course. The state park includes a marina and three boat ramps. Free.

Haskell Indian Nations University. 155 Indian Ave.; (785) 749-8404; haskell.edu. This is one of the oldest educational institutions for Native Americans and Alaska Natives supported by the federal government. Founded in 1884, Haskell has evolved from an elementary school to a university offering a baccalaureate in elementary teacher education. Open only to members of federally recognized Indian nations, enrollment averages 1,000 students a semester.

The Haskell Cultural Center and Museum. 2411 Barker Ave.; (785) 832-6686. This facility houses exhibits on the history of the university and the Native American experience in

Kansas. Cultural performances are held at the adjacent outdoor amphitheater. The grounds include a memorial to Native Americans who have served in the United States military. Walking-tour brochures that explain the history and significance of buildings on campus are available at the center. Closed on Sat.

In the fall Haskell hosts an outdoor Indian Art Market in conjunction with Lawrence's annual Indian Arts Show. In the spring an outdoor powwow attracts hundreds of Native American and Alaska Native dancers and singers from across the United States.

Freedom's Frontier National Heritage Area. 200 W. Ninth St.; (785) 856-5300; freedomsfrontier.org. The headquarters for the Freedom's Frontier is located here in the Carnegie Building. Rotating exhibits explain the struggle for freedom that took place in 29 eastern Kansas and 12 western Missouri counties prior to, during, and immediately following the Civil War. Closed Mon and Tues. Free.

Lawrence Arts Center. 940 New Hampshire; (785) 843-2787; lawrenceartscenter.com. The Lawrence Arts Center is designed specifically for art education. Two visual arts galleries showcase area artists' works, and a gallery gift shop offers additional items for sale. Performing arts presentations are scheduled regularly in the theater. Open seven days a week. Free.

Old West Lawrence Historic District. From Sixth to Ninth Streets between Tennessee and Illinois Streets. The impressive 19th-century architecture here is listed on the National Register of Historic Places. Drive by the Plymouth Congregational Church, 925 Vermont St., for a vision of spires, buttresses, and stained glass.

University of Kansas. Mount Oread Campus. The 1,000-acre campus is one of the prettiest in the country and features a pond called Potter Lake at the bottom of a grassy wooded knoll between the Campanile and Memorial Stadium. From the stop sign at the west end of Memorial Drive, you can turn left onto West Campus Road, where there are some sorority and fraternity houses. This leads to the Chi Omega Fountain. At the south side of the intersection is a large rock marking the site of many Oregon Trail campfires. If you go around the fountain, you'll wind up making a left turn onto Jayhawk Boulevard, the main drag of the campus. If school is in session, you'll need to stop and get a visitor's pass at the booth. Jayhawk Boulevard has some wonderful old buildings, including Strong Hall, Watson Library, and others. Detailed information and a map of the campus can be found at ku.edu. Some stops on your itinerary might include these:

Booth Hall of Athletics. Adjacent to Allen Fieldhouse; (785) 864-7050. If you'd like to get a firsthand look at the original rules of basketball, visit this museum-like facility adjacent to the sports center where some of the country's best basketball is played. But all KU sports are honored here in six different exhibit rooms. Closed Sun. Free.

Helen Foresman Spencer Museum of Art. 1301 Mississippi St. (behind the Kansas Union); (785) 864-4710; spencerart.ku.edu. This gem of a place houses one of the finest university art museums in the country. Eleven galleries offer changing exhibitions and art from the museum's collections that represent more than 4,000 years of world art history and include wonderful European and American paintings, sculptures, and photography. Japanese Edo-period painting and 20th-century Chinese painting are of particular interest. The Spencer also affords art lovers a chance to experience touring exhibitions of remarkable works not found elsewhere in the area. Closed Mon. Free.

KU Biodiversity Institute and Natural History Museum. Dyche Hall, 1345 Jayhawk Blvd.; (785) 864-4450; biodiversity.ku.edu. Listed on the National Register of Historic Places, the museum holds exhibits of Kansas and Great Plains animals and offers a historic panorama of North American plants and animals. On display are live bees, fish, snakes, and minerals. Closed Mon. Donations suggested.

The Lied Center. 1600 Stewart Dr.; (785) 864-2787; lied.ku.edu. This is the home for KU's Concert, Chamber Music, Broadway, and New Directions series. The lobbies here offer a magnificent view of the rolling hills and the Wakarusa Valley. The Lied Center provides a state-of-the-art setting for music, dance, theater, lectures, films, and convocations. Visitors are welcome to view the building during business hours Mon through Fri. Tickets to events can be purchased at the box office.

Robert J. Dole Institute of Public Policy. 2350 Petefish Dr.; (785) 864-4900; doleinstitute .org. Adjacent to the Lied Center, this facility honors the public service of the late Kansas Senator Bob Dole. The interactive exhibits here chronicle the life of the senator who served Kansas for 46 years and ran three times for president of the United States. The state-of-the-art presentations on this history of Kansas, the soaring stained-glass windows, and the Memory Wall honoring World War II veterans make the center worthy of a visit, no matter what your politics. The center hosts political presentations and historic discussions throughout the year. Open daily. Free.

where to shop

1313 Mockingbird Lane Toys. 1027 Massachusetts; (785) 424-7158; 1313mockingbird-toys.com. Don't let the name of the business and the street address confuse you, but do take time to dig through your closets and attic to find old toys and collectibles. Owners Terry and Liz Taylor are always looking for vintage toys for their shop, which is a great place for collectors to find something special. Open Wed through Sat, 11 a.m. to 7 p.m.; Sun, noon to 5 p.m.

Community Mercantile. 901 Iowa St.; (785) 843-8544. "The Merc" has been serving the Lawrence community since 1974. It is cooperatively owned and offers a full selection of organic and local produce in season. It has an extensive bulk department, with an excellent selection of coffees and teas, herbs, dairy products, and more. There are books and housewares, plus a meat department that features locally raised beef and poultry. Freshly baked goods, crafts by area artists, and a deli department round out the fare. Open daily.

mustard madness

March is always a frenzied time in Lawrence thanks to March Madness—that hysterical time of year when college basketball fans overdose on their favorite sport via televised tournaments across the country night and day. The pack of 68 NCAA teams becomes the Sweet Sixteen, which is then pared to the Final Four. And more times than not, the Jayhawks are in that final number.

At the Free State Brewery, which is always packed with red and blue Jayhawk fans on game day, March Madness is not so much about basketball as it is mustard. You have to know Free State Brewery proprietor Chuck Magerl to truly understand the connection between basketball and mustard, and even then, it doesn't make much sense. After seeing a program on public television about the Mustard Museum in Middleton, Wisconsin, Chuck decided to combine mustard tastings at his restaurant with the tournament brackets for basketball, allowing guests to sample 68 flavors, then 16, then select a final 4 of mustards.

(Note: Middleton is in the Madison, Wisconsin, metro area. The Mustard Museum tells the exciting story of this condiment and displays more than 4,000 containers of historic, thought-provoking mustard. The museum gift shop and catalog carry 400 varieties for sale.)

Each February the phone calls and emails fly fast and furious between Lawrence and Mount Horeb, scientifically identifying the precise varieties of mustards that will fill in the tournament brackets. All told, about 200 containers of Wisconsin mustard make their way to the Free State Brewery, a little more or a little less, based on how well the Jayhawks perform.

Farmers' Market. 1000 block of Vermont Street; (785) 865-4499; lawrencefarmersmarket. org. This is the largest and oldest farmers' market in the state. Local growers and farm producers offer products and produce ranging from fresh fruits and veggies to baked goods, herbs, and homemade condiments. Open Sat morning and Tues afternoon, May through Nov.

Phoenix Gallery. 825 Massachusetts St.; (785) 843-0080; phoenixgalleryart.net. Works by local and regional artisans are represented here and include pottery, blown glass, jewelry, weaving, paintings, prints, and textiles. Open daily.

The Raven Bookstore. 809 Massachusetts St.; (785) 749-3300; ravenbookstore.com. In a time when independent bookstores are disappearing, the Raven continues to grow and expand, in large part because of the phenomenal customer service found here and the genius of owner Danny Caine. The Raven specializes primarily in mysteries and hosts two mystery reading groups a month for customers. It also offers a British-import mystery section for many titles that are hard to find in this country. Fiction, history and regional studies, travel, nature, and other works of literature also fill the shelves. Check the calendar for special events. Open daily.

Waxman Candles. 609 Massachusetts St.; (785) 843-8593; waxmancandles.com. Situated at the northern end of Historic Downtown Lawrence, this unique shop produces handmade candles, including the one-of-a-kind "Silhouette," which has a backlit effect as it burns and is quite a showstopper. Three tons of candles wait to be sold here, including clean-burning beeswax and soy candles. Open daily.

where to eat

Note: Lawrence has an extensive selection of ethnic restaurants ranging from small mom-and-pop locations, to food trucks to pop-up eateries that could be romantic or rowdy or indoor/outdoor. The bases are covered. The richness of the Lawrence dining scene is ever changing, so if you see something or smell something good, just jump on in. Listed below are just a few of the longtime favorites in Lawrence. Explore and enjoy.

Culinaria Mediterranean Kitchen. 512 E. Ninth St.; (785) 766-8591; culinariafoodandwine. Combine a little local history with your dinner out In East Lawrence. You've heard so much about Quantrill's raid on Lawrence; this building was constructed shortly after to better protect the city and citizens. Now the lovely patio, gardens, and interior dining space provide an engaging setting in which to enjoy burnt eggplant, chicken shawarma, and other yummy Mediterranean dishes. Open Thur through Sat, 3:30 to 9 p.m. $

Free State Brewing Co. 636 Massachusetts St.; (785) 843-4555; freestatebrewing.com. This is the first brewery to operate in Kansas since the state passed a prohibition law more than a century ago. Located inside a renovated trolley barn, this combination brewery–restaurant produces a small variety of high-quality beer, using fresh, natural ingredients. The restaurant offers an interesting menu that includes everything from stir-fried veggies to fresh fish and steak. Brewery tours are offered Sat at 2 p.m. Open daily. $–$$

Ladybird Diner. 721 Massachusetts; (785) 856-5239; ladybirddiner.com. Even the simple entrées here are served with flare. Try the spicy chicken mac and cheese served with cotija Mexican cheese or the smoked salmon hash. But most people come for the fresh baked goods. A caramel pumpkin pie will show off your Thanksgiving. Open Wed through Sun, 8 a.m. to 3 p.m. $

Sylas and Maddy's Homemade Ice Cream. 1014 Massachusetts St.; (785) 832-8323. This is the place to come for banana splits, sundaes, malts, milkshakes, sodas, and home-made waffle cones filled to the brim with fantastically rich and creamy ice cream made on the premises. Choose from 130 rotating flavors that include Da Bomb (Oreos, chocolate chips, and cookie dough), prairie pumpkin nut, and pineapple cheesecake, or try the chocolate chip and peanut butter chocolate chip made with superior chunks of chocolate. Take a cooler so that you can pack a pint or a quart to go. Yum! Open daily. $

Wheatfield's Bakery and Cafe. 904 Vermont St.; (785) 841-5553. This delightful place features fresh-baked breads made with Kansas wheat. Everything from traditional favorites like sourdough and raisin breads to cookies and truffles are made on the premises, along with soups, sandwiches, and stuffed pastries. Open daily for lunch and dinner; a full breakfast is served until 2 p.m. on Sun and until 11 a.m. on weekdays. $–$$

where to stay

Circle S Guest Ranch & Country Inn. 3325 Circle S Ln.; (785) 843-4124 or (800) 625-2839; circlesranch.com. This charming retreat has been continuously owned and operated through five generations since the late 1800s. The ranch spans more than 1,200 acres and includes more than 400 head of cattle. More than 20 ponds dot the surroundings, and there is abundant wildlife. The inn itself was built to resemble a Kansas barn. Twelve spacious guest rooms offer private baths and views. Some feature claw-foot or whirlpool baths and fireplaces. Breakfast is included in the price of the room. Dinner is available on Sat night by request. $$$

The Eldridge Hotel. 701 Massachusetts St.; (785) 749-5011 or (800) 527-0909; eldridge-hotel.com. This downtown hotel is the only hotel in Lawrence listed as an official Historic Hotel of America. Completely destroyed during Quantrill's Raid in 1863, the structure was promptly rebuilt and named the Hotel Eldridge. After a period of decline in the mid-20th century, the hotel was renovated and reopened in 1986. All 48 rooms are suites, and the hotel restaurant serves a great Sunday brunch. $$

day trip 02

west

a tale of two capitals:
lecompton, ks; topeka, ks

lecompton, ks

The original territorial capital of Kansas, so named in 1855, has much to teach us about the Civil War, politics, and the world we live in today. The tense debate here over Kansas becoming a pro-slavery or free state resulted in a brawl in the nation's capital, the fracturing of the Democratic party, and the election of Abraham Lincoln as our 16th president. Kansas entered the Union on January 29, 1861, and the Civil War began in April of that year.

A more modern or festive reason to visit Lecompton includes the annual Christmas tree displays with more than 200 trees decorated in a variety of colorful and historic ornaments.

getting there

Lecompton is located 50 miles west of Kansas City on I-70. Take exit 197, turn north.

where to go

Constitution Hall. 319 Elmore St.; (785) 887-6520. Built in 1856, this is where the first pro-slavery constitution was drafted. Although it was eventually overturned and Kansas was a free state, the events that took place here changed the United States. See the timeline of events and some of the key players of the day and learn about the federal troops sent to keep the peace. Open Wed through Sat, 9 a.m. to 5 p.m.; Sun, 1 to 5 p.m. Admission fee.

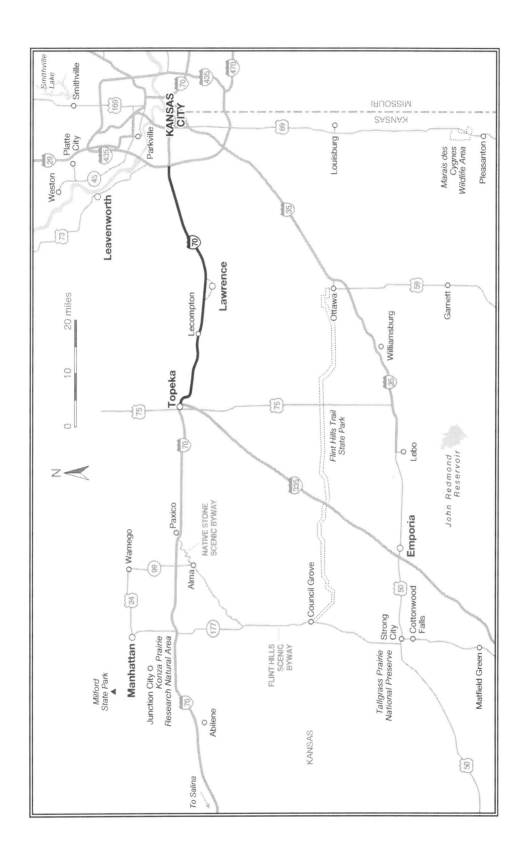

Territorial Capital Museum. 640 E. Woodson; (785) 887-6520. This building was supposed to be the first state capitol in Kansas. Of course, that never happened, but even
the building's construction was marred with the violence of "bleeding Kansas." It eventually
became a university attended by the parents of Dwight Eisenhower. A tour today showcases Civil War artifacts from the region and history of life in this region during the early
days of statehood. Open Wed through Sat, 10 a.m. to 4 p.m.; Sun, 1 to 5 p.m. Donations
suggested.

where to eat

Aunt Netter's Café. 336 Elmore St.; (785) 503-6004. This humble little café and bakery is
a delightful place to hang out and enjoy a cup of coffee, homemade pie, and a sandwich for
lunch. But they are best known for their cupcakes. Even if you don't care about the history
of Lecompton, pull off I-70 anyway for chocolate peanut butter–filled cupcakes, Butterfinger
blizzard cupcakes, lemon glaze with cream cheese frosting. The list goes on and on. Open
Wed through Sun, 7 a.m. to 2 p.m. $

topeka, ks

The capital of Kansas, Topeka lies on rich, sandy river-bottom land where Native Americans
lived for millennia using the Kansas (Kaw) River for navigation. Each year Topeka celebrates
its Native American heritage with the Shawnee Country Allied Tribes All Nations Powwow,
held Labor Day weekend.

The Kaw River also drew to it three French Canadian brothers who started a ferry service across the river in 1842. They married three Kanza (Kansas) Indian sisters whose tribe
had lived in the area for many years. Thus marked the beginnings of Topeka as a stopping
point on the Oregon Trail. Years later, one of the couples celebrated the election of their
grandson, Charles Curtis, as vice president of the United States—the only US vice president
of Native American descent.

Topeka has a rich abundance of attractions, including one of the most extensive rose
gardens in the country, a tropical rain forest, an international raceway offering top-flight
motor sports events, and several interesting museums. Springtime is especially beautiful
in downtown Topeka. About 60 tulip beds with more than 35,000 tulip bulbs line Kansas
Avenue and Topeka Boulevard.

Topeka has 14 electrical vehicle charging stations.

getting there

From Lecompton, take I-70 west for 20 miles to exits for Topeka.

where to go

Topeka Convention & Visitors Bureau. 719 S. Kansas Ave.; (785) 234-2644; visittopeka. com.

***Brown v. Board of Education* National Historic Site.** 1515 SE Monroe St.; (785) 354-4273; nps.gov/brvb. Located in the former Monroe School, one of four African American schools in the Topeka School District prior to 1954, this site represents the segregation of publicly funded schools, the civil rights movement of the time, and the landmark Supreme Court ruling on May 17, 1954, that ended segregation. Oliver Brown, a Topeka minister, was the first of 13 parents in Topeka to file suit on behalf of 20 children, thus, the name Brown on the case. However, the case represents similar lawsuits filed in five states at that time on behalf of more than 150 children. Today the building has been restored to its condition of the early 1950s. Numerous interactive exhibits encourage visitors to explore the concept of racial segregation and record their feelings at the conclusion of the tour. Free.

Cedar Crest. Located off I-70 and Fairlawn Road; (785) 296-3636. The home has been the official residence of the Kansas governor since 1962. Built in 1928, this 12-room French Norman–style home overlooks the Kansas River Valley. It was designed by W. D. Wight of Kansas City and was named for the numerous cedar trees on the property. The home is nestled on 244 acres that include hiking trails, fishing ponds, and nature areas open to the public. Public tours are offered on Mon between 1 and 4 p.m. Groups of eight or more require reservations. Free.

Combat Air Museum. Forbes Field, Hangar 602, at exit 177 off I-70; (785) 862-3303; combatairmuseum.org. Dedicated to restoring, preserving, and displaying aircraft and artifacts, this museum is the only one in the world to display operational aircraft from every armed conflict utilizing powered aircraft. Housed here are surveillance aircraft fighters, missiles, and other military pieces dating to 1917. Visitors can walk through one of the early 1950 radar planes and browse through the many exhibits that include the Women Air Service Pilots, major battles fought by air, and information on other nations' air force programs. Open daily. Admission fee.

Equality House. 1200 SW Orleans St.; (no phone); plantingpeace.org. Directly across the street from the Westboro Baptist Church, known for protesting at military funerals, this brightly colored house celebrates acceptance, tolerance, peace, and equality. Painted the colors of the pride flag, the adjacent house painted red, white, and blue. A communal garden is yours. Pull some weeds, and take a vegetable or two if you need it. Stop in and say hello. Free.

Evel Knievel Museum. 2047 SW Topeka Blvd.; (785) 215-6205; evelknievelmuseum.com. Have you ever wanted to jump across 16 police cars on a motorcycle like Evel Knievel did? Yep, you can in this incredible museum, the only one sanctioned by the Knievel family. It started with the opportunity for this Harley dealership to renovate the Mac truck that transported the Evel Knievel show across the country. Now it's on display permanently, as well as motorcycles, helmets, costumes, and more used by the great showman. Open Tues through Sat, 10 a.m. to 5 p.m. Fee.

Gage Park. 635 SW Gage Blvd.; (785) 368-3838. Topeka's 160-acre Gage Park features many attractions, including the following:

Carousel in the Park. The antique carousel was built around 1908 by New York's Herschell-Spillman Company. It was purchased by the city of Topeka in 1986 and totally restored for the public to enjoy and ride. Open daily in warm weather. Admission fee.

Reinisch Rose Garden. (785) 272-6150. This is one of the most extensive rose gardens in the country, with more than 180 varieties and 4,500 bushes. It is one of 23 test gardens in the nation for hybridizers and has one of the most complete displays of All-American Winners selected since 1940 on public view. Internationally famous for its beauty, the Reinisch Rose Garden was founded in 1930 and named after Topeka's first park superintendent. Today the roses grow in a lovely setting of rock gardens and pools. The red Topeka Rose stands majestically in the center of the garden. Blooming season normally is June through Oct; peak time, early June and mid-Sept. Open daily. Free.

Topeka Zoological Park. 635 SW Gage Blvd.; (785) 368-9180; topekazoo.org. Exhibits include the Tropical Rain Forest (see below) and "Gorilla Encounter," which allows visitors to view the creatures in an open environment from a glass-enclosed area. African lions, Japanese macaques, and Chinese muntjac deer are part of the displays. Warm weather makes the Water Bird Lagoon a pleasant place for bird-watching. The Children's Zoo features a traditional red barn and a series of wooden corrals that create a farm-like setting for visitor-friendly animals. Another nice attraction is Black Bear Woods. A large wood ramp and deck provide viewing areas of the bears' home. There are a pool, tall trees for them to climb, natural berries to eat, and a large area for playing, sleeping, and just being bears. Open daily. Admission fee.

Tropical Rain Forest. Located inside Topeka Zoo. The damp, pungent smell mingles with the sweet odor of rare flowers and plants; coupled with the cries of exotic birds, the rain forest is a rare experience to savor. Housed in a 30-foot-high geodesic dome, 100 feet in diameter, the Tropical Rain Forest supports some of the rarest and most exotic plant and animal life in the world. This is a bird-lover's paradise. The feathered creatures here are so lavishly colored that they look as though they have been dipped in richly textured paints. Many of the other inhabitants are so well camouflaged that most visitors miss them. Many are nocturnal and quite a few move freely about the dome, so be careful not to step on anybody's toes! Exhibits are open daily. Admission fee.

Great Overland Station. 701 N. Kansas Ave.; (785) 251-6945. Topeka's proximity to the Oregon and Santa Fe Trails and the railroads played a key role in the city's development. The museum is housed in a former Union Pacific depot and helps tell the story of life on the rails and how those rails brought Topeka to life. The site now includes a Veteran's Memorial and avenue of 50 American flags. Admission fee.

Heartland Motorsports Park. 7530 SW Topeka Blvd.; (785) 861-7899; heartlandmotorsports.us. All the state-of-the-art elements found here are designed with the spectator in mind, from the 2.5-mile road-race course to the quarter-mile drag strip—one of the fastest in the world. The viewing berms afford spectators an excellent view of the Grand Prix road-race course, while the modern grandstands offer onlookers a look at the pit-stop action. Open for seasonal events. Admission fee.

Kansas Museum of History. 6425 SW Sixth St.; (785) 272-8681; kshs.org. Located on the historic Oregon Trail, the museum holds one of the country's largest prairie collections of memorabilia and historic objects. In the permanent gallery, "Voices from the Heartland: A Kansas Legacy" tells the story of Kansas, from its first inhabitants to modern-day culture. The past comes alive through interactive video displays and exhibits that feature an 1866 log house; a Southern Cheyenne buffalo-hide tepee; a locomotive with coal, dining, and sleeping cars attached; and more. You can catch the pioneer spirit as you browse through special areas, such as a children's Discovery Place, where hands-on discovery is encouraged. Open Wed through Sat. Admission fee.

Kansas State Capitol Building. 10th and Jackson Streets; (785) 296-3966; kshs.org. Original construction of the building began in 1861 but wasn't completed until 1903. The grounds surrounding the building contain monuments of interest, including a statue of Abraham Lincoln located southeast of the capitol. In 1915, Robert Merrell Gage was just out of school and living with his parents when he completed the figure of Lincoln in the barn adjacent to his parents' home.

Southwest of the capitol is another monument by Gage, dedicated to the pioneer women of Kansas. A bronze replica of the Statue of Liberty, at the northwest section of Capitol Square, and a replica of the Liberty Bell, at the east side of Capitol Square, complete the grouping. As you walk, look for the bronze plaques embedded in the sidewalk. This Walk of Honor is a tribute to Kansans who have made great contributions to the nation, including Clyde Cessna, Walter Chrysler, and Fred Harvey.

Inside the building, murals by John Steuart Curry and David Overmyer tell an unusual pioneer story. Check out the huge panel of a furious John Brown on the second floor. Guided tours are offered daily, Mon through Fri. Dome tours are possible June through Dec. The building is also open on weekends just to look around. Free.

Mulvane Art Museum. 1700 SW Jewell St. on the Washburn University campus; (785) 231-1124; washburn.edu. Built in 1922, this is the oldest visual-arts museum in the state. It offers changing exhibits from its permanent collection and focuses on contemporary art from the Mountain–Plains region. The exterior courtyard features sculptures and fountains, along with native wildflowers. Closed Sun and Mon. Free.

Old Prairie Town. 124 NW Fillmore St.; (785) 251-6989. Old-fashioned fun can be had at this unusual city park. It features 5.5 acres of living history that includes a restored 1870 Victorian mansion, a log cabin, a train depot, a one-room schoolhouse, a stone barn, a drugstore, and botanical gardens.

The Potwin Drug Store is worth seeing. A 1920s-style building was designed to house fixtures that were once part of Edelblute's Drug Store in Potwin, Kansas. There is a superb back bar and marble counter perfect for sipping sodas. On the second floor of the Potwin Drug Store, professional, medical, and dental offices appear as they would have a century ago. Also on the park premises is the Mulvane General Store, featuring yesteryear décor and gift items for sale.

Open daily. Admission fee.

Truckhenge. 4124 NE Brier Rd.; (785) 234-3486. A Kansas take on England's famous Stonehenge and Nebraska's well-established Carhenge, Truckhenge is six antique trucks stuck in the ground, surrounded by recycled art and native plants. This is Ron Lessman's family farm, and he is quite proud of his odd art. Siri doesn't always do a great job with directions out here, so if you have any trouble, just call Ron for help. Free.

where to eat

Annie's Place. Gage Shopping Center, 4014 Gage Center Dr.; (785) 273-0848; anniesplacetopeka.com. This family-owned restaurant bakes its buns fresh daily, along with dinner rolls, cinnamon rolls, and desserts. The baker is visible through a "showroom" in the restaurant. Annie's also grinds prime beef to make its famous gourmet burgers. Try the renowned "hot air fries," cooked without grease. Ask for a side order of chicken gravy, which is served with chunks of white-meat chicken. Save time to look around the adjacent gift shop with items all made by local artists. $$

Paisano's Ristorante. Fleming Place, 4043 SW 10th St.; (785) 273-0100; paisanoskansas. com. Paisano's serves superior Italian food. Appetizers include tasty mushroom caps stuffed with sausage and baked in white wine cream sauce. Entrees include veal and chicken dishes, Pesce al Vino Bianco (lobster, shrimp, scallops, crab, and whitefish in a sage and garlic cream sauce), and penne primavera (penne pasta sautéed in extra-virgin olive oil, garlic, and fresh basil sauce, then tossed with vegetables and topped with crumbled Gorgonzola cheese). The portions are large and the prices reasonable. Early-bird lunch special: Entrees are half price before 11:30 a.m. Open daily for lunch and dinner. $$

The Pennant. 915 S. Kansas Ave.; (785) 286-6808; thepennanttopeka.com. Certainly lots of good food is served here, but a lot of people come for the vintage arcade games, the bowling alley, and beer garden. Appreciate the fact that you're in a 100-plus-year-old building where the original tile and woodwork have been saved. Black Angus beef for burgers is a Kansas must, but there's also a good selection of wraps, pastas, and salads. And the dessert menu with weird things happening to ice cream is a lot of fun. Open seven days a week, 11 a.m. to 9 p.m. $

where to stay

Cyrus Hotel. 918 S. Kansas Ave.; (785) 596-0500; cyrushotel.com. This creative boutique hotel brings 109 guest rooms into an old office building in downtown Topeka. The hotel features all the modern amenities and luxuries you expect from a boutique hotel with a very modern, slightly industrial edge to it. An outdoor courtyard with firepit is a nice way to wind down after exploring Topeka. $$

Senate Luxury Suites. 900 SW Tyler St.; (785) 233-5050; senatesuiteshotel.com. As intimate as a bed-and-breakfast and as grand as a first-class hotel, the Senate Luxury Suites was originally built in the 1920s as an elegant apartment building. Today, the location appeals to business and leisure travelers alike, with 52 elegantly furnished suites, some with kitchenettes, and some with hot tubs and fireplaces. Guests are treated to a complimentary breakfast. $$–$$$

day trip 03

west

native stone scenic byway:
wamego, ks; alma, ks

The scene is miles of rolling hills and prairie under a sweeping sky. Native bluestem prairie grass follows vast stretches of virgin land in a seemingly endless vista. At times the expanse is so immense that one can see the curve of the earth. Sky and land merge as one. It takes the breath away.

Where is this? Surely not Kansas. It's supposed to be flat. It shouldn't look like New Mexico or Montana. But it does along Skyline–Mill Creek Drive, an offshoot of the Native Stone Scenic Byway. The drive is clearly marked, and the byway takes you past land covered with stone fences. A historical marker tells you that the 1867 law abolishing open range provided payment to landowners for building and maintaining the venerable stone fences that still stand today. The only sound is your car as it hums along the road, and if you stop along the way and sit quietly, you can almost feel the 1800s surround you: The buffalo, the Native Americans, the pioneers—they were here, and it's hard to tell where the past stops and the present begins.

wamego, ks

A small community of 4,000, the town is located on the Vermillion River, where Louis Vieux, a Potawatomie Indian, operated the first ferry along the Oregon Trail. Wamego is also the birthplace of Walter P. Chrysler, who built the car named after him. The annual Tulip Festival, held in April at the city park, offers a beautiful floral display, along with entertainment and

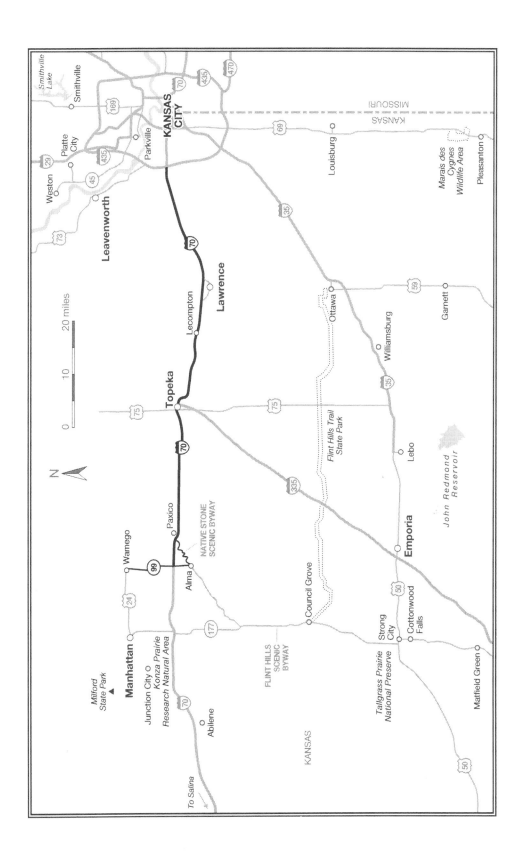

food. Canoers and kayakers appreciate the access point to the Kaw River from the city's riverfront park.

While in town, look for the 15 large statues of Toto the Dog. Share on social media with #TotosAroundTown.

getting there

From downtown Kansas City, drive west on I-70 about 90 miles to exit 328 for Wamego and Alma. Head north on KS 99 to Wamego.

where to go

Wamego Area Chamber of Commerce. 529 Lincoln Ave.; (785) 456-7849; wamego-chamber.com or visitwamego.com. Pick up a map for the Totos Around Town and other information about things happening in the merry old land of Oz.

Columbian Theatre Museum and Art Center. 521 Lincoln Ave.; (785) 456-2029; columbiantheatre.com. In 1994 a $1.8-million renovation restored the luster and elegance to this century-old theater. Rare 1893 murals, the only remaining set of decorative art from the 1893 Chicago World's Fair, grace the walls of the 250-seat theater, which features a guest-artist series, musical concerts, drama and dance productions, educational programs, and regional art exhibits. Docent-guided tours are by appointment. Admission fee (for events).

Dutch Mill. East side of City Park, Fourth Street; (785) 456-2040. This is Kansas's only authentic operating stone Dutch mill. Built in 1879 and listed on the National Register of Historic Places, the mill overlooks the beautiful city park—a perfect place for picnicking. The mill grinds wheat to flour while you watch, and you can purchase products to take back home. An adjacent museum contains historical and American Indian artifacts. Tours of the inside of the mill are available upon request. Fee for the tours.

The Marvelous Land of Oz Museum. 511 Lincoln Ave.; (785) 458-TOTO; ozmuseum .com. A Wamego native began collecting *Wizard of Oz* items as a child and has now donated more than 2,000 pieces to this magical museum. As you enter, you find yourself in the Gale barnyard looking at the weathered farmhouse Dorothy flew in over the rainbow. The museum progresses chronologically through both the movie and the books by L. Frank Baum, taking visitors through Munchkinland, the Haunted Forest, and Emerald City. An in-house theater runs original black-and-white silent *Wizard of Oz* movies. A gift shop should satisfy any cravings you have for *Wizard of Oz* memorabilia. An Oz festival in October features opportunities to learn more about the book and movie. Open daily. Admission fee.

Oregon Trail Nature Park. 20560 Oregon Trail Rd., 10 miles east of Wamego on US 24. Hike along the same trail that carried thousands of pioneers from Kansas City 2,100 miles to Oregon, many of them walking every step of the way. Restrooms and picnic tables available.

where to eat

Friendship House. 507 Ash St.; (785) 456-9616. The bakery items sold here use stone-ground flour from the Dutch Mill and are made from scratch each day along with tasty sandwiches, homemade soups, breads, and pastries that include cookies, muffins, and sweet rolls. Weekly menu items include bread pudding, fresh-baked pie (Fri), and honey wheat bierocks, unique hamburger and cabbage pocket sandwiches. Work by local artists and crafters is also on display and for sale. Open for lunch Tues through Sat. $

Toto's Tacoz! 515 Lincoln Ave.; (785) 456-8090; totostacoz.com. Just because it's fun to say and of course because the food is good, stop in for the Yellow Brick Burro'd and taco sauces like the Smokin' Scarecrow and the Cryin' Lion. Despite the schtick, the food is fresh and authentic Cal-Mex. Join the locals at one of their favorite spots in the region. Open Tues through Wed, 11 a.m. to 2 p.m.; Thur through Sat, 11 a.m. to 7 p.m. $

where to stay

Victory Inn Bed & Breakfast. 710 Eighth St.; (785) 456-1393. Every home should have a front porch like this beautiful curved, flower bedecked porch on this 1867 Victorian home. Francis and Margaret Feyh have five lovely rooms for guests, but also offer tea and tours of their beautiful home if you call ahead. $

alma, ks

Alma is considered the heart of the Native Stone region, and here you can see numerous buildings, fences, and natural formations made out of the limestone. KS 99 and KS 4 are the key routes to follow, but feel free to explore along any public roads to appreciate this region's natural beauty. For information about the Native Stone Scenic Byway, call (785) 765-4655 or visit ksbyways.org.

getting there

From Wamego, head south on KS 99 toward Alma, and you will access the Native Stone Scenic Byway, clearly marked by signs.

where to go

Alma Creamery. 509 E. Third St.; (785) 765-3522; almacreamery.com. For more than 75 years, the Alma Creamery has been making cheese by hand, the old-fashioned way. Today people call it "artisan cheese." The gift shop sells the cheese, along with Kansas wines and other treats appropriate for a picnic, at several area locations. Tours are offered, but advanced notice is requested. Closed Sun.

Grandma Hoerner's Foods. 31862 Thompson Rd.; (785) 765-2300; grandmahoerners .com. You've probably seen the Grandma Hoerner's label in area grocery stores and specialty food shops, but here you can see how the applesauce and other goodies are bottled from all-natural, organic ingredients. Or you can simply pick up some of your favorite items in the outlet store for prices better than you'll find elsewhere. And for the record, there was a real Grandma Hoerner. Just ask her grandson Duane McCoy, who owns the family business. Closed Sun.

Echo Cliff Park. Between Eskridge and Dover on KS 4—watch for signs; (785) 256-6050. Plan a picnic at this beautiful park, and make sure your phone is fully charged for some fabulous scenery and art. You'll feel like you are in Colorado or places more renowned for their natural beauty than Kansas. Look for some of the quirky folk art built from scrap metal by an area farmer. An old iron bridge crosses Mission Creek, and of course, shout or yodel to hear your own echo. Open daily. Free.

day trip 04

west

manhattan, ks

Touting itself as the "Little Apple," this thriving college town has a charm all its own, and quite different from its sunflower rival in Lawrence.

Kansas State University and the K-State Wildcat football team are located here, and home games are held on "Wildcat Weekends," drawing thousands of fans who converge on the city wearing purple to participate in numerous events and activities that are part of the fun.

The university also boasts scientific research that is on the cutting edge of agricultural technology. Thanks to techniques instituted here, K-State has produced great-tasting hormone- and antibiotic-free beef, poultry, pork, bread, pasta, pastry, milk, eggs, and ice cream.

One of K-State's most enthusiastic alums is Emmy Award–winning actor Eric Stonestreet, who makes at least one or two appearances a season at a Wildcat game.

Manhattan is a pretty place to visit. The streets are filled with lovely homes and venerable shade trees that offer respite on a hot Kansas day. Just a short drive from here is the Konza Prairie, a Nature Conservancy Preserve that features a pristine and beautiful landscape with a hiking trail open to the public. Depending on your perspective, Manhattan is either the beginning or the end of one of the most gorgeous scenic drives in the country, the Flint Hills Scenic Byway.

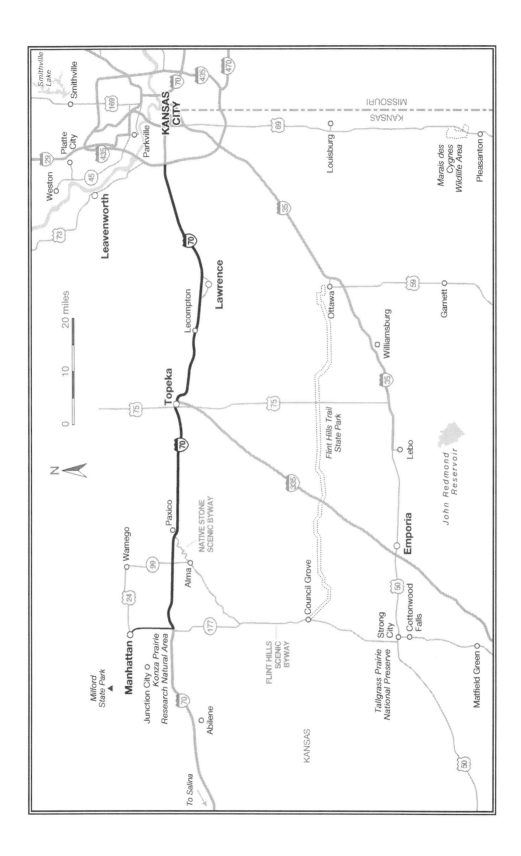

Aggieville, home to dozens of shops and restaurants on the southeast side of the K-State campus, is the oldest shopping center in Kansas.

getting there

Manhattan is about 120 miles west of Kansas City, a straight two-hour drive on I-70. Exit north on KS 177, travel 12 miles. Remember the change for the toll booths.

where to go

Manhattan Convention and Visitors Bureau. 501 Poyntz Ave.; (785) 776-8829; manhattancvb.org.

Flint Hills Discovery Center. 315 S. Third St.; (785) 587-2726; flinthillsdiscovery.org. One of the most exciting developments in Manhattan, Kansas, since the color purple, this 35,000-square-foot facility is dedicated to understanding and appreciating the Flint Hills region. Focusing on 22 counties in central Kansas, the center encompasses the geology and soil science of the Flint Hills. Walk underground under the tallgrass prairie to see the root systems of prairie wildflowers and witness the prairie on fire in order to understand how important such destruction is for the health of the prairie. Numerous hands-on, interactive exhibits help children and adults appreciate the impact of the Flint Hills and the tallgrass prairie on the much larger global environment. Open daily. Admission fee.

Fort Riley. Located 10 miles west of Manhattan at exit 301 on I-70; (785) 239-2737; riley .army.mil. The grounds of historic Fort Riley hold colorful exhibits that showcase the history of the Great Plains. The beautifully restored Custer House stands as the only set of surviving officers' quarters from the fort's early history. Built in 1855 of native limestone, the quarters are nearly identical to the house that George Armstrong Custer and his wife occupied while residing at the fort. The Custer House also depicts military and family life on the western frontier during the Indian wars.

The US Cavalry and First Infantry Division Museums are housed in separate buildings on the Main Post. The US Cavalry Museum, located in Building 205 on Custer Avenue, houses displays that chronicle the years of the American mounted horse soldier from the Revolutionary War to 1950. Adjacent to the US Cavalry Museum, the First Infantry Division Museum offers the history of this decorated division in life-size dioramas that portray the trenches and battlefields of both World War I and World War II, as well as the jungles of Vietnam and the sands of Desert Storm. Buffalo in a nearby corral are a further reminder of the history of America before fast-food franchises and tract housing bulldozed away much of the tallgrass prairie. Open daily. Free. Be prepared to show photo ID when entering the military base.

Kansas State University. 1700 Anderson Ave.; (785) 532-6011; k-state.edu. The 668-acre campus weaves throughout Manhattan. Founded in 1863, K-State has a number of internationally recognized programs that attract teachers and students from around the globe. Its

College of Agriculture offers the only worldwide programs in grain, milling, baking, and feed science and management. The College of Veterinary Medicine is internationally recognized as a center for the study of livestock diseases.

Marianna Kistler Beach Museum of Art. 701 Beach Ln.; (785) 532-7718; beach.k-state .edu. With six galleries, this museum promotes appreciation of the fine arts through exhibitions of works by popular regional artists and through various educational and outreach programs. It also offers displays held in conjunction with other museums of art around the country. As a Lending Affiliate for the National Gallery of Art in Washington, D.C., the museum enables teachers to borrow educational resource materials developed by the National Gallery. Closed Sun, Mon, and during school breaks. Free.

University Gardens. 1500 Dennison Ave.; (785) 532-3271; k-state.edu/gardens. Located at Denison Avenue, north of Claflin Road, the University Gardens features specialty gardens and plant collections that are woven together to provide an invaluable educational resource and learning laboratory for K-State students and a delightful experience for the visiting public. Among the favorites are more than 150 varieties of peonies, a large collection of tall bearded irises and, of course, roses and daylilies. The garden visitor center, located inside the old K-State Dairy Barn, has a number of resources and exhibits to help the home gardener with any issue. Open daily, Mar through Nov. Free.

Milford Lake State Park. Located four miles northwest of Junction City, c/o Milford State Park, 8811 State Park Rd., Milford; (785) 238-3014; ksoutdoors.com. Kansas's largest reservoir is one of the state's most productive for anglers. Walleye, crappie, smallmouth bass, and wiper—a hybrid between white and striped bass—abound in the lake waters. Weighing six to eight pounds, they join up with white bass and cruise together in the early summer to the main part of Milford to search for their favorite food of shad. According to experts, that's the time the wipers and white bass are easy to catch. With more than 16,000 surface acres and 163 miles of shoreline, there are plenty of fish around for the eating. Milford Lake and its surrounding 21,000 acres make up one of Kansas's prime outdoor habitats, and the body of water is one of the more scenic lakes in the area.

The Milford Nature Center/Fish Hatchery is located at the base of Milford Dam and offers displays that explore the surrounding natural area. Free.

SNW Gallery. 406½ Poyntz Ave.; (785) 537-2099; snwgallery.com. This upstairs gallery highlights the work of about 40 local artists whose media include ceramics, silk, and oil. If you enjoy the beauty of the Flint Hills, you will find many of those images reflected in the work here. Closed Sun and Mon.

Sunset Zoo. 2333 Oak St.; (785) 587-2737; sunsetzoo.com. This 56-acre zoo may be small, but it is one of the most romantic zoos in the Midwest. That's because love is always in bloom here and lots of animals grow up healthy thanks to the zoo's excellent breeding program. There are 13 endangered species in the zoo, including snow leopards and red pandas that have managed to thrive in captivity.

Other zoos, including the famed San Diego Zoo, send their animals here for breeding purposes because of the zoo's spectacular success rate at producing healthy zoo babies. The medical care for animals is unique. With K-State's renowned veterinary medical school and exotic medicine program available at all times, two K-State vets are employed by the zoo to monitor and care for the animals and their offspring.

Become mesmerized at the Hummingbird Garden and Butterfly Garden, two of the five beautiful gardens at the zoo. Open daily. Admission fee.

Tuttle Creek Lake. 5020 B Tuttle Creek Blvd.,15 miles north of I-70 on KS 177; (785) 539-7941; ksoutdoors.com. The 12,500-acre lake is surrounded by 104 miles of irregular, wooded shoreline, and its wildlife, water, and climate make it a good spot for outdoor recreation. White bass, crappie, channel catfish, and spawn fishing draw anglers, who come in spring and summer to drop a line in any of the numerous sites around the lake that are available for fishing. Other activities include boating, waterskiing, swimming, hunting, picnicking, camping, and other outdoor sports. Pontoon, kayak, and fishing boat rentals; fishing supplies; fuel; boat-slip rentals; and concessions are available at the marina. The park has 11 cabins available for overnight accommodations, miles of hiking and mountain bike trails, and an 18-hole disc golf course. Dinner cruises aboard a houseboat are offered for small groups. Free.

Wildwood Adventure Park. 375 Johnson Rd.; (785) 477-9543; mhkadventures.com. This 80-acre park is for the adrenaline junkie. Seven zip lines, a two-mile obstacle course, climbing wall, and more challenge every muscle and fiber of your being. Open seasonally and according to weather conditions. Fee.

where to shop

Aggieville. Southeast of the K-State campus, Manhattan; (785) 776-8050; aggieville.org. The first shopping center in Kansas is named for the former K-State Aggies. Today it is a pre- and postgame host to Wildcat sporting events. Aggieville offers more than 100 businesses that feature shopping, dining, dancing, and nightlife, all within walking distance of K-State and concentrated in a little over four blocks. Everything from barbecue to women's clothing can be found here. Part of the fun is trying out the food, which ranges from cappuccino and croissants to Cajun jambalaya and gumbo.

where to eat

AJ's NY Pizzeria. 301 Poyntz Ave.; (785) 587-0700; ajsnypizza.com. Making that connection between the Big Apple and the Little Apple, this pizzeria uses a recipe provided by Mastandos of Brooklyn and ingredients authentic to New York–style pizza. A choice of seven cheeses and five sauces makes creating your own a lot of fun. Buy by the slice or the whole pie. Open daily, 11 a.m. to 10 p.m. $

Call Hall. 918 N. Martin Luther King Jr. Dr. on the K-State campus; (785) 532-1292. Thanks to the scientific laboratories in the Dairy and Poultry Science Building, all the superb-tasting milk, butter, cheese, and ice cream come straight from the cow to your mouth, hormone free with no antibiotics. There are 40 flavors of ice cream that change daily, and each one is better than the one before it. You might want to bring a cooler and plenty of ice to take back some of the terrific cheese and butter sold here. But more than dairy, a limited breakfast and lunch menu is open to the public as well as students. Closed Sun and when classes are not in session. $

Little Apple Brewing Company. 1110 Westloop Shopping Center; (785) 539-5500. Five refreshing handcrafted brews and certified Angus beef steaks are the claim to fame at this friendly restaurant and pub that cater to football lovers. However, if you prefer to grill your steak at home, the restaurant operates a meat market as well, via the website. Open Tues through Sat, 4:30 to 8:30 p.m. $–$$

The Chef Café. 111 S. Fourth St.; (785) 537-6843; thechefcafe.com. Voted the Best Breakfast in Kansas, The Chef has been a presence in Manhattan since shortly after World War II. Despite being closed for a few years, The Chef still draws crowds, particularly for breakfast. The signature item is the fajita scramble, but the stacked French toast with caramel cream cheese is a reason to come back for breakfast again the next day. Open daily for breakfast and lunch. $

Cox Brothers Barbecue. 223 McCall Rd.; (785) 539-0770; coxbbq.com. A little bit Texas, a little bit Carolina and Memphis, but a whole lotta Kansas City influence the barbecue here. Seriously, barbecue is made to satisfy all taste buds. The coleslaw is creamy and the turkey legs are Manhattan style. You'll just have to ask about that. Open daily. $$

day trip 05

west

>>>

flint hills scenic byway:
konza prairie research natural area;
council grove, ks; tallgrass prairie national
preserve; cottonwood falls, ks

Flint Hills Scenic Byway (KS 177) runs for 84 miles meandering from Manhattan to Cassoday, through a region of rounded limestone hills covered with bluestem prairie. Along the way you'll reach the eastern segment of the Konza Prairie Research Natural Area, and from there you can visit the Tallgrass Prairie National Preserve, Kansas's first national park. Keep traveling south and you'll come to the bed-and-breakfast country of Council Grove and Cottonwood Falls. For more information on all eight Kansas scenic byways, visit ksbyways.org.

konza prairie research natural area

Owned by the Nature Conservancy and managed by Kansas State University for the purpose of scientific study of this natural ecosystem, the Konza Prairie is the most intensively studied grassland on earth.

getting there

Just south of Manhattan, the Konza Prairie Research Natural Area is easily viewed from adjacent highways. KS 177 parallels the eastern segment of the preserve, and I-70 runs along most of its southern border. To reach the Konza Prairie entrance from KS 177, drive to the east end of the Kansas River Bridge and turn onto McDowell Creek Road (County Road 901S).

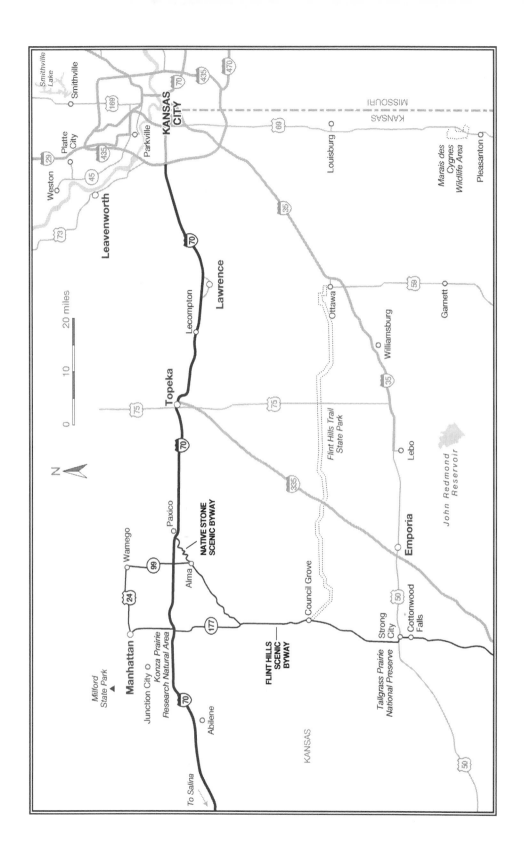

The entrance is about six miles down the road on the left. (From I-70 take exit 307 and drive northeast on McDowell Creek Road. The entrance is approximately five miles on your right.)

where to go

Konza Prairie Research Natural Area. (785) 587-0441; keep.konza.k-state.edu. This scenic area, named for the Kanza Indians who once roamed here, covers more than 8,600 acres of unplowed, uncultivated land filled with 70 species of dominant grasses and more than 500 species of wildflowers, shrubs, and trees.

The bison herd that lives here is part of a scientific effort to study the effect of these native grazers upon the grasslands. Fire, along with innumerable animals who grazed here, shaped the landscape, and it is here at Konza that the effects of both are being investigated. Most of the Konza Prairie Research Natural Area is closed to the public. However, three self-guided nature trails are open daily. Trail maps are available at the front gate. Donation appreciated.

The Fall Visitors Day, offered on even-numbered years, is filled with special tours and presentations. Tour guides are available with advance reservations. Pack your binoculars since deer and hawk sightings are a common occurrence. Open from dawn to dusk year-round. No drones or dogs allowed.

defining the flint hills

Draped in bluestem grasses and colorful wildflowers during warm weather, the Flint Hills are an ancient reminder of our planet's ecological history. This represents the largest tract of tallgrass prairie in North America that has never been broken by a plow or other man-made efforts. The surface of the Flint Hills is composed of limestone sediment and thin layers of chert (commonly known as flint) that were deposited by inland seas more than 200 million years ago.

Centuries of erosion formed the rugged, high escarpments and gently rolling landforms found in Chase County. Woodland Indians once roamed the area, and archaeological digs at Eldorado and Council Grove have unearthed many prehistoric campsites.

The early settlers in the area found that a combination of farming and ranching was not only possible in this region but often necessary for survival. Today's successful farmer–stockman must also use the rich bottomland soil for growing crops such as wheat, soybeans, corn, milo, and alfalfa, while employing the upland prairie with its wonderful native grasses, for grazing cattle.

council grove, ks

The historic town of Council Grove got its name from a negotiated treaty between US commissioners and the Osage Indian chiefs in 1825, an agreement that granted non-natives safe passage along the Santa Fe Trail.

A camping and meeting place for explorers, soldiers, traders, and Native Americans, Council Grove offered ample water, grass, and abundant wood, making it a rendezvous point for wagon trains heading west.

John Fremont's expedition of 1845 and Colonel A. W. Doniphan's troops bound for Mexico in 1846 camped on this site. In 1849 the Overland Mail was established with the supply headquarters at Council Grove, followed the next year by monthly coach service.

Council Grove today offers a quaint shopping district, restaurants, and lodging.

The town has an informative self-guided walking-tour brochure, filled with historic things to see that include the wheel ruts left by the wagon trains heading west; the Custer Elm, where George Armstrong Custer camped; and the Council Oak, named for the treaty signed beneath the tree by the Osage Indians and the US commissioners.

While Council Grove is a modern, thriving community, it is a place steeped in history. The community maintains 25 historic sites, each with a rich story about the growth of our country as it passed through central Kansas. Visit the Council Grove website or the Visitors Bureau offices for a brochure and map to these destinations.

getting there

From Manhattan, follow KS 177 south 35 miles to Council Grove.

where to go

Council Grove/Morris County Visitors Bureau. 207 W. Main St.; (620) 767-5413; councilgrove.com.

Flint Hills Trail State Park. Intersection of Donnon and Walnut Streets. This 117-mile-long trails-to-trails project passes through five counties in central Kansas. The trailhead offers restrooms, fresh water, and information about the trail.

Flint Hills Lavender Farm. 516 H Ave., Alta Vista; (785) 499-6405; flinthillslavender.com. In addition to beautiful lavender fields and products, this little farm has herbs for sale to grow yourself or just to sprinkle on whatever you're cooking. Call before dropping by or look for them at the Council Grove Farmers' Market.

Neosho Riverwalk. Connecting the Flint Hills Trail State Park to the Kaw Mission State Historic Site, this 1.1-mile paved trail on both sides of the Neosho River crosses the Old Santa Fe Trail Road with a highlight of where the wagons crossed the river. Well lit for evening walks, the trail is ADA accessible.

where to shop

Alexander Artworks. 923 W. Main St.; (620) 767-5153; a2wks.com. From delicate stained glass to rugged steel signs and life-size silhouettes, Bob and Christy Alexander are bringing a fresh approach to creativity and entrepreneurship to central Kansas. In addition to creating some really cool items, for sale in their retail shop, they also teach classes in stained glass and metal art. Oh, and if you're looking for the best cup of coffee in Council Grove, word is it's available inside at the Watts Coffee Co. Open Tues through Sat.

where to eat

Hays House 1857 Restaurant and Tavern. 112 W. Main St.; (620) 767-5911; hayshouse .com. This National Historic Landmark was built in 1857 by Seth Hays, great-grandson of Daniel Boone and cousin of Kit Carson. One of the oldest continuously operated restaurants west of the Mississippi, the tavern is an attraction on the Santa Fe National Historic Trail tour. In its early days it was host to theatricals, court proceedings, mail distribution, and church services, as well as serving good food to all.

Now a comfortable stop for modern-day travelers, the Hays House offers delicious foods served in a relaxed atmosphere. Specialties include aged Kansas beef, homemade breads, and desserts. The Victorian-inspired second floor houses the Hays Tavern, which offers a fully stocked bar in the evening. The restaurant also features several private dining rooms. Open seven days a week. $$

where to stay

Cottage House Hotel. 25 N. Neosho St.; (620) 767-6828; cottagehousehotel.com. This restored Victorian hotel is on the National Register of Historic Places and has been serving travelers for more than a century. It features modern comforts in nostalgic surroundings and offers a relaxing atmosphere, with gazebo-style porches, a sauna, and period furnishings. Each of the 26 rooms in the main hotel has a distinctive style. Stained glass and a brass-and-iron bed are featured in the bridal chamber. A continental breakfast is served each morning. $$

tallgrass prairie national preserve

This unique cooperative between the Nature Conservancy and the National Park Service contains 10,894 acres of tallgrass prairie, which is leased to the National Park Service. Expansive rolling hills and wide-open vistas greet you as you experience the beauty of this quiet land. From Apr 10 through Oct 31, a seven-mile bus tour is available to take you through the area. The natural prairie cycle of climate, fire, and animal grazing has sustained this beautiful land, where nearly 400 species of plants, 150 kinds of birds, 31 species of mammals, and assorted reptiles and amphibians reside.

Also at the preserve is the Z-Bar/Spring Hill Ranch, home of the original owner, Stephen F. Jones. The 11-room structure, built with hand-cut native limestone, is characteristic of the Second Empire style of 19th-century architecture. Also on the premises is a massive three-story barn and Lower Fox Creek School, a one-room schoolhouse located on a nearby hilltop. Brochures are available for self-guided tours. Docent tours are given hourly between Apr 10 and Oct 31. Admission fee. Call (620) 273-8494 or visit nps.gov/tapr.

getting there

From downtown Kansas City, follow I-35 south to Emporia approximately 110 miles. Turn west on US 50 and travel about 20 miles to the intersection of KS 177. Turn north and travel two miles.

where to stay

Clover Cliff Ranch. 826A US Highway 50, Elmdale; (620) 273-6698; clovercliffranch.com. Bring your own horse along to ride the trail that runs along this 4,000-acre working cattle ranch located east of Strong City, off US 50. Hiking, fishing, and general all-purpose relaxing are other amenities found at the ranch, which is listed on the National Register of Historic Places. The main house offers four guest rooms, two with private baths. There are also adjacent guest houses that are truly "homes away from home." The larger one features two bedrooms, a loft area with twin beds, a sitting room, twin baths, kitchen facilities, a fireplace, and a television. The smaller guest house has two bedrooms, a sleeper sofa, one bath, kitchen facilities, a fireplace, and a television. Breakfast is served in the main house. $$–$$$

cottonwood falls, ks

The oldest settlement in Chase County, the tiny hamlet of Cottonwood Falls is located in the center of the picturesque Flint Hills. The best time to visit the area is spring, fall, or early summer, rather than during a hot summer scorcher. Don't be fooled by appearances; there are plenty of things to see and do around the town, provided you know where to go. And come on Friday nights for free music in the streets. Every Friday night, musicians from around the region simply gather for an impromptu jam session that goes on for hours.

getting there

When leaving the Tallgrass Prairie, turn south on KS 177 and travel just three miles into Cottonwood Falls.

where to go

Chase County Chamber of Commerce. 318 Broadway; (620) 273-8469; chasecountychamber.org.

Chase County Courthouse. Broadway and Pearl Streets; (620) 273-8469. Built in 1872 of native limestone, the courthouse is an impressive structure. Listed on the National Register of Historic Places, it remains the oldest courthouse in continual use in Kansas. Each year more than 6,000 visitors from around the country visit the structure, marveling at the architectural design, stonework, and spiral staircase. Guided tours of the courthouse can be arranged in advance. Admission fee.

symphony in the flint hills

The best seat in the house for this performance is a hay bale, facing west.

In the most unlikely, but undeniably natural and appropriate setting, the Kansas City Symphony has found a new audience in the annual **Symphony in the Flint Hills**. *Begun in 2006 as a 10th anniversary tribute to the Tallgrass National Prairie, the symphony has become an immediate and sold-out hit.*

The Symphony in the Flint Hills is held the second weekend in June, while the nights are still cool. Eighty-five musicians from the Kansas City Symphony perform under the stars, accompanied by singing cicadas and crickets, as the sun sets dramatically beyond the Flint Hills. Before the performance, visitors can take part in guided nature walks through the prairie, horse-drawn wagon rides, and a musical-instrument petting zoo. The location moves each year, but note that tickets go on sale in March and sell out quickly. Call (620) 273-8955 or visit symphonyintheflinthills .org.

Chase County Historical Society Museum. 301 Broadway; (620) 273-8500. The museum holds historic memorabilia and artifacts of the area, including information about the demise of Knute Rockne, the famous Notre Dame coach who was killed when his airplane crashed in heavy fog near here in 1931. Donation requested. Closed Sun and Mon.

where to shop

Flint Hills and Tallgrass Gallery. 321 Broadway; (620) 273-6454. The gallery features the paintings of Chase County artists, along with custom-made spurs, knives, belt buckles, and hat racks. The shop also sells jewelry, Indian baskets, drums, and stained glass. Closed Sun.

Jim Bell & Son. 322 Broadway; (620) 273-6381. If you're looking for a unique shopping experience, try this place. The restored building was opened in 1927 as a retail store for real cowboys. It still supplies any piece of custom-made tack the working cowboy needs, plus there's a boot and saddle repair shop located in the store's basement in case you decide to gallop into town on your horse. Even nonworking cowboys and cowgirls can find the latest styles in western and casual wear for the entire family, from boots and hats to outdoor wear, hunting apparel, and more. Open daily.

where to eat

Grand Central Hotel and Grill. 215 Broadway; (620) 273-6763; grandcentralhotel.com. Looking for a little espresso, Asti Spumante, champagne, or Carmel Valley sauvignon blanc to perk up your day? What better place to find it than smack in the middle of a vast Midwestern plain.

Located in the center of the Flint Hills, along the one and only main thoroughfare of town, this restaurant specializes in Sterling Silver, a line of Certified Premium USDA Choice steaks so terrific that you'll think you've died and gone to Kansas.

Entrees are served with salad, choice of potato or vegetable, and fresh bread and butter. Dessert can be Grand Central cheesecake topped with cherries or almond amaretto or homemade bread pudding with New Orleans bourbon sauce. The full-service restaurant offers lunch and dinner to the public and an elegant continental breakfast daily to hotel guests. Closed Sun. $$–$$$

Chef Stan's Place or The Little Restaurant on the Prairie. 225 Church St., Strong City; (213) 400-4559. Located in an old one-room schoolhouse/church, built in 1905, Chef Stan Lerner has turned this very simple location into the most adorable little restaurant. He's known for his Mediterranean-style quiche, soups, and salads, but he also has a pulled chicken sandwich and egg salad sandwich served on prairie bread that's quite interesting. Ask him about prairie bread or anything else. Stan is a talker and loves sharing with others his love of culinary history. Ask about the history of magic cookie bars. Oh, and try the lemon tarts. He's added a seared salmon to the dinner menu. It's such an enjoyable, simple Kansas thing to do. Open Thurs through Sun, 11 a.m. to 2 p.m. and 5 to 8 p.m. $

where to stay

Grand Central Hotel. 215 Broadway; (620) 273-6763; grandcentralhotel.com. Definitely not your little roadside prairie motel, the Grand Central Hotel is a must-stop on your way through Kansas. The AAA four-diamond hotel and restaurant opened in 1884 and reopened in 1995; the hotel has been restored beyond its original elegance. Located two miles from the Tallgrass Prairie National Preserve and one block west of scenic KS 177, the Grand Central offers 10 beautifully appointed rooms, all designed with a western flair. Its full-service restaurant offers lunch and dinner to the public and an elegant continental breakfast daily to hotel guests.

For starters, there are queen- and king-size beds draped with Egyptian cotton duvets and sheets purchased in Paris. Plush VIP robes, Jacuzzi showers, full concierge service, complimentary continental breakfast, and meeting rooms for private dining and corporate retreats are offered. A very nice wheelchair-accessible room on the first floor has its own outdoor porch. The hotel is happy to provide guests with a variety of outdoor experiences that include nature hiking, horseback riding, and fishing. $$

day trip 06

west

presidential town:
abilene, ks

abilene, ks

The name Abilene immediately conjures up images of the wild, wild West, with cowboys, cattle herds, and Main Street shootouts at the end of the Chisholm Trail. Although that image was certainly true in the mid-1800s, Abilene is now a quiet town that gave birth to one of the United States' most decorated military officers and beloved presidents.

Abilene comes from a Bible scripture that means "city of the plains," and although "city" may be a stretch, it is certainly a pleasant community on plains worthy of exploration. Too often, Kansas Citians blow by Abilene on I-70 on their way to more glamorous destinations at the other end of the interstate. However, those who stop for just a few moments or a few days will find a town void of many chain restaurants and commercial establishments, but with a vibrant downtown, lovely neighborhoods of historic homes, and a gentler pace of life.

Founded in a small dug-out homestead and stagecoach stop in 1857, Abilene had grown only slightly when the railroads began to reach across the Plains after the Civil War. The railroads meant a way to move cattle to market on the East Coast, and the Chisholm Trail brought cattle and cowboys from southern Texas by the millions beginning in 1867. For the next five years, more than three million cattle arrived in Abilene before being shipped east by rail. Some days as many as 5,000 cowboys received their pay for moving the cattle along the trail, so undoubtedly, things got a little rowdy downtown.

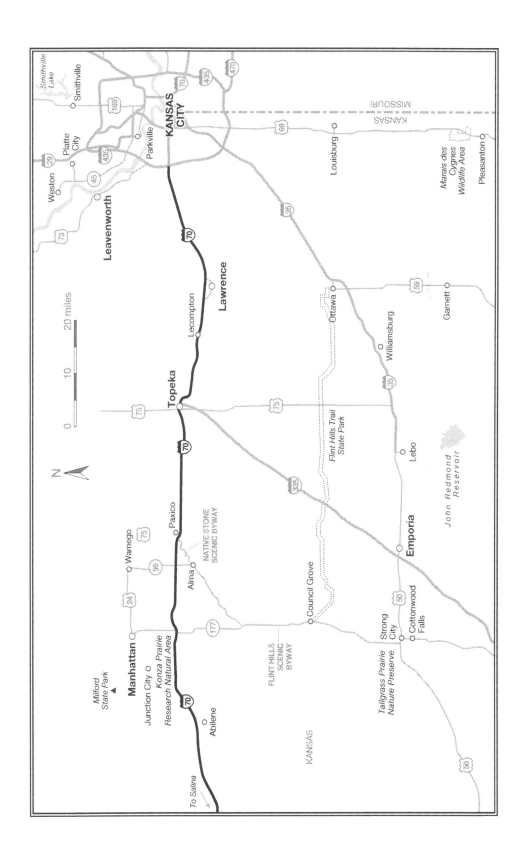

Today you can learn much of the history of Abilene via a trolley ride that departs from the restored train depot. The influx of wealth at the end of the 19th century resulted in several elegant homes, two of which have been restored and are open to tour today. However, Abilene is perhaps best known as the home of Dwight D. Eisenhower, the leader of the Allied Forces in Europe during World War II, who became the 34th president of the United States. He and his five brothers were raised here. A tour of the presidential library and grounds is a must for anyone visiting the community.

Several other museums, restaurants, and a professional theater company provide plenty of activity for a few hours or a few days.

getting there

From Kansas City, take I-70 west 150 miles to exit 275.

where to go

Abilene Convention and Visitors Bureau. 201 NW Second St.; (785) 263-2231; abilenekansas.org. Located in the historic Union Pacific Depot, this is where to find out the latest developments in town, as well as take one of the trolley rides through Historic Downtown.

Abilene Smoky Valley Excursion Train. 200 SE Fifth St.; (785) 263-1077; asvrr.org. Enjoy the Kansas countryside as you ride in a century-old dining car or open-air gondola car, or for a special fare, you can ride in the caboose or the engine. The train is powered by a 1945 ALCO S-1 engine originally designed for World War II submarines. A gift shop in the depot carries all sorts of train memorabilia. Closed Nov through Apr.

Bow Studio and Gallery. 921 S. Buckeye Ave.; (785) 263-7166; bowsart.com. Take a piece of native Kansas home with you after a visit to the studio of Inga and Bob Bow. The wildflower garden that fills their property is for more than show. This is where Inga gathers ideas and materials for her work. You'll find leaves, flowers, wheat, and other designs of nature pressed and painted into original clay designs and fired on-site. Open daily.

Heritage Center of Dickinson County. 412 S. Campbell St.; (785) 263-2681; dickinsoncountyhistoricalsociety.com. Here's where you can learn about the wicked history of Abilene in the days when it was known as one of the wickedest towns in the West. From jail records to antique guns confiscated from rowdy cowboys, the artifacts here tell the story of the conflicts more than a century ago. Within the museum is the Museum of Independent Telephony, which chronicles the early days of telephone service in small, rural towns like Abilene. The little telephone company in Abilene, sold, changed hands, grew up and eventually became what we know today as Sprint. In a separate building behind the museum is an operating C. W. Parker Carousel, one of the original hand-carved track-operated machines created by the Abilene-based entertainment company in the early 1900s. Open Wed through Sat, 10 a.m. to 3 p.m. Admission fee.

Eisenhower Center. 200 SE Fourth St.; (785) 263-6700 or (877) RING-IKE; eisenhower library.gov. This complex tells the remarkable life story of native son Dwight D. Eisenhower, one of America's most honored military leaders and the 34th president of the United States. Historians of all genres and generations will appreciate the details presented from World War II and the D-Day invasion led by then General Eisenhower, as well as the global conflicts that followed World War II. Plan on spending several hours here touring the Eisenhower home, library, museum, and memorial chapel, where the former president and First Lady are buried. Fee for those 16 and older for the museum only. Open daily.

Eisenhower Park and Rose Garden. 500 Pine St.; (785) 263-7288. All the world seemed to watch in 1952 when then General Dwight Eisenhower announced he would run for president from this little municipal stadium. It's now on the National Register of Historic Places. More than 150 types of roses and more than 500 other types of flowers make this a peaceful place to reflect on the events that took place because of the little boy who grew up on the wrong side of the tracks in Abilene and changed the course of human history.

Greyhound Hall of Fame. 407 S. Buckeye Ave.; (785) 263-3000; greyhoundhalloffame .com. Sharon and Chig, two retired racing dogs, will greet you before you begin a self-guided tour, which showcases the "Sport of Queens." You may pet greyhounds and learn about the history of the world's fastest dogs all the way back to prehistoric times. Open Wed through Sun, 10 a.m. to 4 p.m.

Seelye Mansion. 1105 N. Buckeye Ave.; (785) 263-1084; seeleyemansion.org. Step back in time as you are guided through this 1905 Georgian-style mansion built by Dr. and Mrs. A. B. Seelye, the name that for years was associated with rural medical care and patent medicines. Stroll through the gardens and learn about the patent medicine manufacturing business located in Abilene that once rivaled the names of Bayer and Eli Lilly. Built in the early years of the 20th century, the home contains many items and fixtures purchased at the 1904 World's Fair in St. Louis. Thomas Edison worked with the architect to bring lighting and other modern conveniences to the home. A basement-level bowling alley and a third-level ballroom speak to the opulence found on the Great Plains during this period. Christmas is an especially beautiful time to visit the Seelye Mansion to see the 40 decorated Christmas trees and more than 200 poinsettias throughout the home. Open for tours daily. Admission fee.

where to eat

Ike's Place. 100 NW 14th St.; (785) 200-6278; ikesplacegrill.com. Ike never hung out here. This bar and grill has only been a part of the Abilene dining scene since 2018. And he might be a little self-conscious of the décor that celebrates the Supreme Allied Commander and eventual Commander-in-Chief, but we think he would like the burgers, the open-faced prime rib sandwiches, and steaks on the menu. Ike and Mamie would definitely support the local musicians who are a part of most evening's entertainment. Closed Tues.

Mr. K's Farmhouse. 407 S. Van Buren St.; (785) 263-7995; mrksfarmhouse.com. This rambling old farmhouse was a favorite of Dwight and Mamie Eisenhower when they lived in or returned to Abilene, and it's still popular today for homemade pies, roast beef, and huge pork chops. You may want to keep it quiet if you eat here on your birthday. You might just receive a paddling from one of the many wooden paddles hanging from the ceiling, a tradition that was begun when Dwight Eisenhower dined here on his 75th birthday. Closed Mon. $–$$

where to stay

Abilene's Victorian Bed and Breakfast Inn. 820 NW Third St.; (785) 263-7774; abilenesvictorianinn.com. This home dates to 1900 and was once the family home of "Swede" Hazlett, a close, personal friend of President Eisenhower. Today the home has six spacious guest rooms across the street from Eisenhower Park and is within walking distance of downtown. Homemade cookies await your check-in, as well as board games, a video library, and a spacious porch for relaxing. $–$$

worth more time:
salina, ks

As long as you are in Abilene, drive just another 25 miles west on I-70 to Salina. Or on your next trip to Colorado, plan an overnight stop in Salina. Either way, make sure you're wearing your Lee jeans when you come to town. This is where Henry David Lee founded a mercantile company in the late 1800s that eventually became Lee Jeans, now based in Merriam, Kansas.

The **Historic Lee District** in downtown Salina is now a pedestrian-friendly shopping district with more than 300 businesses. A number of festivals and special events take place here throughout the year.

Salina is also home to the **Smoky Hill Vineyards and Winery,** a fabulous wildlife center. And you have to enjoy the best stinkin' burger in Kansas at the century-old Cozy Inn.

For more information, contact the **Salina Chamber of Commerce,** 120 W. Ash St.; (785) 827-9301; salinakansas.org.

northwest

day trip 01

northwest

military memorabilia, mansions, museums & memorials:
leavenworth, ks; atchison, ks; hiawatha, ks

leavenworth, ks

As the "First City of Kansas," Leavenworth was at the forefront of the transportation revolution. From boat to wagon to railroad, the town led the way in opening the vast resources of America. The Leavenworth Landing Park, located adjacent to the Missouri River, features exhibits that portray the town's part in forging a path through the American West.

All along the Overland Trails, US Cavalry fortifications such as Fort Leavenworth sprang up to defend western settlements. Between 1838 and 1845 a military road was constructed through the Indian Territory to connect Fort Leavenworth in Kansas and Fort Gibson in Oklahoma.

Today the old military road no longer exists, but modern US 69 and other connecting pathways located near its original route have been designated the Frontier Military Scenic Byway. Fort Leavenworth and Fort Scott, two of the remaining historic Kansas forts lying along that route, are open to tour today.

Established by Colonel Henry Leavenworth in 1827, Fort Leavenworth was a cantonment to protect wagon trains headed west and to help maintain peace with the Native Americans. Leavenworth was also the starting point for exploration parties. When travel to California began in the 1840s, thousands of prairie schooners passed through the posts.

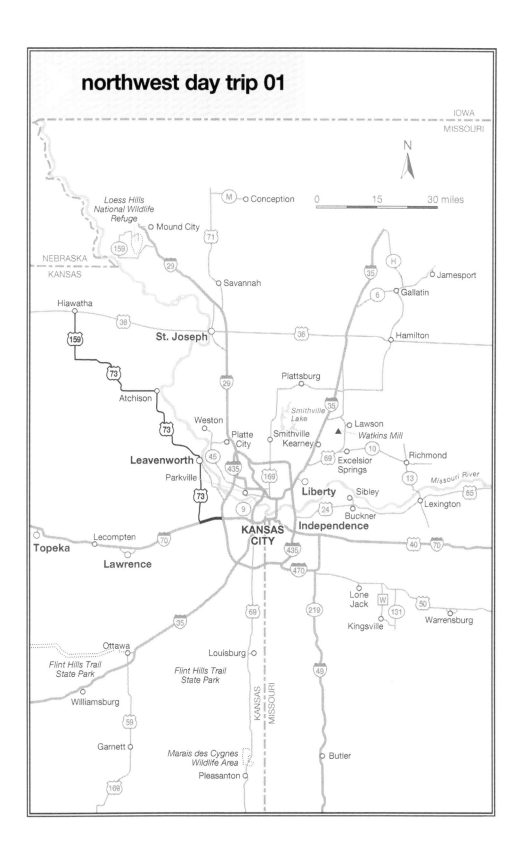

northwest day trip 01

Leavenworth has had its share of the famous and infamous. In 1895, the Fort Leavenworth Military Prison was transferred to the Department of Justice, and Congress authorized 1,000 acres of military reservation for a penitentiary.

The US Penitentiary at Leavenworth was completed in 1906 and has housed infamous criminals within its walls, including Al Capone; "Machine Gun" Kelly; Robert Stroud, the "Birdman of Alcatraz"; and James Earl Ray.

Leavenworth has a long list of good guys too. Civil War General William T. Sherman practiced law here, and restaurateur Fred Harvey built his magnificent home on one of the tree-shaded streets. William F. "Buffalo Bill" Cody, Army scout and showman, moved to Leavenworth with his family in 1854 when he was seven years old. Working for J. B. "Wild Bill" Hickok, he helped outfit trains with supplies for the Overland Stage Company. Leavenworth's US Army Command and General Staff College, on the post, educated such famous students as Douglas MacArthur, George Marshall, John Pershing, Dwight Eisenhower, and Colin Powell.

getting there

From downtown Kansas City, follow I-70 west to exit 224 and turn north. Follow US 73 for 15 miles into Leavenworth.

where to go

Leavenworth Area Convention and Visitors Bureau. 105 N. Fifth St.; (913) 758-2948; visitleavenworthks.com. The visitors bureau can supply you with brochures, self-guided tour booklets, and other information on the city.

Carroll Mansion. 1128 Fifth Ave.; (913) 682-7759. More than a museum, this elegant 1882 Victorian home is a masterpiece of elaborately carved woodwork and stained-glass windows. You can feel the style and spirit of the age as you travel through this 16-room mansion. The parlor contains fine Sevres, Dresden, and Early American porcelain; Steuben glass; and lovely furniture. Elsewhere in the museum you'll see antiques from Leavenworth homes, some of them brought up the river by steamer.

In the kitchen, along with the pitcher pump and woodstove, is a copper sink, a refinement of the period. The bathroom contains a lead tub that supplied both hot and cold water and a shower–bath, newfangled oddities that were probably among the first in the West. The museum is maintained by the Leavenworth County Historical Society. Closed Sun and Mon. Admission fee.

Fort Leavenworth. Seventh and Metropolitan Streets, Fort Leavenworth; (913) 684-3600; leavenworth.army.mil. Established in 1827, this is the oldest military installation in continuous service west of the Mississippi River. In the early part of the 19th century, it played an important role for wagon trains heading west. Generals George Custer, William Sherman,

Robert E. Lee, Douglas MacArthur, Dwight D. Eisenhower, George S. Patton, Omar Bradley, Norman Schwarzkopf, and Colin Powell were stationed here. Today it is home to the Combined Arms Center, the Command and General Staff College, and the US Disciplinary Barracks. A self-guided tour booklet is available in the Frontier Army Museum Gift Shop on the premises. Visitors are welcome to drive through the fort year-round, but be prepared to present photo identification for anyone 16 and older and have your vehicle searched upon entering the gates. There are restaurants open to the public within the fort. Here are a few places worth seeing:

Berlin Wall Monument. Three sections of the destroyed Berlin Wall were donated to Fort Leavenworth because of the worldwide influence of the US Army Command and General Staff College. The design of the memorial expresses three themes: a "falling position," representing the crumbling of the wall; a horizontal position, depicting the wall's destruction; and a vertical position, symbolizing democracy.

Buffalo Soldier Monument. Grant Avenue and the south bank of Smith Lake, Fort Leavenworth. This monument, dedicated July 25, 1992, honors the Black soldiers who served in the 9th and 10th Cavalry Regiments from 1866 until the armed services were integrated following World War II.

The Frontier Army Museum. Off Reynolds Avenue, Fort Leavenworth; (913) 651-7440. The museum blends the history of Fort Leavenworth with that of the Frontier Army from 1817 to 1917. The outstanding exhibits graphically relate the history of the US Army and its role in western expansion beginning with the Lewis and Clark Expedition of 1804–1806. The carriage used by Abraham Lincoln on his visit to Kansas in December 1859 is displayed here.

Fort Leavenworth National Cemetery. (913) 684-5604. More than 20,000 veterans representing every war since 1812 are buried here. The large monument near the flagpole marks the grave of Colonel Henry Leavenworth, for whom the fort and the city of Leavenworth are named.

Rookery. 12–14 Sumner Place, Fort Leavenworth. This was the temporary home of the first territorial governor of Kansas and is the oldest continuously occupied house in the state, built in 1834. A National Historic Landmark, it once housed First Lieutenant Douglas MacArthur, who lived here as a bachelor officer. The Rookery is not open to tour.

C. W. Parker Carousel Museum. 320 Esplanade St.; (913) 682-1866. The C. W. Parker Amusement Company, which began in Abilene in 1896, later moved to Leavenworth, where it operated successfully until the start of the Great Depression. The museum to this amusement company houses a carousel from 1913 that is considered unique because of its two hand-carved rabbits used as a focal point. The carousel also has 24 hand-carved horses, three ponies, and a lovers' cup to ride in. Hometown girl Melissa Etheridge donated an organ to the museum. Open Fri through Sat. Admission fee.

First City Museum. 734 Delaware St.; (913) 682-1866. Here you can find a collection of early frontier memorabilia and artifacts, as well as artifacts from Buffalo Bill Cody's family and prison-related items. Open Thurs afternoons or by appointment. Admission fee.

glaciers & guitars

Enjoy a drive along the Kansas Scenic Byway Program, KS 7 from Leavenworth, and north through Atchison, all the way to the Nebraska border. Also called the Glacial Hills Scenic Byway because of the region's glacier-created rolling hills and valleys, this part of Kansas looks more like "Little Switzerland" than it does flatland.

In downtown Leavenworth, KS 7 is also known as Fourth Street, and it's where you'll find two guitar-shaped signs proclaiming Leavenworth to be the hometown of Melissa Etheridge. The Grammy Award–winning singer was born here in 1961, graduated from Leavenworth High School in 1979, and returns often for benefit concerts and other events to support the community. Pick up a brochure of sites important to Melissa's childhood here, including the shop where she took guitar lessons, from the convention and visitors bureau office.

Leavenworth Landing Park. Missouri River and Esplanade; (913) 651-2132. This transportation-themed park is decorated with sculptures depicting different modes of transportation throughout Leavenworth's history. The Paddle Wheel Plaza is reminiscent of the actual riverboat landing located in this same area. The Roundhouse Plaza uses inlaid paving stones depicting the railroad roundhouse that was located at the eastern end of the downtown area. Another unique feature is a raised four-state map constructed of terrazzo and brass; it locates the rivers, trails, and railroads that were an important part of Kansas's history. A diorama explains the scientific value of plant specimens gathered during the Lewis and Clark Expedition. Open daily. Free.

National Fred Harvey Museum. 624 Olive St.; (913) 682-1866. In the early days of railroading, passengers on the Santa Fe stopped at Fred Harvey restaurants for good food. Fred Harvey, founder of the chain, lived in the house until his death in 1901. The home is closed indefinitely while seeking funding for renovation.

Performing Arts Center. 500 Delaware St.; (913) 682-7557. This 1938 theater is an interesting example of American art deco architecture. Now on the National Register of Historic Places, the structure was donated to the city by Durwood, Inc., and today hosts live performances by Leavenworth's River City Community Players. A schedule of performances is at rccplv.com.

Richard Allen Cultural Center and Museum. 412 Kiowa St.; (913) 682-8772; raccm.org. Located in the home of a former Buffalo solider, this center showcases the Black heritage of Leavenworth and eastern Kansas, including the region's role in the Underground Railroad. General Colin Powell's family has donated items to the museum. Open daily. Admission fee.

where to eat

The Corner Pharmacy. 429 Delaware St.; (913) 682-1602. The pharmacy has been around since 1871. Its old-fashioned soda fountain and lunch counter are a throwback to the days when you could get good food and medicine all in one trip. Breakfast and lunch are served at the Victorian-style soda fountain, which comes complete with mahogany bentwood swivel stools and a mirrored back bar. The shakes, malts, and sodas are served in glass containers with the cans from the mixer alongside. The Corner also features home-made chili and an assortment of sandwiches, plus terrific fresh-squeezed limeades and homemade lemonades. Closed Sun. $

Harbor Lights Coffeehouse & Café. 316 Shawnee St.; (913) 682-2303; harborlight-scoffeehouse.com. Satisfy your sweet tooth or grab something healthy at this lovely, locally owned spot. So many good salads, sandwiches, and wraps for lunch, and then there's the dessert counter. Choose from seasonal cheesecakes, so many pies, cakes, cookies, cupcakes, and more. You imagine it and they have made it. Open for breakfast and lunch. Closed Mon. $

Homer's Drive-In. 1320 S. Fourth St.; 913-651-3500. Homer's has been an institution in Leavenworth since just about the time the first automobile arrived on the streets here and needed someplace to drive. It's not quite that old, but it is a classic burger drive-in, with a nice dining area indoors as well. Old pictures on the walls document that Homer's has been here a long, long time. Open daily. $ (no cards)

Meriwether's Café & Market. 702 Cherokee St.; (913) 240-9686; meriwetherscoffeeshop. com. Part coffee shop and café, part market for locally produced goods, and an occasional place for live music and a game of cards, Meriwether's is the essence of community. Closed Sun. $

Metropolitan Steak House. 1501 Metropolitan Ave.; (913) 651-6624. Nothing overly fancy in the décor, but you'll find a great steak and good service. In addition to steak, they have roast turkey, chicken fried steak, and just a good variety to choose from. Open for lunch and dinner daily. $$

where to shop

Dad's Toys & Trains. 417 Delaware St.; (913) 682-1786. This is a wonderful, old-fashioned toy store with lots of model trains set up and chugging their way around the showroom. Find some classic arcade games in the back and lots of sugary treats to up their energy level. Check the Facebook page for fun activities throughout the year. Closed Mon.

atchison, ks

It was here on July 4, 1804, that Lewis and Clark and the Corps of Discovery camped and celebrated the 28th birthday of the United States by firing their cannon. Independence Creek, the waterway that runs through Atchison into the Missouri River where Lewis and Clark camped, received its name that day. Today, a bridge that crosses the Missouri River here is named for the city's most famous resident, Amelia Earhart. A festival each July celebrates her birth with fireworks over the bridge.

During the mid-19th century, Atchison was an important center of overland freighting. In 1859 the Atchison, Topeka, Santa Fe Railway Company was founded here. A renovated 1880s-era freight depot now houses the Santa Fe Depot Visitors Center, historical museum, and gift shop.

Atchison is filled with history, museums, antiques and specialty shops, and magnificent 19th-century mansions, many of which are located on the beautiful Missouri River bluffs. The city is proud of its reputation as one of the most haunted cities in North America. Book early for ghost tours in October. There are three electric car charging stations in Atchison.

getting there

From Leavenworth, follow US 73 north for a scenic 30 miles to Atchison.

where to go

Atchison Chamber of Commerce. 200 S. 10th St.; (913) 367-2427; visitatchison.com. Located in the former Santa Fe Depot, this visitor center includes a nice exhibit on Amelia Earhart along with other aspects of the city's history. This is where the trolley tours start as well.

Amelia Earhart Birthplace Museum. 223 N. Terrace St.; (913) 367-4217; ameliaearhartmuseum.org. This historic home, where Amelia Earhart was born in 1897, is listed on the National Register of Historic Places. Interpretive displays, newspaper and magazine clippings, and family belongings tell the story of the legendary aviatrix. Open Wed through Sat, Mar through mid-Dec, by appointment from mid-Dec through Feb. Admission fee.

Amelia Earhart Earthwork. 17862 274th Rd., Warnock Lake; (913) 367-2427. This one-acre portrait of Amelia Earhart is on a hillside near Warnock Lake on the city's south side. It comprises live plantings, stone, and other natural materials. It is the first perpetual crop artwork created by famed Kansas artist Stan Herd and was designed to commemorate

Earhart's 100th birthday. A nearby viewing deck offers a good look at the earthwork and photographic displays that illustrate how the artist created his unusual portrait. Free.

Amelia Earhart Hangar Museum. 16701 286th Rd.; (913) 372-0021; ameliaearharthang-armuseum.org. Located at the small airport named for Atchison's most famous resident, this museum includes the only remaining Lockheed Electra L-10 in the world. This is the model of the plane Amelia and navigator Fred Noonan were flying when they disappeared on their round-the-world flight. Although you can't touch the airplane, 10 hands-on exhibits around the hangar allow visitors to learn some of the principles of flight, to navigate by the stars and learn more about trailblazing women in aviation. Open daily. $

Atchison County Historical Society. 200 S. 10th St.; (913) 367-6238; atchisonhistory .org. Located in a restored Santa Fe Depot, this museum hosts some interesting exhibits on Amelia Earhart, Lewis and Clark, and other events, large and small, in the area. It is also home to the unofficial David Rice Atchison Presidential Library. Atchison served as president for a 24-hour period in March 1849. (see Day Trip 01, Northeast)

Benedictine College. 1020 N. Second St.; (800) 467-5340; benedictine.edu. Founded more than 165 years ago by the joint Catholic communities of Mount St. Scholastica and St. Benedict's Abbey, the entire Second Street complex is listed on the National Register of Historic Places. Visitors can tour the campus, which is located above a river bluff affording a breathtaking autumn view.

International Forest of Friendship. South of Atchison on KS 7 near Warnock Lake; (913) 367-1419; ifof.org. Trees from all 50 states and 30 countries grow here. Spend a pleasant afternoon walking along a path engraved with the names of famous aviators, and spend a minute or two reflecting at a memorial for the astronauts who died aboard the space shuttle *Challenger*. There's no charge here, but donations are welcome.

Muchnic Art Gallery. 704 N. Fourth St.; (913) 367-4278; atchisonart.org. Monthly displays by regional artists are exhibited amid the elegant furnishings of one of Atchison's most spectacular Victorian mansions. The interior features rich woodwork, fine hand-tooled leather, brilliant stained-glass windows, and elaborate fireplaces. Open Wed, Sat, and Sun afternoon.

Providence Hill Farm. 8096 Pratt Rd.; (913) 360-0497; providencehillfarm.net. Is there anything more adorable than baby goats? This is the place to surround yourself with their playfulness and furry love. From goat yoga to hikes with goats to goat university, you'll never be the same after a day at Providence Hill Farm. Also, take classes and workshops on making soap, cheese, and candles. The farm also has a wood-fired brick oven, so plan a day making pizza. Bring your own wine if you like. $

St. Andre Orchard. 5443 Rawlins Rd.; (813) 702-6588; standreorchard16.wixsite.com. If you are passionate about fresh fruit, you'll love the selection here: peaches, apples, nectarines, plums, cherries, blackberries, and raspberries. Follow the website to see when crops are ready and then make an appointment to pick your own.

where to shop

Backroad Atlas. 517 Commercial St.; (913) 426-2470; backroad-atlas.com. Find furniture and other home goods that have been refurnished and given a new life by Angela Harris-Spurlock. You'll also find one-of-a-kind items from local artists and designers. Sign up for classes to give your own home that professional designer's touch. Open Tues through Sat, 9:30 a.m. to 5 p.m.

where to eat

Paolucci's. 115 S. Third; (913) 367-1241. The Paolucci family immigrated from southern Italy to Atchison in the 1890s and have been in business ever since, operating a grocery and deli, as the business evolved over the generations. For almost 40 years, Paolucci's Restaurant has been serving up authentic Italian dishes, as well as American steaks and burgers. Visit for Sunday brunch. Open daily, hours vary. $$

Cedar Ridge. 17028 318th St.; (913) 367-4357; cedar-ridge-restaruant.com. Enjoy a family-style dinner out in the country in this renovated barn. Boasting home-cooked meals, Cedar Ridge is open only on Saturday evening and for Sunday brunch. $

Jerry's Again. 125 N. Fifth St.; (913) 367-0577. Jerry's was in business for 40 years in Atchison and closed for a few years. Then they opened again, thus the name of the classic American restaurant. The menu includes lots of homemade everything from meatloaf to pork tenderloin, soups and sandwiches, and oh, the pies. Homemade fresh every day. Hours vary. $$

hiawatha, ks

The streets of little Hiawatha each fall host the oldest Halloween parade in the country. Started in 1914, the parade often calls for early dismissal from school. There's a Halloween queen. The governor is often in attendance. It's a big deal in Hiawatha. Join the parade! There is no entry fee and everyone is welcome! For more information: Hiawatha Chamber of Commerce, 801 Oregon St.; (913) 742-7136; hiawathaks.com.

getting there

Head north on US 73 from Atchison to US 159 and on to Hiawatha.

where to go

Brown County Agriculture Museum. 301 E. Iowa; (785) 742-3330; browncountyhistoricalsociety.com. Nothing says rural Kansas like a windmill, and this museum has more than 40 collected from around the region, all lined up in a colorful lane you can walk or drive along. There's also a collection of antique tractors, buggies and cars, and an old country schoolhouse from the 1900s. Open May through Dec, Mon through Fri, 10 a.m. to 4 p.m.

The Davis Memorial. Mount Hope Cemetery, Hiawatha. From Horton take US 159/73 north to Hiawatha. Or if you're coming from St. Joseph, take US 36 West. It's worth the drive to see one of the most unusual monuments ever built. Each year thousands of people come to see the tomb and sign their names on the guest register mounted at the site of this strange rendering of love and loss.

When Sarah Davis of Hiawatha died in 1930, her husband, John M. Davis, perpetuated her memory by building a memorial that contains 11 life-size figures depicting the couple at various stages of their married life. Davis spent a whopping sum of $500,000 to have the imported marble and granite figures carved by Italian craftsmen. He died penniless in a county home for the aged in 1947. A statue of Sarah, complete with angel wings, was positioned over the vault in which his coffin was placed. Her body rests in the crypt next to his. Atop that stone slab is a kneeling statue of Davis.

Although Davis's death and funeral were written up in *Life* magazine, few people attended the service. Only one man, Horace England, the tombstone salesman, seemed genuinely concerned by Davis's passing. Open daily. Free. No phone.

where to eat

The Bread Bowl. 100 Oregon St.; (785) 288-1480. Daily specials here include a massive pork tenderloin sandwich, open-faced roast beef sandwiches, and cheeseburgers. But there is always hardy soup served in a bread bowl. But the reason to plan lunch or dinner at the Bread Bowl is the bakery. A massive selection of homemade pies, cinnamon rolls, and more keep the place smelling like heaven all day long. Closed Sun. $

day trip 02

northwest

history at the river's edge:
parkville, mo; weston, mo;
platte city, mo

parkville, mo

The land for the town of Parkville was purchased in 1840 by Colonel George S. Park, a veteran of Sam Houston's cavalry who recognized the value of riverfront land for steamboat trade. As trade and commerce grew along the river, so did Parkville.

Downtown shops combine specialty items with antiques, crafts, clothing, home furnishings, and art. Remember to cross the railroad tracks to the shops and restaurants located there.

Park University was founded in 1875 and sits high on a bluff overlooking the town. It has always been an integral part of city activities, frequently opening its facilities to the community.

The town's amenities include English Landing Park, a short block from downtown. The walking trail by the river, picnic facilities, basketball goals, disc golf, and a volleyball court are popular with people all over the metro. The unusual Waddell A-Frame Bridge, listed on the National Register of Historic Places, is located within the park. Look for the marker that shows where passengers from the Arabia Steamboat came ashore in 1856, the basis of the Arabia Steamboat Museum in Kansas City's River Market. Parkville also boasts a nature sanctuary that makes for a pleasant retreat, as well as a popular farmers' market on Wed afternoons and Sat mornings.

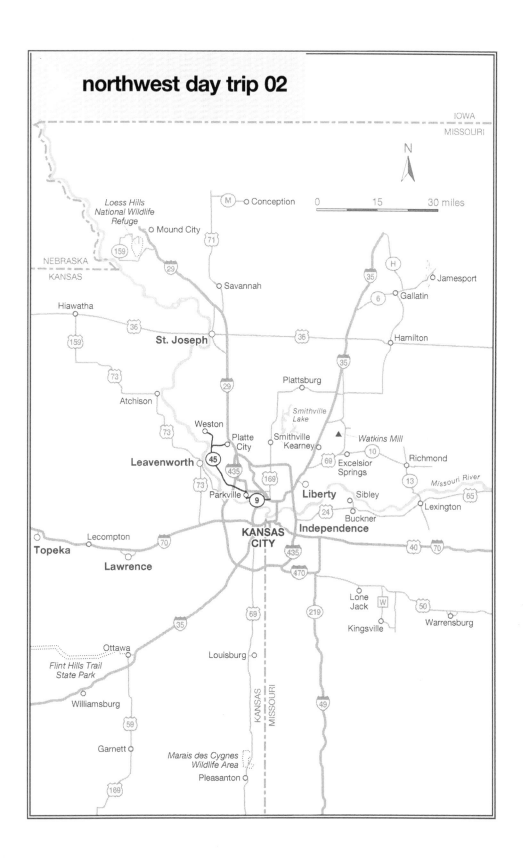

northwest day trip 02

Christmas on the River in Dec and cruise nights throughout the warm-weather months are among the many events that bring energy to this community all year long. Information on Parkville, as well as a walking-tour brochure, can be obtained at the Main Street Parkville office. Step into the alley south of the American Legion for your best selfie spot in Parkville.

getting there

From downtown, cross the Buck O'Neil Bridge, or US 169, heading north and follow MO 9 about eight miles into downtown Parkville.

where to go

Main Street Parkville. 104 Main St.; (816) 214-8477; parkvillemo.org.

Park University. 8700 NW River Park Dr.; (816) 741-2000, ext. 6211; park.edu. The university has a unique and contrasting campus that boasts buildings listed on the National Register of Historic Places. Be sure to visit the underground library and the Campanella Gallery, which highlights the work of students, faculty, and some community members. The Jenkin and Barbara David Theatre hosts six impressive performances each year, and the Graham Tyler Memorial Chapel is home to musical performances by the Northland Community Choir and other community groups. Stop by for a soccer or softball game on the fields on the north side of town on MO 9.

Parkville Mini Golf. 7 Mill St.; (816) 505-9555; parkvilleminigolf.com. This challenging 18-hole miniature golf course is great for families with children. There is room for private parties and birthday groups. Located on the bluff overlooking downtown Parkville, the course offers an unbeatable view of the town below and a clubhouse that houses a full-service snack bar and video game entertainment. Hours change seasonally.

Parkville Nature Sanctuary. Main entrance behind Platte County Health Department, 1201 East St.; (816) 741-7676; parkvillemo.com. Featuring more than 115 acres of natural fields, woodlands, ponds, and small waterfalls, the sanctuary makes a wonderful getaway from the stress of the city. A picnic shelter is located along the trail. The volunteer staff offers guided nature hikes and special events. Halloween week is always a good time. Bring live Christmas trees here for recycling. Open daily. Free.

where to shop

Cathy Kline Art Gallery. 8701 NW River Park Dr.; (913) 449-4460; cathyklineartgallery. com. Located in the wonderful, old train depot, built in 1840, which also served as city hall and survived the Great Flood of 1993, the fine art gallery shows some of the Kansas City area's top oil and acrylic painters. Special shows throughout the year bring blown glass, stained glass, photography, and pottery to Parkville. This gallery sponsors the Paint Parkville

Plein Air Event each spring and workshops throughout the year. Open Mon through Fri, 10 a.m. to 6 p.m., or by appointment.

The Farm House Collection. 109 Main St.; (816) 656-5190. This inviting shop carries a wide variety of candles and kitchenware and plenty of odds and ends that make for a lovely gift basket or a pick-me-up for your home. And it really smells good in here. Ask about the scent of the day.

Samsara. 12 East St.; (816) 505-1615; samsara-home.square.site. One of metro Kansas City's most popular home furnishings store is filled to overflowing with artwork, vases, planters, lamps, floral, and adorable seasonal gnomes, among other items. The four guys who own the shop love to refurbish old furniture and enjoy vintage décor. Stop in for a glass of sangria and leave with a new look for your home.

Wines by Jennifer. 405 Main St.; (816) 505-9463; winesbyjennifer.com. Located in a former residence on Main Street, Wines by Jennifer is as comfy, cozy as enjoying a glass of your favorite wine in your own living room. Wine tastings and pairings are often held on the back patio, also as casual as getting together with your favorite friends in your own backyard. Check the schedule of events or just drop in. Jennifer and gang will welcome you like family.

where to eat

Café des Amis. 112½ Main St.; (816) 587-6767; cafedesamiskc.com. Fine French cuisine is available in the upper level of a building built in 1844. The restaurant has built a reputation for delicious crepes, but daily specials run the gamut of everything delectable from the French. Order Champagne and watch as they slice the top off the bottle with a sword, a French tradition. This has become a popular spot to celebrate Bastille Day each July 14. Open for lunch, Thurs through Sat; dinner, Tues through Sat. Reservations helpful on Fri and Sat nights. $$

The Craic. 12 Main St.; (816) 599-4012; thecraiconmain.com. This Irish pub gets its name from a Gaelic word that basically means "good times." With a pint of Guinness, enjoy your fish 'n chips, poutine, or shepherd's pie and other pub fare. Stop in Fri and Sat nights for live Celtic music. $

Parkville Coffeehouse. 103 Main St.; (816) 216-6560; parkvillecoffee.com. This wonderful old building has exposed stone walls that date to the earliest days of Parkville. A nice quiet spot to read or watch the foot traffic on Main Street, the coffeehouse offers multiple choices in coffee, tea, and baked goods, as well as a limited breakfast and lunch menu. On a hot day, check out the smoothies, lemonade, and Italian soda. Open daily. $

Stone Canyon Pizza Co. 15 Main St.; (816) 746-8686. Appetizers, pizza, pasta, salads, and sandwiches are served at this popular Parkville establishment. Everyone raves over the salads, but come on Tuesdays for an amazing pork tenderloin sandwich. Open for lunch and dinner. $

where to stay

Main Street Inn. 504 Main St.; (816) 272-9750; mainstreetinnparkville.com. This 1886 home, built from bricks kilned by Park College students in the 1880s, has three warm and cheery guest rooms that reflect the history of Parkville. Two of the rooms have large, in-room hot tubs. One room has a private entrance. Breakfast is delivered to your room. $$–$$$

weston, mo

Founded in 1837, Weston still preserves its antebellum homes, which rest peacefully on hillsides and bluffs that once overlooked the Missouri River. It seems that the mighty Missouri changed its course after the flood of 1884. This left Weston drained of its bustling potential as a river town, with the river diverted to a channel two miles away. Long before that, the Lewis and Clark Expedition camped at what is now the foot of Main Street during the summer of 1804. A marker identifies the significance of the explorers' presence in Platte County.

Weston's many shops contain a treasure trove of goodies. Everything from handcrafted clothing and jewelry, country primitives, home décor, European furniture, and locally produced spirits can be found along Main Street. Check the city's website and Facebook page for pop-up events featuring antiques or other fun products.

getting there

From Parkville, follow MO 9 north four miles to the intersection of MO 45. Turn left, or west, and travel 22 miles into downtown Weston.

where to go

Weston Chamber of Commerce. 526 Main St.; (816) 640-2909; westonmo.com. Stop in while exploring Main Street for a map of the walking and driving tours of the area.

National Silk Art Museum. 423 Main St.; (816) 536-5955; nationalsilkdartmuseum.com. This unusual museum houses a collection of 700 silk tapestries dating to 1872. It's the largest private collection of such works in the world and is the result of John Pottie's fascination with the intricate art form. See weaving looms and historic punch cards that allowed for such intricate work. Open Tues through Sun. Free.

Pirtle's Winery. 502 Spring St.; (816) 640-5728; pirtlewinery.com. Long before there was a winery or two in every community in the US, there was Pirtle's in Weston. One of the first vineyards to be planted in northwest Missouri after state law changed in 1965, Pirtle's has been winning awards since 1978. Mead (honey wine) is a specialty here. Stop in for wine and cheese tastings in this former German Lutheran Church. Grab a picnic basket full of sausages, bread, and cheese to enjoy at an area park. Open daily.

Red Barn Farm. 16300 Wilkerson Rd.; (816) 386-5437; westonredbarnfarm.com. Get the kids and yourself into life on a real working farm. Turkeys, geese, and chickens roam the property along with goats, pigs, and cows in pens. Take a hayride through corn and soybean fields, or pick apples and pumpkins during the autumn months. Pick strawberries in May and June. There's a small gift shop in the big red barn and barbeque available on weekends. The farm is open daily, Memorial Day through Halloween, or by appointment. Free admission; fee for some activities.

Riverwood Winery. 22200 MO 45 North; (816) 579-9797; riverwoodwinery.com. Located in an old schoolhouse, Riverwood offers nine varieties of dry and sweet wines. There's always something going on—from programs highlighting regional foods and cheeses, to book signings, to musical events. Open Wed through Sun, Mar through Oct.

Snow Creek, Inc. Snow Creek Drive, five miles north of Weston on MO 45; (816) 640-2200; skisnowcreek.com; Snow Report Line: (816) 589-SNOW. Kansas City's only downhill ski area includes 30 acres of skiable terrain, a 300-foot vertical drop, 12 runs, and seven chair-lifts. The longest run is about one-fifth of a mile. There are intermediate trails, chairlifts, and beginner areas with rope tows. The Tornado Alley Tube Park is fun for people of any skill level and age range, including those with mobility issues. A day lodge features a cafeteria-style restaurant, a lounge, ski rentals, a ski school, and ticket sales. Open daily and at night from mid-Dec through Mar, depending on the weather. Admission fee.

Weston Historical Museum. 601 Main St.; (816) 386-2977; westonhistoricalmuseum.org. Located in the former Baptist Church, this museum offers displays depicting life in Platte County from prehistoric days through World War II. Exhibits include household items, tools, glassware, china, furniture, historic documents, and other items. Open afternoons, Thurs through Sun, mid-Mar through mid-Dec. Free.

Weston Bend State Park. 16600 Highway 45; (816) 640-5443; mostateparks.com. This lovely state park gets its name from a bend in the Missouri River, a feature that you can easily appreciate from an overlook above the river. On a clear day, you can easily see 10 miles into Kansas. The park includes a paved biking trail, a couple of good hiking trails, a playground, a dog park, and a historic tobacco barn. The birding is particularly good here. The camp-ground has modern restrooms and laundry facilities. Open daily, 7 a.m. until sunset.

where to shop

Backroads Art Gallery. 416 Main St.; (816) 386-0140; backroadsartgallery.com. If you're looking to spruce up the outside of your home, you'll find lots of high-quality metal and outdoor art here, as well as Native American and wildlife art indoors from talented artists around the country. Closed Mon.

Celtic Ranch. 404 Main St.; (816) 640-2881; celticranch.com. The Irish in all of us finds a voice in this shop that carries clothing imported directly from shops in the United Kingdom, along with teas, jewelry, and books. There's a whiskey-tasting room in the back. But mixed right in are a large number of items that satisfy the cowboy in us, such as leather vests, horsehair bracelets, and cowhide rugs. Open daily.

Farmer's House Market. 415 Main St.; (816) 640-3276; thefarmershouse.org. This shop is filled with homemade jams, jellies, breads, pies, candles, and more, all made by adolescents and adults with developmental disabilities. They manage the shop and hone their skills at a nearby farm, which sells additional goodies (23200 Highway 273 North; 816-800-9390). Check the website for events throughout the year, like flower sales, special dinners, and autumn festivals. Open daily.

McCormick on Main. 420 Main St.; (816) 640-3149. Founded in 1856, McCormick Distilling Company is best known for being the oldest continuously active distillery still operating on its original site. The store sells McCormick products and other Weston memorabilia. Closed Mon.

Missouri Bluffs Boutique. 512 Main St.; (816) 640-2770; missouribluffs.com. Clothes hounds looking for something nobody else has will love this place. You'll find a variety of styles here, from Native American, Asian, and African to vintage-inspired, contemporary, and locally made natural fiber garments. Like most other customers, you may wind up spending a lot of time trying on various ensembles and playing with the unusual baubles. Open daily.

The Coal House. 201 Welt St.; (913) 669-8519. This interesting property is part architectural salvage, part wedding venue, part general store, and part bed-and-breakfast inn, as well as a place to rent vintage bicycles for a ride on the adjacent Weston Bluffs bike trail. Jeff and Tracy Turney love architectural salvage and have lots of plans for how to add even more fun to this intriguing spot.

where to eat

America Bowman Restaurant. Short and Welt Streets; (816) 640-5235. This is the place to find a fine home-cooked lunch and dinner, served in a pre–Civil War setting. Inside this restaurant is Pat O'Malley's Pub. It was patterned after Granary Tavern in Limerick, Ireland. $$

Avalon Cafe. 608 Main St.; (816) 640-2835; avaloncafeweston. The restaurant is located inside an 1847 antebellum home and features Continental cuisine prepared by French-trained chefs and co-owners. Choose from beef tenderloin in Missouri bourbon sauce to American lamb chops in burgundy butter. Desserts are excellent. Closed Mon. $$

Tin Kitchen. 509 Main St.; (816) 640-0100; tin-kitchen.com. So named because of the original tin ceiling in the historic building, The Tin Kitchen uses pecan wood to smoke its barbecue. The coleslaw is vinegar based; the full bar features lots of local wines and spirits. Meet new friends at the long communal table in the center or enjoy a private booth elsewhere. Open daily. $

where to stay

Benner House Bed-and-Breakfast. 645 Main St.; (816) 640-2616; bennerirish.com. This beautiful Victorian home, overlooking downtown Weston, offers four guest rooms with two private baths. A main parlor, a sitting room, and a wraparound front porch are available for relaxing. $$

The Hatchery House. 618 Short St.; (816) 640-5700; hatcherybb.com. This 1845 antebellum bed-and-breakfast has four guest rooms with queen-size beds, gas-burning fireplaces, and private baths, as well as an adjacent cottage. A large outside garden is available for teas and weddings. Ask why this wonderful old home is called "The Hatchery House." You might be surprised. $$–$$$

The Inn at Weston Landing. 526 Welt St.; (816) 640-5788; westonirish.com. Located at the end of a block lined with pre–Civil War homes, the inn offers deluxe accommodations with the ambience of a mid-19th-century Irish cottage. A high-pitched roof, low-set dormers, and gables define Celtic and rural British Isles influences. A full authentic Celtic breakfast features rashers, kippers, trifle cakes, and bramble jelly. An 1842 Irish pub is a favorite for private parties. $$

The St. George Hotel. 500 Main St.; (816) 640-9902; westonirish.com. A fixture on Main Street Weston since 1845, this hotel has been renovated and returned to its original luxury. The hotel offers much more than overnight accommodations in one of its 26 boutique guest rooms. It is a destination in itself that includes fine dining at Charlemagne's Restaurant, a wine bar, and gift shop. $$$

platte city, mo

The seat of Platte County is often considered all business around the courthouse, but look a little more closely and you'll find lots to love in this little town.

getting there

From Weston, follow MO 92 to the east, just about 10 miles into Platte City.

where to go

Fulk Christmas Tree Farm. 23400 Highway 92; (816) 225-8809; fulkfarms.com. This farm has been in the Fulk family since 1889, growing corn and soybeans, but it was not until 1987 that they started growing Christmas trees on 25 acres. Cut your own Scotch or white pine, pick up a live wreath and other holiday décor, and of course, have a chat with Santa. Dennis Fulk also has a collection of vintage farm equipment he's glad to show you. Opens Thanksgiving weekend until all trees are sold.

Ben Ferrel Platte County Museum. 220 Ferrel St.; (816) 431-5121. If this building looks familiar, that's because it is an 1881 replica of the Missouri Governor's Mansion in Jefferson City. As home to the Platte County Historical Society, it offers lots to learn about Platte County. The building is on the National Register of Historic Places. Open mid-Apr through mid-Oct. $

Jowler Creek Winery. 16905 Jowler Creek Rd.; (816) 858-5528; jowlercreek.com. Bring a picnic lunch or grab a picnic sack already prepared for you at the Platte County winery. Just remember you can't bring outside beverages. That's because Jason and Colleen Gerke sell at least 10 flavors of wine from grapes they have grown right here on their property. They also carry beer if you like, as well as soft drinks. Take a stroll through the vineyards and chat with the sheep who are working hard to keep the weeds down. Jowler Creek has a number of musical events and other special programs throughout the year. Traveling in an electric car? There are a couple of car charging stations for your use. Open seven days a week in the warm-weather months.

Wild Rose Equine Center. 17105 Old Pike Rd., Dearborn; (816) 450-8636; wildrose-equinecenter.com. Located about halfway between Platte City and Dearborn at exit 25 off of I-29. If you've never ridden a horse and want to give it a try in a low-stress environment with gentle animals and understanding trainers, here's your place. Dez Mallonee and his family have led trail rides on this 60-acre property since 1992. If you're wanting to become more experienced, lessons are available. Kids as young as four years old are welcome to come enjoy time with the horses and a petting zoo. A food truck serves snacks so you can sit on the deck and enjoy this tranquil atmosphere in rural Platte County. $$

where to eat

Roxanne's Cafe. 1126 Branch St.; (816) 858-7027; roxannescafe.com. One of the best places for a hardy, stick-to-your-ribs breakfast you'll find anywhere, Roxanne's will get your day started right. Roxanne Gray honed her skills at the Corner Café before opening her own location in Parkville and this location in Platte City. The rolls are to die for as is Mom's Meatloaf and pork chops. Open daily for breakfast and lunch. $

Suzie's Cafe. 1302-A Platte Falls Rd.; (816) 858-6050. For the best breakfast in Platte County, Suzie's is the place to go. Serving all-natural ingredients from local vendors, Suzie makes everything you eat in her restaurant. It's a great coffee shop, with more than 100 different types of drinks available. And if you're in a hurry, zip through the drive-through window. $

where to stay

Basswood Country Resort. 15880 Interurban Rd.; (816) 858-5556; basswoodresort.com. Accommodations are available for just about all sizes and tastes here. This place started out as a very nice RV park and campground, but slowly over the years cabins have been added, as well as a fishing pond, swimming pool, playground, volleyball courts, walking trails, and a fitness center. Oh, there's also a house with traditional guest rooms, each named for a celebrity who has actually stayed at the property. You'll find Bing Crosby, Harry Truman, Rudy Vallee, and Matthew McConaughey. A country store and pizza parlor leave you with no reason to leave this resort for quite a while. $–$$

day trip 03

northwest

the start of snail mail:
st. joseph, mo; savannah, mo;
conception, mo

st. joseph, mo

When the Lewis and Clark Expedition camped here in 1804 and 1806, they named the area St. Michael's Prairie.

Founded in 1826 by Joseph Robidoux as a fur-trading post located in the Blacksnake Hills along the Missouri River, the town later became the starting point for settlers heading west over the Oregon Trail. In 1843 the community was named St. Joseph in honor of Robidoux's patron saint. Five years later gold was discovered in California, and in 1849 more than 20,000 forty-niners migrated through St. Joseph, buying food and supplies to sustain them on their journey.

Steamboats made this an important river town, but with the coming of the railroad in 1859, St. Joseph became the farthest point west to be reached by rail. Trains eventually eclipsed steamboats as the prevailing mode of transportation, but still a fast mail service was needed to the West Coast. Thousands of people turned out to watch the first run of the Pony Express on April 3, 1860. St. Joseph's Golden Age began in 1875, after the Civil War. You can pick up pieces of the past by strolling down streets lined with elegant mansions and restored buildings that were built at a time when raising hemp and selling supplies to wagon trains made fortunes. The Victorian years made fortunes for many that would last several generations. Many of the luxurious dwellings still stand and are on the National Register of

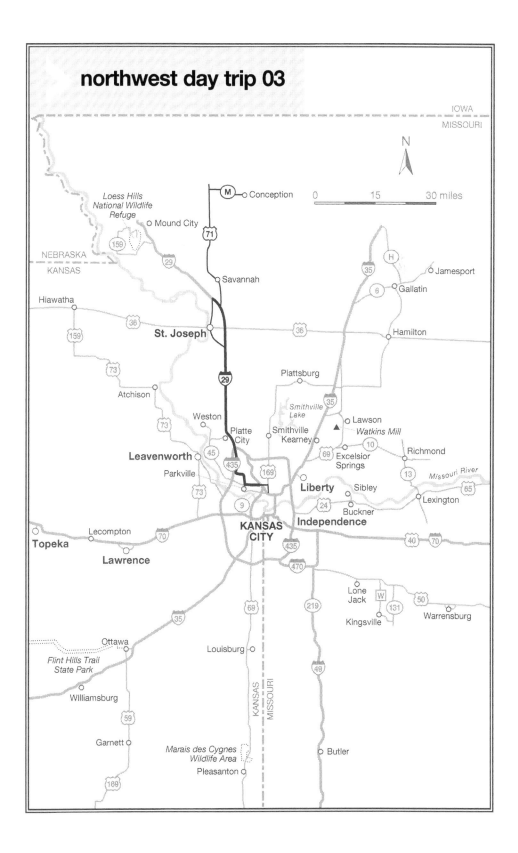

northwest day trip 03

Historic Places. If you are a home flipper, you'll find a number of remarkable buildings here ready for a loving hand.

For many history buffs, St. Joseph will forever be associated with the infamous outlaw Jesse James, who was gunned down here by a member of his own gang in April 1882.

However, since the Kansas City Chiefs summer training camp moved to Missouri Western University, St. Joseph is now better known as the August home of their favorite football team. St. Joseph has 71 car charging stations.

getting there

From downtown, head north across the Buck O'Neil Bridge, otherwise known as US 169, to I-29. Travel about 50 miles to the St. Joseph area.

where to go

St. Joseph Visitors Center. 502 N. Woodbine St.; (816) 232-1839; stjomo.com. Located adjacent to the public library, this is a bit more than your average visitor center. Interactive maps allow you to track the trails that moved west from St. Joseph. Pick up maps of your own, or print them out from computers available to the public. And look closely at the backs of the chairs you're using. You'll see Walter Cronkite, Jesse James, Aunt Jemima, and other figures associated with St. Joseph.

Albrecht-Kemper Museum of Art. 2818 Frederick Blvd.; (816) 233-7003; albrecht-kemper.org. The museum holds one of the finest and most comprehensive collections of 18th-, 19th-, and 20th-century American art in the Midwest. Included here are works by Thomas Hart Benton, Albert Bierstadt, George Caleb Bingham, George Catlin, and others. The museum is housed in a 1935 Georgian-style mansion designed by architects Edward Buehler Delk and Eugene Meyer for William Albrecht, founder of the Western Tablet Company. For guided tours call in advance. Wine tastings are held on the third Thurs of each month. Closed Mon. Admission fee.

Glore Psychiatric Museum. 3406 Frederick St.; (816) 364-1209. The permanent display covers 400 years of psychiatric history and includes exhibits such as the Bath of Surprise, O'Halloran's Swing, the Tranquilizer Chair, and the Hollow Wheel. There are also displays from St. Joseph State Hospital's history. However interesting this museum is, it is not necessarily for children or those easily upset by the human condition. Please tour with appreciation for the evolution of mental health care. Open daily. Admission fee.

Jesse James Home Museum. 12th and Penn Streets; (816) 232-8206. The outlaw Jesse James was only 34 when he was killed by Bob Ford, a member of the former James Gang. James was living in the house with his wife and two children, under the assumed name of Tom Howard. Ford shot him from behind while James stood on a chair to straighten a picture. The bullet passed through his head and entered the wall. Visitors today can still see the bullet hole. Exhibits include artifacts obtained from the outlaw's grave when he was exhumed in 1995 for DNA tests, which showed a 99.7 percent certainty that it was Jesse James who was killed in his home on April 3, 1882. Open daily. Admission fee.

Krug Park. 3500 St. Joseph Ave.; (816) 271-5500. The oldest and largest of the many public spaces in St. Joseph, Krug Park is a visual playground as well as a space for exercise and entertainment in the outdoors. Designed by landscape architect George Burnap, who also designed Washington, D.C.'s park system, Krug Park greets visitors with a beautiful lagoon filled with ducks, an amphitheater, and geometric flower gardens. With 165 acres, there's plenty of room for bike trails, playgrounds, and just wide open spaces to sit and breathe. Be sure to drive the loop road to enjoy the tunnels and rolling landscape. At Christmas, Krug Park is decorated with thousands of lights and holiday displays. Open daily.

Patee House Museum National Historic Landmark. 12th and Penn Streets; (816) 232-8206. Opened in 1858 by John Patee, this was a luxurious hotel built at a cost of $180,000, a substantial sum for that era. It contained 140 guest rooms. Later it served as headquarters for the Pony Express. Exhibits feature a restored 1860 Pony Express headquarters, a replica of the first railway mail car invented for the Pony Express, and other Pony Express memorabilia. Railroad displays include an 1860 Hannibal and St. Joseph locomotive. The 1854 Buffalo Saloon on the premises serves soft drinks and ice cream. Kids will also enjoy a ride on the Wild Things Carousel, a vintage 1941 merry-go-round. Open daily. Admission fee.

Paramount Theatre. 717 Edmond St.; (816) 271-4717; stjoearts.org. Built in 1927 by the Paramount Film Company, this 1,200-seat theater is one of only four remaining in the US from the glory days of Hollywood Oriental Theaters.

Although it is called an Oriental Theater, the building is very Middle Eastern in design with a Bedouin tent–style design hanging from the ceiling and marble carvings and gold features throughout. The theater served as a working movie theater until 1977, when it was closed and scheduled for demolition. However, the Allied Arts Organization rallied to save and restore it, and it reopened in 2002. Live performances continue to fill the stage today.

Pony Express National Museum. 914 Penn St.; (816) 279-5059 or (800) 530-5930; pony express.org. On April 3, 1860, a lone rider on horseback left from this stable to begin his historic ride. Now on the National Register of Historic Places, the Pony Express National Memorial features state-of-the-art exhibits that tell the dramatic story of the creation and operation of the Pony Express. Visitors can take a walk along the 70-foot diorama of the Pony Express Trail. Among the many hands-on displays is the mochila (mailbag), which can be changed from one saddle to another. Visitors can also pump water from the original stable well. Open daily; closed holidays. Admission fee.

Remington Nature Center. 1502 MacArthur Dr.; (816) 271-5499. A monstrous woolly mammoth greets you at the door of this center located on the banks of the Missouri

River. Dedicated to explaining the animal and plant life of this area, the center includes a 7,000-gallon fish tank and numerous hands-on exhibits that kids love. With both indoor and outdoor features, this center could keep any family entertained and better educated for hours. Open daily. Admission fee.

St. Joseph Museum. 1100 Charles St.; (816) 232-8471; stjosephmuseum.org. This 1879 Gothic-style mansion turned museum was copied after a castle on the Rhine and decorated later by the famed Tiffany Company of New York. The 5,000-piece Native American ethnographic collection is the largest in Missouri and represents more than 300 North American tribes. Items in the collection range from Pomo feather baskets to Haida copper masks. There are also local and natural history exhibits of interest. Open daily. Admission fee.

Walter Cronkite Memorial. 4525 Downs Dr.; (816) 271-4200; wcm.missouriwestern.edu. The most trusted man in America was born in St. Joseph, Missouri. While his name may not be as common as it once was, Walter Cronkite was the anchor of the CBS Evening News for nearly 20 years, and a regular broadcast figure long before that. There is no one today that can compare to what Walter Cronkite was to America. If he said it was so, no one questioned it. A replica of his newsroom and anchor desk are the highlights of the exhibit located In Spratt Hall. Open Mon through Fri, 8 a.m. to 5 p.m. Free.

where to shop

Penn Street Square. 12th and Penn Streets; (816) 232-4626. Located in the heart of the city's historic museum area, Penn Street Square offers more than 20,000 square feet of antiques and collectibles on three levels of a historic building.

Stetson Factory Outlet Store. 3601 S. Leonard Rd.; (816) 233-3286. Abraham Lincoln was the nation's president when John B. Stetson made his first western fur–felt hat. The St. Joseph–based company still makes a wide selection of world-famous western felt, straw, and dress hats at direct-from-the-manufacturer prices. This is the nation's only Stetson outlet store. Closed Sun.

where to eat

Boudreaux's Louisiana. 224 N. Fourth St.; (816) 387-9911; boudreauxstjoe.com. Located in a beautiful old historic warehouse downtown, Boudreaux's celebrates Mardi Gras and all things Cajun 365 days a year. With creaky old wood floors and high ceilings, it gets a bit noisy when crowded, which is often, and with flat-screen TVs showing numerous sporting events and friends gathering with friends, yes, it's a lively place. Open for lunch and dinner. In addition to Cajun and seafood, you can find good pasta and bread pudding on the menu. Open Mon through Sat, 11 a.m. to 9 p.m. $$

Cabana Grill. 2131 St. Joseph Ave.; (816) 279-9643; cabanaicecream.com. This locally owned fast food joint offers your basic burgers, hot dogs, tenderloins, and BLTs, but what they are most known for is the tallest ice cream cones ever! The large cone stands 12 inches high above the cone, so you're getting about 16 inches of ice cream. And it comes in swirly flavors such as strawberry, blueberry, and mint. Open daily, 11 a.m. until late. $

The Old Hoof and Horn Steakhouse. 429 Illinois St.; (816) 238-0742; hoofandhorn-steakhouse.net. Located in the heart of the Stockyards, this venerable restaurant has been serving good prime rib, steaks, and seafood since 1896. However, if you prefer Mexican, the carne asada is as good as you can find anywhere and Maria's Fajita Burrito is absolutely perfect. Open Tues through Fri, 11 a.m. to 9 p.m.; Sat, 3 p.m. to 9 p.m. Closed Sun. $$

J. C. Wyatt House. 1309 Felix St.; (816) 676-1004; jcwyatt.net. The beautiful home was built in 1891 by J. C. Wyatt, who was a principal in a major dry goods store of the city. It was a private home for many years, then an apartment building, and then sat empty for a long time waiting for the wrecking ball, until two guys from New York stepped in to save it. The house is fully restored and occasionally open for tour. Reservations are required for dinner Thurs through Sat, as well as the cooking classes that are offered seasonally. $$

savannah, mo

If you love animals, Kewpie dolls, or the family farm, you'll find a lot to love in Savannah. For more information: Savannah Chamber of Commerce, 411 Court St.; (816) 324-3976; savannahmochamber.com.

getting there

From St. Joseph, continue north on I-29 to US 71 just another 15 miles to Savannah.

where to go

Andrew County Museum. 202 E. Duncan Dr.; (816) 324-4720; andrewcountymuseum .org. Explore an old-fashioned general store, a collection of Navajo rugs, and a larger collection of Kewpie dolls. This museum also provides a well-produced explanation of the value of the family farm, which dominates life in Andrew County. Staff can help you with genealogy research. Closed Sun and Mon. Admission fee.

Huckleberry Gardens. 9229 Hwy 59; (816) 332-3563. This lovely garden supply store also carries a fun selection of home décor in addition to traditional garden plants. Sign up for a class on flower arranging, watercolors, and more. Open daily in warm weather.

M'shoogy's Famous Emergency Animal Rescue World Headquarters. 11519 State Route C; (816) 324-5824; mshoogys.com. Nestled on 22 acres of hilly country, M'shoogy's is both an animal rescue facility and a veterinary clinic. More than 750 dogs, cats, and other assorted creatures are kept at this roadside haven, which is the largest no-kill animal shelter in the country. M'shoogy's compassionate owners, Gary and Lisa Silverglat, group all the dogs by temperament in well-maintained outdoor runs. Each animal gets its turn to play in a large, fenced area that surrounds a pond. About 3,000 of M'shoogy's residents are adopted out each year, which evens the odds that they're going to live much happier lives. The Angels Vet Clinic is open to anyone, providing basic shots and other medical procedures at a fraction of the cost of most facilities in the metropolitan area. M'shoogy's is also a Federal Migratory Rehabilitation Center, which attempts to restore injured birds to the wild. Open Sat for adoptions.

conception, mo

The village of Conception is really little more than that, barely a reduced speed sign on US 136 that many people associate with a trip to Maryville and Northeast Missouri State a little farther north. The primary attraction is the Abbey, a peaceful retreat in what is already a peaceful rural community of northwest Missouri.

getting there

From Savannah, continue north on US 71 23 miles to Highway M. You'll see a sign for Conception Abbey.

where to go

Conception Abbey. 37174 State Hwy. VV; (660) 944-3100; conceptionabbey.org. Located just south of Maryville off US 71, the monastery is an architectural masterpiece designed in the Romanesque style. Also on the premises is Conception Seminary College, a four-year seminary established in 1886.

Founded in 1873, Conception Abbey was dedicated in 1891 and was designated a Minor Basilica on its 50th anniversary by Pope Pius XII, becoming the fifth Minor Basilica in the US. The Basilica of the Immaculate Conception is breathtaking in design and, for those of any faith, represents a place to sit and contemplate.

Many come here on weekend retreats to sit or walk the grounds in quiet meditation. The basilica is open each day to "pilgrims" for prayer and meditation and serves as a house of prayer for people of all faiths who enter its impressive wooden doors. It is open to the public during prayer services, including the evening vesper services, when the joyful and spirited harmony of the monks' voices becomes a welcome respite from the cacophony of the world.

Lodging rates are inexpensive. The abbey is not a resort, so don't expect fancy rooms and amenities. Do expect shared baths, long walks, beautiful sunsets, and plenty of fresh air.

Visit the gift shop, where you can buy unique cards and gifts from the abbey's Printery House. Art from the Holy Land, carved by artists from around the city of Bethlehem; porcelain and hand-carved nativity scenes; and limited offerings of gold-plated and polished bronze jewelry are also offered. Open daily. Fee for overnight accommodations and meals.

day trip 04

northwest

bird heaven & haven:
loess bluffs national wildlife refuge

loess bluffs national wildlife refuge

Established in 1935, Loess Bluffs provides more than 7,000 acres of man-made marshes where waterfowl and other creatures can find food, water, and shelter. The refuge is located five miles south of Mound City, a town that gets its name from the loess mounds that bound Squaw Creek to the east. The loess bluffs are a rare geologic formation of wind-deposited soil from the past glacial period. The stuff is crumbly and falls apart in your fingers.

If you are making your first visit to Loess Bluffs, you may want to ask some questions at the refuge headquarters, where you'll also find brochures about area wildlife. The refuge itself is open year-round from sunrise to sunset. Poaching has forced stricter adherence to the refuge's opening and closing hours. If you're found on the refuge after closing time, you risk receiving a stiff fine for trespassing.

getting there

You can reach the refuge by taking I-29 North to exit 79, then onto US 159. Follow US 159 West for 2.5 miles, and it will take you in front of the refuge headquarters. The drive is about 90 miles and takes around two hours.

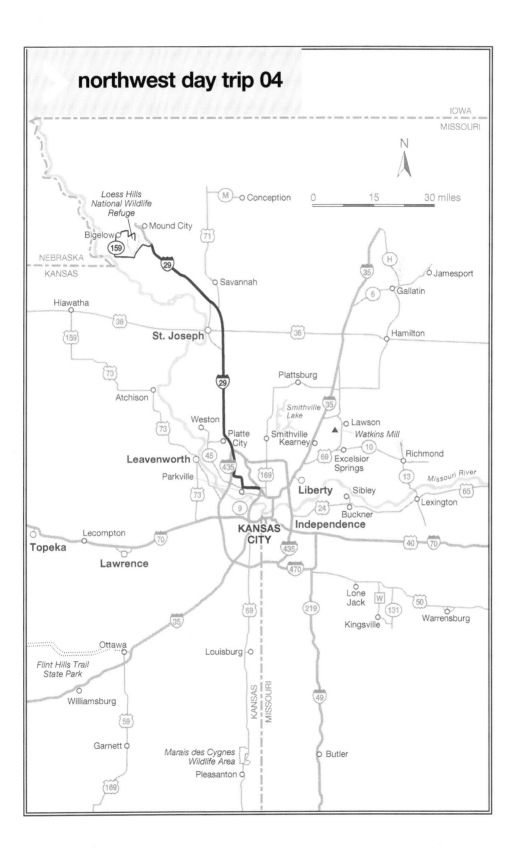

northwest day trip 04

where to go

Loess Bluffs National Wildlife Refuge. Mound City; (660) 442-3187; fws.gov/refuge/loess-bluffs. Birding is good year-round, although fall and spring are the most spectacular times. White pelicans are present during Sept and Apr. In Nov and Dec the refuge offers visitors a special treat when bald eagles migrate to the area. During winter, Loess Bluffs is said to have one of the highest concentrations of eagles in the United States, and eagle counts on the refuge have soared beyond 300 in the past.

The refuge holds an annual Eagle Days the first full weekend in Dec. The event includes a live eagle program, special viewing sites, an auto tour, handouts, and various other programs—every hour on the hour. Open-house weekends are held in spring and fall and center on the bird migrations.

After leaving the headquarters, take the bridge directly in front of it to the first observation tower you see, then turn left. An auto-tour route completes a 10-mile loop going through a variety of habitats. Follow the road around to Eagle Overlook, which is clearly marked on a sign. This is a split of land that extends into Eagle Pool, where you can mingle with the birds firsthand.

In warm weather look for red-tailed hawks, ring-necked pheasants, sandpipers, ring-billed gulls, terns, and owls. Fall and spring migrations often bring close to 200,000 snow geese, 150,000 ducks, and millions of blackbirds. Be sure to bring along a pair of binoculars to search for eagles, which perch along rows of high trees that border the water.

Mammals are more difficult to see than birds because of their nocturnal habits and the dense habitats they choose. But if you are patient and interested enough to wait and watch, you might observe white-tailed deer, opossums, raccoons, and coyotes along the roads.

Hunting and camping aren't allowed. Bring your own snacks, especially energy foods and a thermos of something warm to drink on a cold day. The refuge temperature is about 10 degrees colder than it is in Kansas City and there's always a windchill factor, so wear a sweater, plus a parka, hat, gloves, and boots in winter.

The refuge headquarters is open daily, except for federal holidays. Free.

where to eat

Quackers Bar & Grill. 1012 State St., Mound City; (660) 442-5502. If you're visiting the Mound City area, you're probably bird-watching at the Loess Bluff Wildlife Area, so you might as well enjoy a meal at a place called Quackers. Known for their wings, burgers, and salads, you'll find friendly staff and a casual environment. Open Mon through Sat, 10:30 a.m. until late. Closed Sun. $

Toad Hollar Bar & Grill. 1710 Nebraska St.; (660) 442-1033; toadhollarbarandgrill.com. A local community favorite because of the live music, the sand volleyball leagues, and other activities that invite locals and visitors to enjoy the day together. Toad Hollar is open for breakfast, lunch, and dinner, seven days a week.

where to stay

Big Lake State Park Resort. Located 11 miles northeast of Mound City, on MO 111 and US 159, Craig; (660) 771-6341; mostateparks.com/biglake.htm. Located on a natural oxbow lake, this lovely state park offers cabins with fireplaces, a meeting room, a dining room, and motel rooms and suites with kitchenettes. There's a swimming pool and fishing available as well. The resort closes at the end of Oct through the last weekend in Mar. A minimum of two nights' stay is required, but you'll want to spend at least that or more enjoying the tranquility of the area. $–$$

regional information

northeast

Excelsior Springs Chamber of Commerce.
461 S. Thompson, Excelsior Springs, MO 64024; (816) 630-6161; exspgschamber.com.

Hamilton Missouri Tourism.
visithamiltonmo.com.

Jamesport Community Association.
Jamesport, MO 64648; (660) 684-6146; jamesportmissouri.org.

Kearney Chamber of Commerce.
PO Box 242, Kearney, MO 64060; (816) 628-4229; kearneymo.com.

Liberty Chamber of Commerce.
1170 W. Kansas St., #H, Liberty, MO 64068; (816) 781-5200; libertychamber.com.

Plattsburg Chamber of Commerce.
114 W. Maple St., Plattsburg, MO 64477; (816) 539-2148; plattsburgchamber.com.

Richmond Chamber of Commerce.
104 N. Main St., Richmond, MO 64085; (816) 776-6919; richmondchamber.org.

Smithville Chamber of Commerce.
105 W. Main St., Smithville, MO 64089; (816) 532-0946; smithvillechamber.org.

east

Benton County Chamber of Commerce. 181 Harrison St., Warsaw, MO 65355; (660) 438-5922 or (660) 438-2090; welcometowarsaw.com.

Boonville Tourism. 100 Spring St.; Boonville, MO 65233; (660) 882-3967; goboonville.com.

City of Independence Tourism Department. 210 W. Truman Rd., Independence, MO 64050; (816) 325-7890; visitindependence.com.

Columbia Convention and Visitors Bureau. 300 S. Providence, Columbia, MO 65205; (573) 874-2489; visitcolumbiamo.com.

Friends of Arrow Rock. (660) 837-3231; friendsofarrowrock.org.

Friends of Rocheport.
rocheport-mo.com.

Jefferson City Convention and Visitors Bureau. 700 E. Capitol Ave., Jefferson City, MO 65101 (573) 632-2820; visitjeffersoncity.com.

Lexington Tourism Bureau.
111 S. 11 St., Lexington, MO 64067; (660) 251-3270; visitlexingtonmo.com.

New Franklin City Hall. 130 E. Broadway, New Franklin, MO 65274; (660) 848-2288; newfranklinmo.org.

Sedalia Chamber of Commerce. 600 E. Third St., Sedalia, MO 65301; (800) 827-5295; visitsedaliamo.com.

St. Clair County Economic Development. 301 S. Main St.; Lowry City, MO 64763; (417) 309-9662; stclairbusiness.com.

Warrensburg Chamber of Commerce. 100 S. Holden St., Warrensburg, MO 64093; (660) 747-3168; warrensburg.org.

south

Carthage Convention and Visitors Bureau. 116 W. Third St., Carthage, MO 64836; (417) 359-8181; visitcarthage.com.

southwest

Chanute Chamber of Commerce. 21 N. Lincoln St., Chanute, KS 66720; (620) 431-3350; chanutechamber.com.

Crawford County Convention and Visitors Bureau. 117 W. Fourth St., Pittsburg, KS 66762; (620) 231-1212; explorecrawfordcounty.com.

Emporia County Convention and Visitors Bureau. 719 Commercial St., PO Box 703, Emporia, KS 66801; (620) 342-1600; visitemporia.com.

Fort Scott Chamber of Commerce. 231 E. Wall St., Fort Scott, KS 66701; (620) 670-2750; visitfortscott.com.

Franklin County Convention and Tourism Bureau. 2011 K-68 Highway, Ottawa, KS 66067; (785) 242-1411; franklincountyks.com.

Garnett Area Chamber of Commerce. 419 S. Oak St., Garnett, KS 66032; (785) 448-6767; simplygarnett.com.

Humboldt Chamber of Commerce. 725 Bridge St., Humboldt, KS 66748; (620) 473-3232; humboldtkansas.com.

Osawatomie Chamber of Commerce. 509 Fifth St., Osawatomie, KS 66064; (913) 755-4114; osawatomiechamber.org.

Wichita Convention and Visitors Bureau. 515 S. Main St., Wichita, KS 67202; (316) 265-2800; visitwichita.com.

west

Abilene Convention and Visitors Bureau. 201 NW Second St., Abilene, KS 67410; (800) 569-5915; abilenekansas.org.

Bonner Springs/Edwardsville Chamber of Commerce. 129 N. Nettleton, Bonner Springs, KS 66012; (913) 422-5044; lifeisbetter.org.

Chase County Chamber of Commerce. 318 Broadway, Cottonwood Falls, KS 66845; (800) 431-6344; chasecountyks.org.

Council Grove/Morris County Visitors Bureau. 207 W. Main St., Council Grove, KS 66846; (800) 732-9211 or (620) 767-5882; councilgrove.com.

Lawrence Convention and Visitors Bureau. 785 Vermont St., Ste. 101, Lawrence, KS 66044; (785) 865-4499; visitlawrence.com.

Manhattan Convention and Visitors Bureau. 501 Poyntz Ave., Manhattan, KS 66502; (785) 776-8829; manhattan.org.

Topeka Convention and Visitors Bureau. 1275 SW Topeka Blvd., Topeka, KS 66612; (785) 234-1030; visittopeka.us.

Wamego Area Chamber of Commerce. PO Box 34, Wamego, KS 66547; (785) 456-7849; wamego.org.

northwest

Atchison Chamber of Commerce. Santa Fe Depot Visitors Center, 200 S. 10th St., Atchison, KS 66002; (913) 367-2427; visitatchison.com.

Hiawatha Chamber of Commerce. 801 Oregon St., Hiawatha, KS 66434; (913) 742-7136; hiwawathaks.com.

Leavenworth Area Convention and Visitors Bureau. 100 N. Fifth St., Leavenworth, KS 66048; (913) 758-2948; visitleavenworthks.com.

Main Street Parkville. 104 Main St. Parkville, MO 64152; (816) 214-8477; parkvillemo.org.

Platte County Convention and Visitors Bureau. 11724 NW Plaza Circle, #200, Kansas City, MO 64152; (816) 270-3979; visitplatte.com.

Plattsburg Chamber of Commerce. 114 W. Maple St., Plattsburg, MO 64477; (816) 539-2148; plattsburgchamber.org.

Savannah Chamber of Commerce. 411 Court St.; (816) 324-3976; savannahmochamber.com.

St. Joseph Visitors Center. 502 N. Woodbine, St. Joseph, MO 64502; (816) 232-1839; stjomo.com.

Weston Development Company. 526 Main St., Weston, MO 64098; (816) 640-2909; westonmo.com.

missouri wineries

For a complete list of Missouri wineries, visit missouriwine.org.

Baltimore Bend Winery. 27150 US 24, Waverly; (660) 493-0258; baltimorebend.com.

Belvoir Winery. 1325 Odd Fellows Rd., Liberty; (816) 200-1811.

Bristle Ridge Vineyards. P Highway and US 50, Montserrat; (660) 422-5646.

Jowler Creek Vineyard & Winery. 16905 Jowler Creek Rd., Platte City; (816) 858-5528; jowlercreek.com.

Les Bourgeois Vineyards. I-70 and Highway BB, Rocheport; (573) 698-2133.

Montserrat Vineyards. 104 NE 641, Knob Noster; (660) 747-9463.

Pirtle's Winery. 502 Spring St., Weston; (816) 640-5728; pirtlewinery.com.

Primitive Olde Crow and Winery. 32 SE Highway AA, Clinton; (660) 885-2051.

Red Fox Winery and Vineyards. 1422 NW 800 Rd., Urich; (816) 918-8161; redfoxwinery.com.

Riverwood Winery. 22200 MO 45 North, Rushville; (816) 579-9797; riverwoodwinery.com.

Terra Vox Winery. 1099 Welt St., Weston; (816) 354-4903; terravox.com.

kansas wineries

For a complete list of Kansas wineries, visit kansaswinerytrail.com.

456 Wineries. 503 Miller Dr., Wamego; (785) 456-9463.

Bourgmont Winery. 20299 Quivira Rd., Bucyrus; (913) 708-8505; bourgmont.com.

Holy-Field Vineyard & Winery. 18807 158th St., Basehor; (913) 724-9463; holyfieldwinery.com.

Isinglass Estate Vineyard & Winery. 16241 W. 381st St., La Cygne; (913) 259-9411; isinglass-estate.com.

Oz Winery. 417 Lincoln Wave., Wamego; (785) 456-7417; ozwinerykansas.com.

Pome on the Range. 2050 Idaho Rd., Williamsburg 66095; (785) 746-5492; pomeontherange.com.

Prairie Fire Winery. 20250 Hudson Ranch Rd., Paxico; (785) 636-5533; prairiefirewinery.com.

Somerset Ridge Vineyard. 29725 Somerset Rd., Paolo; (913) 491-0038; somersetridge.com.

Vinedo Del Alamo Winery. 2304 Poplar Rd., Fort Scott; (620) 215-6311.

festivals & celebrations

march

True/False Film Festival. Columbia, MO; (573) 442-8783; truefalse.org.

april

Dynamic Discs Open. Emporia, KS. Last weekend of April. dynamicdiscsopen.com.

Gatsby Days Festival. Excelsior Springs, MO. Second weekend in April. (816) 637-2811.

Tulip Festival. Wamego, KS. Third Saturday and Sunday of April. (785) 456-7849; visit-wamego.com.

may

Apple Blossom Festival and Parade. St. Joseph, MO. First weekend in May. (800) 785-0360; appleblossomparade.com.

Arrow Rock Annual Antique Show. Arrow Rock, MO. Third weekend in May. (816) 837-3470; arrowrock.org.

Big Muddy Folk Festival. Boonville, MO. Two-day event in mid-May. (660) 882-2721; bigmuddy.org.

Fort Leavenworth Homes Tour. Fort Leavenworth, KS. First Saturday in May. (800) 444-4114; ffam.us.

May Day Festival. Jamesport, MO. Early May event. (816) 684-6682; jamesport-mo.com.

Mushroom Festival. Richmond, MO. First weekend in May. (816) 776-6684; mushroom-festival.net.

june

Art in the Park. Columbia, MO. First weekend in June. (573) 443-8838; columbiaartleague. org.

Flint Hills Rodeo. Strong City, KS. (620) 273-6480; flintshillsrodeo.org.

Good Ol' Days. Fort Scott, KS. First weekend in June. (620) 215-3631; fortscottgoodol-days.com.

Juneteenth Celebration. Lexington, MO. Mid-June celebration. (660) 259-3082; visitlexingtonmo.com.

Lavender Fest. Fort Scott, KS. Mid-June. (620) 223-1364.

Old Drum Festival. Warrensburg, MO. Second Saturday in June. (660) 262-4611; visitwarresnburg.com.

Scott Joplin Ragtime Festival. Sedalia, MO. First week in June. (660) 826-2271; scottjoplin.org.

Sunflower Music Festival. Topeka, KS. Third week in June. (785) 670-1396; sunflowermusicfestival.org.

Symphony in the Flint Hills. Flint Hills, KS. (620) 273-8955; symphonyintheflinthills.org.

Wah-Shun-Gah Days. Council Grove, KS. Third weekend in June, in even-numbered years. (620) 767-5882; councilgrove.com.

Waterfest. Excelsior Springs, MO. Third weekend in June. (816) 630-6161; exspgschamber.com.

july

Amelia Earhart Festival. Atchison, KS. Annual festival in late July. (800) 234-1854; visitatchison.com.

Fiesta Mexicana Week. Topeka, KS. Weeklong mid-July festival. (785) 221-9253; oldfiestamexican.org.

Fort Osage Independence Day. Sibley, MO. July 4. (816) 650-3278.

Fourth of July Celebration. Wamego, KS. (785) 456-7849; wamego.org.

Kaw Valley Rodeo and Riley County Fair. Manhattan, KS. Last week in July. (785) 770-7714; kawvalleyrodeo.com.

Missouri State Powwow. Sedalia, MO. Mid-July event. (800) 827-5295; visitsedaliamo.com.

Mulvane Art Fair. Topeka, KS. First weekend in June. (785) 670-1010; mulvaneartmuseum.org.

Platte County Fair. Tracy, MO. Third weekend in July. (816) 431-3247; plattecountyfair.com.

Sunflower State Games. Topeka, KS. Two weekends in late July. (785) 235-2295; sunflowergames.com.

Wild Bill Hickok Rodeo and Western Heritage Festival. Abilene, KS. Last weekend of July. (800) 569-5915; wildbillhickockrodeo.com.

august

Collins Pie Festival. Collins, MO. Third weekend in August. (417) 309-3155.

Missouri River Festival of the Arts. Boonville, MO. Second week of August. (660) 882-2721; goboonville.com.

Missouri State Fair. Sedalia, MO. (800) 422-FAIR; mostatefair.com.

Water Wars. Humboldt, KS. It's a big water fight the third Saturday in August. (620) 473-3232; humboldtkansas.com.

september

Annual Ciderfest. Louisburg Cider Mill, Louisburg, KS. Last week in September and first week in October. (913) 837-5202; louisburgcidermill.com.

Apple Jubilee. Waverly, MO. Mid-September event. (660) 493-2616.

Cider Days. Topeka, KS. Last weekend of September. (785) 230-5226; ciderdays.com.

Chisholm Trail Day Festival. Abilene, KS. First Saturday of September. (785) 263-2681; abilenekansas.org.

Haskell Indian Art Market. Lawrence, KS. September and October. (785) 749-8467; haskell.edu.

Heritage Day "Step Back in Time" Festival. Jamesport, MO. (660) 684-6682; jamesport-mo.com.

Jesse James Festival. Kearney, MO. Mid-September event. (816) 628-4229; jessejames festival.com.

Little Balkans Days. Pittsburg, KS. Annual September event. (620) 704-7369; littlebalkans .com.

Ozark Ham and Turkey Festival. California, MO. Third Saturday in September. (573) 796-3040.

Power of the Past Antique Engine and Tractor Show. Ottawa, KS. Second weekend of September. (785) 242-1411; powerofthepast.net.

Treeline Music Festival. Columbia, MO. Second weekend in September. (573) 442-5862; treelinemusicfest.com/.

Santa-Cali-Gon Days Festival. Independence, MO. Labor Day weekend. (816) 325-7111; santacaligon.com.

october

Apple Fest. Weston, MO. Early October event. (816) 640-2909; westonmo.com.

Apple Festival. Topeka, KS. Early October celebration. (785) 368-3888; visittopeka.us.

Arrow Rock Heritage Festival. Arrow Rock, MO. Second weekend in October. (660) 837-3335; arrowrock.org.

Fort Osage Rendezvous and Trade Fair. Sibley, MO. Second weekend in October. (816) 650-3278.

Halloween Frolic. Hiawatha, KS. Halloween night. (913) 742-7136.

Haunted Atchison Tours. Atchison, KS. Every night in September and October. (800) 234-1854; atchisonkansas.net.

Lake Garnett Grand Prix Revival. Garnett, KS. First weekend in October. lggpr.org.

Maple Leaf Festival. Carthage, MO. Third weekend of the month. (417) 358-2373; visit-carthage.com.

Oktoberfest. Atchison, KS. First weekend of the month. (800) 234-1854; atchison.org.

OztoberFest. Wamego, KS. First Saturday of October. (866) 458-TOTO; oztoberfest.com.

november

Annual Christmas Lighting Ceremony. Carthage, MO. Mid-November event. (800) 543-7975; visit-carthage.com.

Step Back in Time Christmas Festival. Jamesport, MO. Last week in November. (816) 684-6682; jamesport-mo.com.

Veterans Day Tribute. Emporia, KS. Early November. (800) 279-3730.

december

Christmas in Weston Candlelight Homes Tour. Weston, MO. First weekend in December. (816) 640-2909; westonmo.com.

Christmas on the River. Parkville, MO. First Thursday through Sunday in December. (816) 505-2227; parkvillemo.com.

Frontier Candlelight Tour. Fort Scott, KS. First weekend in December. (800) 245-FORT; fortscott.com.

Loess Bluffs National Wildlife Refuge Eagle Days. Mound City, MO. First full weekend in December. (660) 442-3187; fws.gov/midwest.

ICE PLANET
BARBARIANS